The Works

OF

Francis Bacon

The Wisdom of the Ancients and Other Essays

REG U S PAT OFF

BLACK'S READERS SERVICE

ROSLYN, NEW YORK

CONTENTS

ESSAYS; OR, COUNSELS CIVIL AND MORAL.

THE WISDOM OF THE ANCIENTS; A SERIES OF MYTHOLOGICAL FABLES.

INTRODUCTION

Few careers as public as Francis Bacon's retain so many dark corners and obstinate secrets, few characters that have been so exposed to the searchlight of investigation remain as difficult to understand. Seldom is one called upon to admire a man, as one must admire the author of "The Advancement of Learning," and at the same time to despise him, as one must despise the betrayer of Essex; seldom is it possible to admire at all when it is so obviously impossible either to love or like; seldom has fortune dealt so variously with a man as it dealt with the disappointed servant of Elizabeth and the proud Chancellor of James I. His character is a study in contradictions, his life a study in contrasts. In the world of the intellect he was an unswerving idealist, devoted to a noble cause; in the world of practical affairs, he was a calculating sychophant and an unscrupulous opportunist. Equally startling are the contrasts exhibited by his career. Baffled in his quest of place and power until he was almost fifty, he was suddenly elevated to the heights, and then as suddenly cast down again in ruin and disgrace. It is not easy to pass judgment on such a man and such a life; but his contemporaries, even when they respected his talents, mistrusted him, and posterity has confirmed their opinion by condemning him, even while fully acknowledging the quality and range of his genius.

When Francis Bacon was born, on the 22nd of January, 1561, at York House in the Strand, he drew his first breath among the chosen of the earth. His father was Sir Nicholas Bacon, Elizabeth's Lord Keeper; his mother was the daughter of Sir Antony Cook and the sister of Lady Cecil; his uncle by marriage was William Cecil, later the great Lord Burghley. "This means," writes Dean Church, "that his boyhood from the first was passed among the high places of the world—at one of the greatest crises of English history—in the very centre and focus of its agitations. He was brought up among the chiefs and leaders of the rising religion, in the houses of the greatest and most powerful persons of the State, and naturally, as their child, at times in the Court of the Queen, who joked with him, and called him 'her young Lord Keeper'."

No child, it seemed, could be born in more promising circumstances; none, granted even average talents, could be surer of future favor, advancement, and position. His father was a faithful and honored servant of the Queen, his near relatives held the keys of power. But Bacon, whose talents were so far above the average, was destined to be rebuffed year after long year, to be held down in an obscurity which he scorned and a comparative poverty which he detested. Year after year he paid vain suit to all who might assist him. Elizabeth, however much she might have joked with the child, would do nothing for the young man when the death of his father, in 1579, called him back from Cambridge to make his own way in the world. Burghley had nothing for him but fair words, and words were all that he could ever get from his powerful cousin Robert Cecil. When he had already passed thirty he found a beneficent patron in Essex, but even that imperious favorite, who was accustomed to have his way in all things, was baulked when he sought to assist Bacon. It would almost seem that an authority against which there was no appeal had decreed that Francis Bacon should be shown no favor. Whatever the explanation, the fact is that so long as Elizabeth reigned he had to be content with minor legal duties and with small rewards. The one major use that the Queen found for him was as an instrument in the destruction of Essex, and it is probable that Bacon lost more than he gained by his ready and base compliance in this affair. It is unlikely that Elizabeth, who had loved Essex, could forgive the willing assistant in a judicial murder for which she could scarcely forgive herself. The mere sight of Bacon must have been to her a reminder and a reproach. And, Elizabeth's feelings in the case apart, he had branded himself as a Judas before all the world.

So the years passed by. in an era when youth rose swiftly

to places of responsibility and power, and Francis Bacon, whom posterity was to know as one of the great men of his day, slipped into middle age without position or distinction. Even the accession of James I brought no immediate change in his fortunes; it is true that he was knighted two days before the coronation, but this was an honor which he shared, to his disgust, with three hundred others. Not until Bacon was forty-seven, and James had discovered how useful an advocate he could be in upholding the royal prerogative, did he secure the first post on which he had set his heart, that of Solicitor-General. Not until he was fifty-two did George Villiers, Duke of Buckingham, effect his appointment as Attorney-General, the position which another royal favorite had vainly begged for him twenty years before. Thereafter, success and its outward signs came fast; he was named Lord Chancellor in 1617, Baron Verulam in 1618, Viscount St. Alban's in 1621. But disaster followed on feet as swift. Barely two months after the last honor was bestowed upon him, he was charged with corruption on a grand scale; against these charges, pressed by old enemies with Sir Edward Coke at their head, he entered no defence. He was convicted without trial, at his own request, and without any offense which custom did not sanction being really proved against him; he was deposed from office, fined a huge sum, banished from the Court, and condemned to imprisonment in the Tower during the King's pleasure. Actually he was imprisoned only a few days, and his fine was largely remitted, but in his public capacity at least he was a broken man; and death followed disgrace at a distance of only five years, on Easter morning, the ninth of April, 1626.

This then was the reward of long waiting, tireless scheming, and unflagging ambition. It is a strange story; but there is another very different story, more important to us to-day, that is interwoven with it,—the history of Bacon's intellectual life and literary productions. When Bacon, at the age of thirty-one, announced to Burghley that he had taken all knowledge to be his province, he dedicated himself to a task which he never abandoned despite vicissitudes of fortune. Believing that "the sovereignty of man lieth hid in knowledge," he was determined that Francis Bacon should lead man into his kingdom. To that end he worked tirelessly at the accumulation and arrangement of human knowledge, at the destruction of false science and the establishment of true. To that end all his writings were ultimately directed,—"The Advancement of Learning," the "Essays," the "Novum Organum," and the rest. Even in disgrace and declining health his mind and pen did not falter. And, because of his devotion to this great cause, his worldly conduct has not lacked defenders. He sought wealth and power, we are told, only because he could not do his work without them. Other men have acted as he did for meaner ends, none has done so for a nobler. The defence is plausible, but it breaks down when we recall what men living in obscurity and poverty have done for literature and learning. Seen clearly and simply, Francis Bacon was a great man of bad character. No more can be said, and no defence however plausible need be offered, for posterity has no intimate or active concern with his character. Our business is with what he wrote, no line of which would be altered had he betrayed a hundred great lords instead of one, or accepted a million brides. Bacon the man went down into the dust with Essex three hundred years ago; but the words of the writer are alive.

Essays

I.—OF TRUTH.

WHAT is truth? said jesting Pilate;[1] and would not stay for an answer. Certainly, there be that delight in giddiness; and count it a bondage to fix a belief; affecting freewill in thinking as well as in acting. And though the sects of philosophers of that kind be gone, yet there remain certain discoursing wits which are of the same veins, though there be not so much blood in them as was in those of the ancients. But it is not only the difficulty and labor which men take in finding out of truth; nor again, that, when it is found, it imposeth upon men's thoughts, that doth bring lies in favor; but a natural though corrupt love of the lie itself. One of the later schools[2] of the Grecians examineth the matter, and is at a stand to think what should be in it that men should love lies; where neither they make for pleasure, as with poets; nor for advantage, as with the merchant, but for the lie's sake. But I cannot tell; this same truth is a naked and open daylight, that doth not show the masks, and mummeries, and triumphs of the world,

[1] He refers to the following passage in the Gospel of St. John, xviii. 38: "Pilate saith unto him, What is truth? And when he had said this, he went out again unto the Jews, and saith unto them, I find in him no fault at all."

[2] He probably refers to the "New Academy," a sect of Greek philosophers, one of whose moot questions was, "What is truth?" Upon which they came to the unsatisfactory conclusion, that mankind has no criterion by which to form a judgment.

1

half so stately and daintily as candle-lights. Truth may perhaps come to the price of a pearl, that showeth best by day, but it will not rise to the price of a diamond or carbuncle, that showeth best in varied lights. A mixture of a lie doth ever add pleasure. Doth any man doubt, that if there were taken out of men's minds vain opinions, flattering hopes, false valuations, imaginations as one would, and the like, but it would leave the minds of a number of men poor shrunken things, full of melancholy and indisposition, and unpleasing to themselves? One of the fathers,[3] in great severity, called poesy "vinum dæmonum,"[4] because it filleth the imagination, and yet it is but with the shadow of a lie. But it is not the lie that passeth through the mind, but the lie that sinketh in, and settleth in it, that doth the hurt, such as we spake of before. But howsoever these things are thus in men's depraved judgments and affections, yet truth, which only doth judge itself, teacheth that the inquiry of truth, which is the love-making, or wooing of it, the knowledge of truth, which is the presence of it, and the belief of truth, which is the enjoying of it, is the sovereign good of human nature. The first creature of God, in the works of the days, was the light of the sense;[5] the last was the light of reason;[6] and his sabbath work, ever since, is the illumination of his Spirit. First, he breathed light upon the face of the matter, or chaos; then he breathed light into

[3] Perhaps he was thinking of St. Augustine.—See *Aug. Confess.* i. 25, 26.

[4] "The wine of evil spirits."

[5] Genesis i. 3: "And God said, Let there be light, and there was light."

[6] At the moment when "The Lord God formed man out of the dust of the ground, and breathed into his nostrils the breath of life; and man became a living soul."—*Genesis* ii. 7.

the face of man; and still he breatheth and inspireth light into the face of his chosen. The poet[7] that beautified the sect,[8] that was otherwise inferior to the rest, saith yet excellently well: "It is a pleasure to stand upon the shore, and to see ships tossed upon the sea; a pleasure to stand in the window of a castle, and to see a battle, and the adventures thereof below; but no pleasure is comparable to the standing upon the vantage-ground of truth" (a hill not to be commanded, and where the air is always clear and serene), "and to see the errors, and wanderings, and mists, and tempests, in the vale below;"[9] so always

[7] Lucretius, the Roman poet and Epicurean philosopher, is alluded to.—*Lucret.* ii. *init.* Comp. *Adv. of Learning,* i. 8, 5.

[8] He refers to the sect which followed the doctrines of Epicurus. The life of Epicurus himself was pure and abstemious in the extreme. One of his leading tenets was, that the aim of all speculation should be to enable men to judge with certainty what course is to be chosen, in order to secure health of body and tranquillity of mind. The adoption, however, of the term "pleasure," as denoting this object, has at all periods subjected the Epicurean system to great reproach; which, in fact, is due rather to the conduct of many who, for their own purposes, have taken shelter under the system in name only, than to the tenets themselves, which did not inculcate libertinism. Epicurus admitted the existence of the Gods, but he deprived them of the characteristics of Divinity, either as creators or preservers of the world.

[9] Lord Bacon has either translated this passage of Lucretius from memory or has purposely paraphrased it. The following is the literal translation of the original: " 'Tis a pleasant thing, from the shore, to behold the dangers of another upon the mighty ocean, when the winds are lashing the main; not because it is a grateful pleasure for any one to be in misery, but because it is a pleasant thing to see those misfortunes from which you yourself are free: 'tis also a pleasant thing to behold the mighty contests of warfare, arrayed upon the plains, without a share in the danger; but nothing is there more delightful than to occupy the elevated temples of the wise, well fortified by tranquil learning, whence you may be able to look down upon others, and see them straying in every direction, and wandering in search of the path of life."

that this prospect be with pity, and not with swelling or pride. Certainly it is heaven upon earth, to have a man's mind move in charity, rest in providence, and turn upon the poles of truth.

To pass from theological and philosophical truth to the truth of civil business; it will be acknowledged, even by those that practise it not, that clear and round dealing is the honor of man's nature, and that mixture of falsehood is like alloy in coin of gold and silver, which may make the metal work the better, but it embaseth it. For these winding and crooked courses are the goings of the serpent; which goeth basely upon the belly, and not upon the feet. There is no vice that doth so cover a man with shame, as to be found false and perfidious; and therefore Montaigne[10] saith prettily, when he inquired the reason why the word of the lie should be such a disgrace, and such an odious charge; saith he, "If it be well weighed, to say that a man lieth, is as much as to say that he is brave towards God and a coward towards men. For a lie faces God, and shrinks from man;" surely, the wickedness of falsehood and breach of faith cannot possibly be so highly expressed, as in that it shall be the last peal to call the judgments of

[10] Michael de Montaigne, the celebrated French Essayist. His *Essays* embrace a variety of topics, which are treated in a sprightly and entertaining manner, and are replete with remarks indicative of strong native good sense. He died in 1592. The following quotation is from the second book of the *Essays*, c. 18: "Lying is a disgraceful vice, and one that Plutarch, an ancient writer, paints in most disgraceful colors, when he says that it is 'affording testimony that one *first* despises God, and then fears men;' it is not possible more happily to describe its horrible, disgusting, and abandoned nature; for, can we imagine anything more vile than to be cowards with regard to men, and brave with regard to God?"

God upon the generations of men: it being foretold, that, when "Christ cometh," he shall not "find faith upon the earth." [11]

II.—OF DEATH.[1]

MEN fear death as children fear to go in the dark; and as that natural fear in children is increased with tales, so is the other. Certainly, the contemplation of death, as the wages of sin, and passage to another world, is holy and religious; but the fear of it, as a tribute due unto nature, is weak. Yet in religious meditations there is sometimes mixture of vanity and of superstition. You shall read in some of the friars' books of mortification, that a man should think with himself, what the pain is, if he have but his finger's end pressed or tortured; and thereby imagine what the pains of death are, when the whole body is corrupted and dissolved; when many times death passeth with less pain than the torture of a limb, for the most vital parts are not the quickest of sense. And by him that spake only as a philosopher and natural man, it was well said, "Pompa mortis magis terret, quam mors ipsa." [2] Groans and convulsions, and a discolored face, and friends weeping, and blacks[3] and obsequies, and the like, show death terrible. It is worthy the observing, that there is no passion in

[11] St. Luke xviii. 8: "Nevertheless, when the Son of man cometh, shall he find faith upon the earth?"

[1] A portion of this *Essay* is borrowed from the writings of Seneca. See his *Letters to Lucilius*, B. iv. Ep. 24 and 82.

[2] "The array of the death-bed has more terrors than death itself." This quotation is from Seneca.

[3] He probably alludes to the custom of hanging the room in black where the body of the deceased lay, a practice much more usual in Bacon's time than at the present day.

the mind of man so weak, but it mates and masters
the fear of death; and therefore death is no such terrible enemy when a man hath so many attendants
about him that can win the combat of him. Revenge
triumphs over death; love slights it; honor aspireth
to it; grief flieth to it; fear preoccupateth it; nay, we
read, after Otho the emperor had slain himself, pity
(which is the tenderest of affections) provoked many
to die out of mere compassion to their sovereign, and
as the truest sort of followers.[4] Nay, Seneca[5] adds
niceness and satiety: "Cogita quamdiu eadem feceris;
mori velle, non tantum fortis, aut miser, sed etiam
fastidiosus potest."[6] A man would die, though he
were neither valiant nor miserable, only upon a weariness to do the same thing so oft over and over. It is
no less worthy to observe, how little alteration in
good spirits the approaches of death make: for they
appear to be the same men till the last instant. Augustus Cæsar died in a compliment: "Livia, conjugii
nostri memor, vive et vale."[7] Tiberius in dissimulation, as Tacitus saith of him, "Jam Tiberium vires et
corpus, non dissimulatio, deserebant:"[8] Vespasian in
a jest, sitting upon the stool,[9] "Ut puto Deus fio;"[10]
Galba with a sentence, "Feri, si ex re sit populi

[4] Tacit, Hist. ii. 49.

[5] Ad Lucil. 77.

[6] "Reflect how often you do the same things; a man may wish
to die, not only because either he is brave or wretched, but even
because he is surfeited with life."

[7] "Livia, mindful of our union, live on, and fare thee well."—
Suet. Aug. Vit. c. 100.

[8] "His bodily strength and vitality were now forsaking Tiberius, but not his duplicity."—*Ann.* vi. 50.

[9] This was said as a reproof to his flatterers, and in spirit is
not unlike the rebuke administered by Canute to his retinue.—
Suet. Vespas. Vit. c. 23.

[10] "I am become a Divinity, I suppose."

Romani," [11] holding forth his neck; Septimus Severus in dispatch, "Adeste, si quid mihi restat agendum," [12] and the like. Certainly, the Stoics [13] bestowed too much cost upon death, and by their great preparations made it appear more fearful. Better, saith he, "qui finem vitæ extremum inter munera ponit naturæ." [14] It is as natural to die as to be born; and to a little infant, perhaps, the one is as painful as the other. He that dies in an earnest pursuit, is like one that is wounded in hot blood, who, for the time, scarce feels the hurt; and therefore a mind fixed and bent upon somewhat that is good, doth avert the dolors of death; but, above all, believe it, the sweetest canticle is "Nunc dimittis," [15] when a man hath obtained worthy ends and expectations. Death hath

[11] "If it be for the advantage of the Roman people, strike."—*Tac. Hist.* i. 41.

[12] If aught remains to be done by me, dispatch."—*Dio Cass.* 76, *ad fin.*

[13] These were the followers of Zeno, a philosopher of Citium, in Cyprus, who founded the Stoic school, or "School of the Portico," at Athens. The basis of his doctrines was the duty of making virtue the object of all our researches. According to him, the pleasures of the mind were preferable to those of the body, and his disciples were taught to view with indifference health or sickness, riches or poverty, pain or pleasure.

[14] "Who reckons the close of his life among the boons of nature." Lord Bacon here quotes from memory; the passage is in the tenth Satire of Juvenal, and runs thus:—

> "Fortem posce animum, mortis terrore carentem,
> Qui spatium vitæ extremum inter munera ponat
> Naturæ"—

"Pray for strong resolve, void of the fear of death, that reckons the closing period of life among the boons of nature."

[15] He alludes to the song of Simeon, to whom the Holy Ghost had revealed, "that he should not see death before he had seen the Lord's Christ." When he beheld the infant Jesus in the temple, he took the child in his arms and burst forth into a song of thanksgiving, commencing, "Lord, now lettest thou thy servant depart in peace, according to thy word, for mine eyes have seen thy salvation."—*St. Luke* ii. 29.

this also, that it openeth the gate to good fame, and
extinguisheth envy: "Extinctus amabitur idem." [16]

III.—OF UNITY IN RELIGION.

RELIGION being the chief band of human society,
it is a happy thing when itself is well contained within
the true band of unity. The quarrels and divisions
about religion were evils unknown to the heathen.
The reason was, because the religion of the heathen
consisted rather in rites and ceremonies, than in any
constant belief; for you may imagine what kind of
faith theirs was, when the chief doctors and fathers of
their church were the poets. But the true God hath
this attribute, that he is a jealous God; and therefore
his worship and religion will endure no mixture nor
partner. We shall therefore speak a few words concerning the unity of the church; what are the fruits
thereof; what the bounds; and what the means.

The fruits of unity (next unto the well-pleasing of
God, which is all in all), are two; the one towards
those that are without the church, the other towards
those that are within. For the former, it is certain
that heresies and schisms are, of all others, the greatest scandals, yea, more than corruption of manners;
for as in the natural body a wound or solution of continuity is worse than a corrupt humor, so in the
spiritual; so that nothing doth so much keep men out
of the church, and drive men out of the church, as
breach of unity; and therefore, whensoever it cometh
to that pass that one saith, "Ecce in Deserto," [1] an-

---

[16] "When dead, the same person shall be beloved."—*Hor. Ep.*
ii. 1, 14.
[1] "Behold, he is in the desert."—*St. Matthew* xxiv. 26.

other saith. "Ecce in penetralibus;"[2] that is, when
some men seek Christ in the conventicles of heretics,
and others in an outward face of a church, that voice
had need continually to sound in men's ears, "nolite
exire," "go not out." The doctor of the Gentiles (the
propriety of whose vocation drew him to have a special care of those without) saith: "If a heathen[3]
come in, and hear you speak with several tongues, will
he not say that you are mad?" and, certainly, it is
little better: when atheists and profane persons do
hear of so many discordant and contrary opinions in
religion, it doth avert them from the church, and
maketh them "to sit down in the chair of the scorn-
ers."[4] It is but a light thing to be vouched in so
serious a matter, but yet it expresseth well the deformity. There is a master of scoffing, that, in his
catalogue of books of a feigned library, sets down
this title of a book, "The Morris-Dance[5] of Heretics;" for, indeed, every sect of them hath a diverse

[2] "Behold, he is in the secret chambers."—*Ib.*
[3] He alludes to 1 Corinthians xiv. 23: "If, therefore, the whole
church be come together into one place, and all speak with
tongues, and there come in those that are unlearned, or unbe-
lievers, will they not say that ye are mad?"
[4] Psalm i. 1: "Blessed is the man that walketh not in the
counsel of the ungodly, nor standeth in the way of sinners, nor
sitteth in the seat of the scornful."
[5] This dance, which was originally called the Morisco dance
is supposed to have been derived from the Moors of Spain; the
dancers in earlier times blackening their faces to resemble
Moors. It was probably a corruption of the ancient Pyrrhic
dance, which was performed by men in armor, and which is
mentioned as still existing in Greece, in Byron's "Song of the
Greek Captive:"—

"You have the Pyrrhic dance as yet."

Attitude and gesture formed one of the characteristics of the
dance. It is still practised in some parts of England.—*Rabelais,
Pantag.* ii. 7.

posture, or cringe, by themselves, which cannot but move derision in worldlings and depraved politicians, who are apt to contemn holy things.

As for the fruit towards those that are within, it is peace, which containeth infinite blessings; it establisheth faith; it kindleth charity; the outward peace of the church distilleth into peace of conscience, and it turneth the labors of writing and reading of controversies into treatises of mortification and devotion.

Concerning the bounds of unity, the true placing of them importeth exceedingly. There appear to be two extremes; for to certain zealots all speech of pacification is odious. "Is it peace, Jehu?"—"What hast thou to do with peace? turn thee behind me."[6] Peace is not the matter, but following, and party. Contrariwise, certain Laodiceans[7] and lukewarm persons think they may accommodate points of religion by middle ways, and taking part of both, and witty reconcilements, as if they would make an arbitrament between God and man. Both these extremes are to be avoided; which will be done if the league of Christians, penned by our Saviour himself, were in the two cross clauses thereof soundly and plainly expounded: "He that is not with us is against us;"[8] and again, "He that is not against us, is with us;" that is, if the points fundamental, and of substance in religion, were truly discerned and distinguished from points not

[6] 2 Kings ix. 18.

[7] He alludes to the words in Revelation, c. iii. v. 14, 15, 16. "And unto the angel of the church of the Laodiceans write: These things saith the Amen, the faithful and true Witness, the beginning of the creation of God; I know thy works, that thou art neither cold nor hot.—I will spue thee out of my mouth." Laodicea was a city of Asia Minor. St. Paul established the church there which is here referred to.

[8] St. Matthew xii. 30.

merely of faith, but of opinion, order, or good intention. This is a thing may seem to many a matter trivial, and done already; but if it were done less partially, it would be embraced more generally.

Of this I may give only this advice, according to my small model. Men ought to take heed of rending God's church by two kinds of controversies; the one is, when the matter of the point controverted is too small and light, not worth the heat and strife about it, kindled only by contradiction; for, as it is noted by one of the fathers, "Christ's coat indeed had no seam, but the church's vesture was of divers colors;" whereupon he saith, "In veste varietas sit, scissura non sit," [9] they be two things, unity and uniformity; the other is, when the matter of the point controverted is great, but it is driven to an over-great subtilty and obscurity, so that it becometh a thing rather ingenious than substantial. A man that is of judgment and understanding shall sometimes hear ignorant men differ, and know well within himself, that those which so differ mean one thing, and yet they themselves would never agree; and if it come so to pass in that distance of judgment, which is between man and man, shall we not think that God above, that knows the heart, doth not discern that frail men, in some of their contradictions, intend the same thing, and accepteth of both? The nature of such controversies is excellently expressed by St. Paul, in the warning and precept that he giveth concerning the same: "Devita profanas vocum novitates, et oppositiones falsi nominis scientiæ." [10] Men create oppositions which are

[9] "In the garment there may be many colors, but let there be no rending of it."

[10] "Avoid profane and vain babblings, and oppositions of science, falsely so called."—1 *Tim.* vi. 20.

not, and put them into new terms, so fixed as, whereas the meaning ought to govern the term, the term in effect governeth the meaning. There be also two false peaces, or unities; the one, when the peace is grounded but upon an implicit ignorance; for all colors will agree in the dark; the other, when it is pieced up upon a direct admission of contraries in fundamental points; for truth and falsehood, in such things, are like the iron and clay in the toes of Nebuchadnezzar's image; [11] they may cleave, but they will not incorporate.

Concerning the means of procuring unity, men must beware that, in the procuring or muniting of religious unity, they do not dissolve and deface the laws of charity and of human society. There be two swords amongst Christians, the spiritual and temporal, and both have their due office and place in the maintenance of religion; but we may not take up the third sword, which is Mahomet's sword, [12] or like unto it; that is, to propagate religion by wars, or, by sanguinary persecutions, to force consciences; except it be in cases of overt scandal, blasphemy, or intermixture of practice against the state; much less to nourish seditions, to authorize conspiracies and rebellions, to put the sword into the people's hands, and the like, tending to the subversion of all government, which is the ordinance of God; for this is but to dash the first table against the second, and so to consider men as Christians, as we forget that they are men. Lucretius the poet, when he beheld the act of Agamemnon,

[11] He alludes to the dream of Nebuchadnezzar, significant of the limited duration of his kingdom.—See *Daniel* ii. 33, 41.

[12] Mahomet proselytized by giving to the nations which he conquered, the option of the Koran or the sword.

that could endure the sacrificing of his own daughter, exclaimed;—

"Tantum religio potuit suadere malorum." [13]

What would he have said, if he had known of the massacre in France,[14] or the powder treason of England? [15] He would have been seven times more epicure and atheist than he was; for as the temporal sword is to be drawn with great circumspection in cases of religion, so it is a thing monstrous to put it into the hands of the common people; let that be left unto the Anabaptists, and other furies. It was great blasphemy when the devil said, "I will ascend and be like the Highest;" [16] but it is greater blasphemy to personate God, and bring him in saying, "I will descend, and be like the prince of darkness;" and what is it better, to make the cause of religion to descend to the cruel and execrable actions of murdering princes, butchery of people, and subversion of states and governments? Surely, this is to bring down the Holy Ghost, instead of the likeness of a dove, in the shape of a vulture or raven; and to set out of the bark of a Christian church a flag of a bark of pirates and assassins; therefore, it is most necessary that the

[13] "To deeds so dreadful could religion prompt." The poet refers to the sacrifice by Agamemnon, the Grecian leader, of his daughter Iphigenia, with the view of appeasing the wrath of Diana.—*Lucret.* i. 95.

[14] He alludes to the massacre of the Huguenots, or Protestants, in France, which took place on St. Bartholomew's day, August 24, 1572, by the order of Charles IX. and his mother, Catherine de Medici. On this occasion about 60,000 persons perished, including the Admiral De Coligny, one of the most virtuous men that France possessed, and the main stay of the Protestant cause.

[15] More generally known as "The Gunpowder Plot."

[16] Isa. xiv. 14.

church by doctrine and decree, princes by their sword, and all learnings, both Christian and moral, as by their Mercury rod,[17] do damn and send to hell forever those facts and opinions tending to the support of the same, as hath been already in good part done. Surely, in counsels concerning religion, that counsel of the apostle would be prefixed: "Ira hominis non implet justitiam Dei;"[18] and it was a notable observation of a wise father, and no less ingenuously confessed, that those which held and persuaded pressure of consciences, were commonly interested therein themselves for their own ends.

IV.—OF REVENGE.

REVENGE is a kind of wild justice, which the more man's nature runs to, the more ought law to weed it out; for as for the first wrong, it doth but offend the law, but the revenge of that wrong, putteth the law out of office. Certainly, in taking revenge, a man is but even with his enemy, but in passing it over, he is superior; for it is a prince's part to pardon; and Solomon, I am sure, saith, "It is the glory of a man to pass by an offence." That which is past is gone and irrevocable, and wise men have enough to do with things present and to come; therefore they do but trifle with themselves that labor in past matters. There is no man doth a wrong for the wrong's sake,

[17] Allusion is made to the "caduceus," with which Mercury, the messenger of the Gods, summoned the souls of the departed to the infernal regions.

[18] "The wrath of man worketh not the righteousness of God." —*James* i. 20.

but thereby to purchase himself profit, or pleasure, or honor, or the like; therefore, why should I be angry with a man for loving himself better than me? And if any man should do wrong merely out of ill-nature, why, yet it is but like the thorn or briar, which prick and scratch, because they can do no other. The most tolerable sort of revenge is for those wrongs which there is no law to remedy; but then, let a man take heed the revenge be such as there is no law to punish, else a man's enemy is still before-hand, and it is two for one. Some, when they take revenge, are desirous the party should know whence it cometh. This is the more generous; for the delight seemeth to be not so much in doing the hurt as in making the party repent; but base and crafty cowards are like the arrow that flieth in the dark. Cosmus, Duke of Florence,[1] had a desperate saying against perfidious or neglecting friends, as if those wrongs were unpardonable. "You shall read," saith he, "that we are commanded to forgive our enemies; but you never read that we are commanded to forgive our friends." But yet the spirit of Job was in a better tune: "Shall we," saith he, "take good at God's hands, and not be content to take evil also?"[2] and so of friends in a proportion. This is certain, that a man that studieth revenge keeps his own wounds green, which otherwise would heal and do well. Public revenges[3] are for the most part fortu-

[1] He alludes to Cosmo de Medici, or Cosmo I., chief of the Republic of Florence, the encourager of literature and the fine arts.

[2] Job. ii. 10.—"Shall we receive good at the hand of God, and shall we not receive evil?"

[3] By "public revenges," he means punishment awarded by the state with the sanction of the laws.

nate; as that for the death of Cæsar; [4] for the death
of Pertinax; for the death of Henry the Third of
France; [5] and many more. But in private revenges
it is not so; nay, rather, vindictive persons live the
life of witches, who, as they are mischievous, so end
they unfortunate.

V.—OF ADVERSITY.

It was a high speech of Seneca (after the manner
of the Stoics), that "the good things which belong
to prosperity are to be wished, but the good things
that belong to adversity are to be admired." ("Bona
rerum secundarum optabilia, adversarum mirabilia.")[1]
Certainly, if miracles be the command over nature,
they appear most in adversity. It is yet a higher
speech of his than the other (much too high for a
heathen), "It is true greatness to have in one the
frailty of a man, and the security of a God." ("Vere
magnum habere fragilitatem hominis securitatem
Dei.") [2] This would have done better in poesy,

[4] He alludes to the retribution dealt by Augustus and Anthony
to the murderers of Julius Cæsar. It is related by ancient his-
torians, as a singular fact, that not one of them died a natural
death.

[5] Henry III. of France was assassinated in 1599, by Jacques
Clement, a Jacobin monk, in the frenzy of fanaticism. Although
Clement justly suffered punishment, the end of this bloodthirsty
and bigoted tyrant may be justly deemed a retribution dealt by
the hand of an offended Providence; so truly does the Poet
say:—

> "neque enim lex æquior ulla
> Quam necis artifices arte perire suâ."

[1] Sen. Ad Lucil. 66.

[2] Ibid. 53.

where transcendencies are more allowed, and the poets, indeed, have been busy with it; for it is, in effect, the thing which is figured in that strange fiction of the ancient poets,[3] which seemeth not to be without mystery; nay, and to have some approach to the state of a Christian, "that Hercules, when he went to unbind Prometheus (by whom human nature is represented), sailed the length of the great ocean in an earthen pot or pitcher," lively describing Christian resolution, that saileth in the frail bark of the flesh through the waves of the world. But to speak in a mean, the virtue of prosperity is temperance, the virtue of adversity is fortitude, which in morals is the more heroical virtue. Prosperity is the blessing of the Old Testament, adversity is the blessing of the New, which carrieth the greater benediction, and the clearer revelation of God's favor. Yet even in the Old Testament, if you listen to David's harp, you shall hear as many hearse-like airs[4] as carols; and the pencil of the Holy Ghost hath labored more in de-

[3] Stesichorus, Apollodorus, and others. Lord Bacon makes a similar reference to this myth in his treatise "On the Wisdom of the Ancients." "It is added with great elegance, to console and strengthen the minds of men, that this mighty hero (Hercules) sailed in a cup or 'urceus,' in order that they may not too much fear and allege the narrowness of their nature and its frailty; as if it were not capable of such fortitude and constancy; of which very thing Seneca argued well, when he said, 'It is a great thing to have at the same time the frailty of a man, and the security of a God.'"

[4] Funereal airs. It must be remembered that many of the Psalms of David were written by him when persecuted by Saul, as also in the tribulation caused by the wicked conduct of his son Absalom. Some of them, too, though called "The Psalms of David," were really composed by the Jews in their captivity at Babylon; as, for instance, the 137th Psalm, which so beautifully commences, "By the waters of Babylon there we sat down." One of them is supposed to be the composition of Moses.

scribing the afflictions of Job than the felicities of
Solomon. Prosperity is not without many fears and
distastes; and adversity is not without comforts and
hopes. We see, in needleworks and embroideries, it
is more pleasing to have a lively work upon a sad
and solemn ground, than to have a dark and melancholy work upon a lightsome ground: judge, therefore, of the pleasure of the heart by the pleasure of
the eye. Certainly, virtue is like precious odors,
most fragrant when they are incensed, or crushed;
for prosperity doth best discover vice, but adversity
doth best discover virtue.[5]

VI.—OF SIMULATION AND DISSIMULATION

DISSIMULATION is but a faint kind of policy, or
wisdom; for it asketh a strong wit and a strong heart
to know when to tell truth, and to do it; therefore it
is the weaker sort of politicians that are the great
dissemblers.

Tacitus saith, "Livia sorted well with the arts of
her husband, and dissimulation of her son;[1] attributing arts or policy to Augustus, and dissimulation to
Tiberius:" and again, when Mucianus encourageth
Vespasian to take arms against Vitellius, he saith,

[5] This fine passage, beginning at "Prosperity is the blessing,"
which was not published till 1625, twenty-eight years after the
first Essays, has been quoted by Macaulay, with considerable
justice, as a proof that the writer's fancy did not decay with
the advance of old age, and that his style in his later years
became richer and softer. The learned critic contrasts this
passage with the terse style of the Essay of Studies (Essay 50),
which was published in 1597.

[1] Tac. Ann. v. 1.

`We rise not against the piercing judgment of Augustus, nor the extreme caution or closeness of Tiberius." [2] These properties of arts or policy, and dissimulation or closeness, are indeed habits and faculties several, and to be distinguished; for if a man have that penetration of judgment as he can discern what things are to be laid open, and what to be secreted, and what to be showed at half-lights, and to whom and when (which indeed are arts of state, and arts of life, as Tacitus well calleth them), to him a habit of dissimulation is a hinderance and a poorness. But if a man cannot obtain to that judgment, then it is left to him generally to be close, and a dissembler; for where a man cannot choose or vary in particulars, there it is good to take the safest and wariest way in general, like the going softly by one that cannot well see. Certainly, the ablest men that ever were, have had all an openness and frankness of dealing, and a name of certainty and veracity: but then they were like horses well managed, for they could tell passing well when to stop or turn; and at such times, when they thought the case indeed required dissimulation, if then they used it, it came to pass that the former opinion spread abroad, of their good faith and clearness of dealing, made them almost invisible.

There be three degrees of this hiding and veiling of a man's self: the first, closeness, reservation, and secrecy; when a man leaveth himself without observation, or without hold to be taken, what he is: the second, dissimulation in the negative; when a man lets fall signs and arguments, that he is not that he is: and the third, simulation in the affirmative; when a

[2] Tac. Hist. ii. 76.

man industriously and expressly feigns and pretends
to be that he is not.

For the first of these, secrecy, it is indeed the
virtue of a confessor; and assuredly the secret man
heareth many confessions; for who will open himself
to a blab or a babbler? But if a man be thought
secret, it inviteth discovery, as the more close air
sucketh in the more open; and, as in confession, the
revealing is not for worldly use, but for the ease of a
man's heart, so secret men come to the knowledge of
many things in that kind; while men rather discharge
their minds than impart their minds. In few words,
mysteries are due to secrecy. Besides (to say truth),
nakedness is uncomely, as well in mind as body; and
it addeth no small reverence to men's manners and
actions, if they be not altogether open. As for talkers
and futile persons, they are commonly vain and cred-
ulous withal; for he that talketh what he knoweth,
will also talk what he knoweth not; therefore set it
down, that a habit of secrecy is both politic and
moral: and in this part it is good that a man's face
give his tongue leave to speak; for the discovery of a
man's self by the tracts[3] of his countenance, is a
great weakness and betraying, by how much it is
many times more marked and believed than a man's
words.

For the second, which is dissimulation, it followeth
many times upon secrecy by a necessity; so that he
that will be secret must be a dissembler in some degree; for men are too cunning to suffer a man to
keep an indifferent carriage between both, and to be
secret, without swaying the balance on either side.
They will so beset a man with questions, and draw

[3] A word now unused, signifying the "traits," or "features."

him on, and pick it out of him, that without an absurd silence, he must show an inclination one way; or if he do not, they will gather as much by his silence as by his speech. As for equivocations, or oraculous speeches, they cannot hold out long: so that no man can be secret, except he give himself a little scope of dissimulation, which is, as it were, but the skirts or train of secrecy.

But for the third degree, which is simulation and false profession, that I hold more culpable and less politic, except it be in great and rare matters; and, therefore, a general custom of simulation (which is this last degree) is a vice rising either of a natural falseness, or fearfulness, or of a mind that hath some main faults; which because a man must needs disguise, it maketh him practise simulation in other things, lest his hand should be out of use.

The advantages of simulation and dissimulation are three: first, to lay asleep opposition, and to surprise; for, where a man's intentions are published, it is an alarum to call up all that are against them: the second is, to reserve to a man's self a fair retreat; for if a man engage himself by a manifest declaration, he must go through or take a fall: the third is, the better to discover the mind of another; for to him that opens himself men will hardly show themselves adverse; but will (fair) let him go on, and turn their freedom of speech to freedom of thought; and therefore it is a good shrewd proverb of the Spaniard, "Tell a lie, and find a troth;" [4] as if there were no way of discovery but by simulation. There be also three disadvantages to set it even; the first, that simulation and dissimulation commonly

[4] A truth.—*A. L.* II. xxiii, 14.

carry with them a show of fearfulness, which, in any business, doth spoil the feathers of round flying up to the mark; the second, that it puzzleth and perplexeth the conceits of many, that, perhaps, would otherwise coöperate with him, and makes a man walk almost alone to his own ends: the third, and greatest, is, that it depriveth a man of one of the most principal instruments for action, which is trust and belief. The best composition and temperature is, to have openness in fame and opinion, secrecy in habit, dissimulation in seasonable use, and a power to feign if there be no remedy.

VII.—OF PARENTS AND CHILDREN.

THE joys of parents are secret, and so are their griefs and fears; they cannot utter the one, nor they will not utter the other. Children sweeten labors, but they make misfortunes more bitter; they increase the cares of life, but they mitigate the remembrance of death. The perpetuity by generation is common to beasts; but memory, merit, and noble works, are proper to men: and surely a man shall see the noblest works and foundations have proceeded from childless men, which have sought to express the images of their minds where those of their bodies have failed; so the care of posterity is most in them that have no posterity. They that are the first raisers of their houses are most indulgent towards their children, beholding them as the continuance, not only of their kind, but of their work; and so both children and creatures.

The difference in affection of parents towards their

several children is many times unequal, and sometimes unworthy, especially in the mother; as Solomon saith, "A wise son rejoiceth the father, but an
ungracious son shames the mother." [1] A man shall
see, where there is a house full of children, one or two
of the eldest respected, and the youngest made wan-
tons; [2] but in the midst some that are, as it were,
forgotten, who many times, nevertheless, prove the
best. The illiberality of parents, in allowance towards their children, is a harmful error, makes them
base, acquaints them with shifts, makes them sort
with mean company, and makes them surfeit more
when they come to plenty; and, therefore the proof [3]
is best when men keep their authority towards their
children, but not their purse. Men have a foolish
manner (both parents, and schoolmasters, and servants), in creating and breeding an emulation between brothers during childhood, which many times
sorteth [4] to discord when they are men, and disturbeth
families. [5] The Italians make little difference between
children and nephews, or near kinsfolk; but so they
be of the lump, they care not, though they pass not
through their own body; and, to say truth, in nature

[1] Proverbs x. 1: "A wise son maketh a glad father, but a foolish son is the heaviness of his mother."
[2] Petted—spoiled.
[3] This word seems here to mean "a plan," or "method," as
proved by its results.
[4] Ends in.
[5] There is considerable justice in this remark. Children should
be taught to do what is right for its own sake, and because it is
their duty to do so, and not that they may have the selfish
gratification of obtaining the reward which their companions
have failed to secure, and of being led to think themselves superior to their companions. When launched upon the world, emulation will be quite sufficiently forced upon them by stern
necessity.

it is much a like matter; insomuch that we see a nephew sometimes resembleth an uncle or a kinsman more than his own parent, as the blood happens. Let parents choose betimes the vocations and courses they mean their children should take, for then they are most flexible; and let them not too much apply themselves to the disposition of their children, as thinking they will take best to that which they have most mind to. It is true, that if the affection, or aptness of the children be extraordinary, then it is good not to cross it; but generally the precept is good, "Optimum elige, suave et facile illud faciet consuetudo." [6] —Younger brothers are commonly fortunate, but seldom or never where the elder are disinherited.

VIII.—OF MARRIAGE AND SINGLE LIFE.

He that hath wife and children hath given hostages to fortune; for they are impediments to great enterprises, either of virtue or mischief. Certainly the best works, and of greatest merit for the public, have proceeded from the unmarried or childless men, which, both in affection and means, have married and endowed the public. Yet it were great reason that those that have children should have greatest care of future times, unto which they know they must transmit their dearest pledges. Some there are who, though they lead a single life, yet their thoughts do end with themselves, and account future times impertinences;

[6] "Select *that course of life* which is the most advantageous; habit will soon render it pleasant and easily endured."

nay, there are some other that account wife and children but as bills of charges; nay more, there are some
foolish, rich, covetous men, that take a pride in having no children, because they may be thought so
much the richer; for, perhaps they have heard some
talk, "Such an one is a great rich man," and another
except to it, "Yea, but he hath a great charge of children;" as if it were an abatement to his riches.   But
the most ordinary cause of a single life is liberty, especially in certain self-pleasing and humorous minds,
which are so sensible of every restraint, as they will
go near to think their girdles and garters to be bonds
and shackles.   Unmarried men are best friends, best
masters, best servants; but not always best subjects,
for they are light to run away, and almost all fugi-
tives are of that condition.   A single life doth well
with churchmen, for charity will hardly water the
ground where it must first fill a pool.[1]   It is indifferent for judges and magistrates; for if they be facile
and corrupt, you shall have a servant five times worse
than a wife.   For soldiers, I find the generals commonly, in their hortatives, put men in mind of their
wives and children; and I think the despising of marriage amongst the Turks maketh the vulgar soldier
more base.   Certainly, wife and children are a kind
of discipline of humanity; and single men, though they
be many times more charitable, because their means
are less exhaust, yet, on the other side, they are more
cruel and hard-hearted (good to make severe inquisi-
tors), because their tenderness is not so oft called
upon.   Grave natures, led by custom, and therefore

[1] His meaning is, that if clergymen have the expenses of a
family to support, they will hardly find means for the exercise
of benevolence toward their parishioners.

constant, are commonly loving husbands, as was said
of Ulysses, "Vetulam suam praetulit immortalitati."[2]
Chaste women are often proud and froward, as pre-
suming upon the merit of their chastity. It is one of
the best bonds, both of chastity and obedience, in the
wife, if she think her husband wise, which she will
never do if she find him jealous. Wives are young
men's mistresses, companions for middle age, and old
men's nurses, so as a man may have a quarrel[3] to
marry when he will; but yet he was reputed one of the
wise men that made answer to the question when a
man should marry, "A young man not yet, an older
man not at all."[4] It is often seen that bad husbands
have very good wives; whether it be that it raiseth the
price of their husbands' kindness when it comes, or
that the wives take a pride in their patience; but this
never fails, if the bad husbands were of their own
choosing, against their friends' consent, for then they
will be sure to make good their own folly.

IX.—OF ENVY.

THERE be none of the affections which have been
noted to fascinate or bewitch, but love and envy.
They both have vehement wishes; they frame themselves readily into imaginations and suggestions, and
they come easily into the eye, especially upon the
presence of the objects which are the points that conduce to fascination, if any such thing there be. We

[2] "He preferred his aged wife Penelope to immortality." This
was when Ulysses was entreated by the goddess Calypso to give
up all thoughts of returning to Ithaca, and to remain with her
in the enjoyment of immortality.—*Plut. Gryll.* 1.

[3] "May have a pretext," or "excuse."

[4] Thales, *Vide* Diog. Laert. i. 26.

see, likewise, the Scripture calleth envy an evil eye;[1] and the astrologers call the evil influences of the stars evil aspects; so that still there seemeth to be acknowledged, in the act of envy, an ejaculation, or irradiation of the eye; nay, some have been so curious as to note that the times, when the stroke or percussion of an envious eye doth most hurt, are, when the party envied is beheld in glory or triumph, for that sets an edge upon envy; and besides, at such times, the spirits of the person envied do come forth most into the outward parts, and so meet the blow.

But, leaving these curiosities (though not unworthy to be thought on in fit place), we will handle what persons are apt to envy others; what persons are most subject to be envied themselves; and what is the difference between public and private envy.

A man that hath no virtue in himself, ever envieth virtue in others; for men's minds will either feed upon their own good, or upon others' evil; and who wanteth the one will prey upon the other; and whoso is out of hope to attain to another's virtue, will seek to come at even hand[2] by depressing another's fortune.

A man that is busy and inquisitive, is commonly envious; for to know much of other men's matters cannot be, because all that ado may concern his own es-

[1] So prevalent in ancient times was the notion of the injurious effects of the eye of envy, that, in common parlance, the Romans generally used the word *"præfiscini,"*—"without risk of enchantment," or "fascination," when they spoke in high terms of themselves. They supposed that they thereby averted the effects of enchantment produced by the evil eye of any envious person who might at that moment possibly be looking upon them. Lord Bacon probably here alludes to St. Mark vii. 21, 22: "Out of the heart of men proceedeth—deceit, lasciviousness, an evil eye." Solomon also speaks of the evil eye, Prov. xxiii. 6, and xxviii. 22.

[2] To be even with him.

tate; therefore, it must needs be that he taketh a kind
of play-pleasure in looking upon the fortunes of
others; neither can he that mindeth but his own business find much matter for envy; for envy is a gadding
passion, and walketh the streets, and doth not keep
home: "Non est curiosus, quin idem sit malevolus." [3]

Men of noble birth are noted to be envious towards
new men when they rise, for the distance is altered;
and it is like a deceit of the eye, that when others come
on they think themselves go back.

Deformed persons and eunuchs, and old men and
bastards, are envious; for he that cannot possibly
mend his own case, will do what he can to impair another's; except these defects light upon a very brave
and heroical nature, which thinketh to make his natural wants part of his honor; in that it should be said,
"That a eunuch, or a lame man, did such great matters," affecting the honor of a miracle; as it was in
Narses[4] the eunuch, and Agesilaus and Tamerlane,[5]
that were lame men.

[3] "There is no person a busybody, but what he is ill-natured
too." This passage is from the Stichus of Plaütus.

[4] Narses superseded Belisarius in the command of the armies
of Italy, by the orders of the Emperor Justinian. He defeated
Totila, the king of the Goths (who had taken Rome), in a deci-
sive engagement, in which the latter was slain. He governed
Italy with consummate ability for thirteen years, when he was
ungratefully recalled by Justin the Second, the successor of
Justinian.

[5] Tamerlane, or Timour, was a native of Samarcand, of which
territory he was elected emperor. He overran Persia, Georgia,
Hindostan, and captured Bajazet, the valiant Sultan of the
Turks, at the battle of Angora, 1402, whom he is said to have
inclosed in a cage of iron. His conquests extended from the
Irish and Volga to the Persian Gulf, and from the Ganges to
the Grecian Archipelago. While preparing for the invasion of
China, he died, in the 70th year of his age, A. D. 1405. He was
tall and corpulent in person, but was maimed in one hand, and
lame on the right side.

The same is the case of men that rise after calamities and misfortunes; for they are as men fallen out with the times, and think other men's harms a redemption of their own sufferings.

They that desire to excel in too many matters, out of levity and vainglory, are ever envious, for they cannot want work; it being impossible but many, in some one of those things, should surpass them; which was the character of Adrian the emperor, that mortally envied poets and painters, and artificers in works, wherein he had a vein to excel.[6]

Lastly, near kinsfolk and fellows in office, and those that have been bred together, are more apt to envy their equals when they are raised; for it doth upbraid unto them their own fortunes, and pointeth at them, and cometh oftener into their remembrance, and incurreth likewise more into the note[7] of others; and envy ever redoubleth from speech and fame. Cain's envy was the more vile and malignant towards his brother Abel, because when his sacrifice was better accepted, there was nobody to look on. Thus much for those that are apt to envy.

Concerning those that are more or less subject to envy: First, persons of eminent virtue, when they are advanced, are less envied, for their fortune seemeth but due unto them; and no man envieth the payment of a debt, but rewards and liberality rather. Again, envy is ever joined with the comparing of a man's self; and where there is no comparison, no envy; and therefore kings are not envied but by kings. Nevertheless, it is to be noted, that unworthy persons are most envied at their first coming in, and after-

[6] Spartian Vit. Adrian, 15.
[7] Comes under the observation.

wards overcome it better; whereas, contrariwise, persons of worth and merit are most envied when their
fortune continueth long; for by that time, though their
virtue be the same, yet it hath not the same lustre;
for fresh men grow up that darken it.

Persons of noble blood are less envied in their rising; for it seemeth but right done to their birth: besides, there seemeth not so much added to their fortune; and envy is as the sunbeams, that beat hotter
upon a bank or steep rising ground, than upon a flat;
and, for the same reason, those that are advanced by
degrees are less envied than those that are advanced
suddenly, and *per saltum.*[8]

Those that have joined with their honor great
travels, cares, or perils, are less subject to envy; for
men think that they earn their honors hardly, and pity
them sometimes, and pity ever healeth envy. Where-
fore you shall observe, that the more deep and sober
sort of politic persons, in their greatness, are ever be-
moaning themselves what a life they lead, chanting
a quanta patimur;[9] not that they feel it so, but only to
abate the edge of envy; but this is to be understood
of business that is laid upon men, and not such as they
call unto themselves; for nothing increaseth envy
more than an unnecessary and ambitious engrossing
of business; and nothing doth extinguish envy more
than for a great person to preserve all other inferior
officers in their full rights and preëminences of their
places; for, by that means, there be so many screens
between him and envy.

Above all, those are most subject to envy, which
carry the greatness of their fortunes in an insolent and

[8] "By a leap," *i.e.* over the heads of others.
[9] "How vast *the evils* we endure."

proud manner; being never well but while they are showing how great they are, either by outward pomp, or by triumphing over all opposition or competition. Whereas wise men will rather do sacrifice to envy, in suffering themselves, sometimes of purpose, to be crossed and overborne in things that do not much concern them. Notwithstanding, so much is true, that the carriage of greatness in a plain and open manner (so it be without arrogancy and vainglory), doth draw less envy than if it be in a more crafty and cunning fashion; for in that course a man doth but disavow fortune, and seemeth to be conscious of his own want in worth, and doth but teach others to envy him.

Lastly, to conclude this part, as we said in the beginning that the act of envy had somewhat in it of witchcraft, so there is no other cure of envy but the cure of witchcraft; and that is, to remove the lot (as they call it), and to lay it upon another; for which purpose, the wiser sort of great persons bring in ever upon the stage somebody upon whom to derive the envy that would come upon themselves; sometimes upon ministers and servants, sometimes upon colleagues and associates, and the like; and, for that turn, there are never wanting some persons of violent and undertaking natures, who, so they may have power and business, will take it at any cost.

Now, to speak of public envy: there is yet some good in public envy, whereas in private there is none; for public envy is as an ostracism,[10] that eclipseth men when they grow too great; and therefore it is a bridle also to great ones, to keep them within bounds.

[10] He probably alludes to the custom of the Athenians, who frequently ostracized or banished by vote their public men, lest they should become too powerful.

This envy, being in the Latin word *invidia*,[11] goeth in the modern languages by the name of discontentment, of which we shall speak in handling sedition. It is a disease in a state like to infection; for as infection spreadeth upon that which is sound, and tainteth it, so, when envy is gotten once into a state, it traduceth even the best actions thereof, and turneth them into an ill odor; and therefore there is little won by intermingling of plausible actions; for that doth argue but a weakness and fear of envy, which hurteth so much the more, as it is likewise usual in infections, which, if you fear them, you call them upon you.

This public envy seemeth to beat chiefly upon principal officers or ministers, rather than upon kings and estates themselves. But this is a sure rule, that if the envy upon the minister be great, when the cause of it in him is small; or if the envy be general in a manner upon all the ministers of an estate, then the envy (though hidden) is truly upon the state itself. And so much of public envy or discontentment, and the difference thereof from private envy, which was handled in the first place.

We will add this in general, touching the affection of envy, that, of all other affections, it is the most importune and continual; for of other affections there is occasion given but now and then; and therefore it was well said, "Invidia festos dies non agit:" [12] for it is ever working upon some or other. And it is also noted, that love and envy do make a man pine, which other affections do not, because they are not so continual. It is also the vilest affection, and the most

---

[11] From *in* and *video*,—"to look upon;" with reference to the so-called "evil eye" of the envious.

[12] "Envy keeps no holidays."

depraved; for which cause it is the proper attribute of the devil, who is called "The envious man, that soweth tares amongst the wheat by night;"[13] as it always cometh to pass that envy worketh subtilely, and in the dark, and to the prejudice of good things, such as is the wheat.

X.—OF LOVE.

THE stage is more beholding[1] to love than the life of man; for as to the stage, love is ever matter of comedies, and now and then of tragedies; but in life it doth much mischief, sometimes like a Siren, sometimes like a Fury. You may observe, that, amongst all the great and worthy persons (whereof the memory remaineth, either ancient or recent), there is not one that hath been transported to the mad degree of love, which shows that great spirits and great business do keep out this weak passion. You must except, nevertheless, Marcus Antonius, the half partner of the empire of Rome, and Appius Claudius,[2] the decemvir and lawgiver; whereof the former was indeed a voluptuous man, and inordinate, but the latter was an austere and wise man; and therefore it seems (though rarely) that love can find entrance, not only into an open heart, but also into a heart well fortified, if watch

[13] See St. Matthew xiii. 25.

[1] Beholden.

[2] He iniquitously attempted to obtain possession of the person of Virginia, who was killed by her father Virginius, to prevent her from falling a victim to his lust. This circumstance caused the fall of the Decemviri at Rome, who had been employed in framing the code of laws afterwards known as "The Laws of the Twelve Tables." They narrowly escaped being burned alive by the infuriated populace.

be not well kept. It is a poor saying of Epicurus, "Satis magnum alter alteri theatrum sumus;"[3] as if man, made for the contemplation of heaven and all noble objects, should do nothing but kneel before a little idol, and make himself subject, though not of the mouth (as beasts are) yet of the eye, which was given him for higher purposes. It is a strange thing to note the excess of this passion, and how it braves the nature and value of things, by this, that the speaking in a perpetual hyberbole is comely in nothing but in love, neither is it merely in the phrase; for whereas it hath been well said, "That the arch flatterer, with whom all the petty flatterers have intelligence, is a man's self;" certainly, the lover is more; for there was never proud man thought so absurdly well of himself as the lover doth of the person loved; and therefore it was well said, "That it is impossible to love and to be wise."[4] Neither doth this weakness appear to others only, and not to the party loved, but to the loved most of all, except the love be reciprocal; for it is a true rule, that love is ever rewarded, either with the reciprocal, or with an inward and secret contempt; by how much the more men ought to beware of this passion, which loseth not only other things, but itself. As for

[3] "We are a sufficient theme for contemplation, the one for the other."—*Sen. Epist. Mor.* 1. 7. (A. L. l. iii. 6.) Pope seems, notwithstanding this censure of Bacon, to have been of the same opinion with Epicurus:—

"Know then thyself, presume not God to scan,
The proper study for mankind is man."
Essay on Man, Ep. ii. 1. 2.

Indeed, Lord Bacon seems to have misunderstood the saying of Epicurus, who did not mean to recommend man as the sole object of the bodily vision, but as the proper theme for mental contemplation.

[4] Amare et sapere vix Deo conceditur.—*Pub. Syr. Sent.* 15. A. L. ii. proœ. 10.)

the other losses, the poet's relation[5] doth well figure
them: "That he that preferred Helena, quitted the
gifts of Juno and Pallas;" for whosoever esteemeth
too much of armorous affection, quitteth both riches
and wisdom. This passion hath his floods in the very
times of weakness, which are, great prosperity and
great adversity, though this latter hath been less observed; both which times kindle love, and make it
more fervent, and therefore show it to be the child of
folly. They do best who, if they cannot but admit
love, yet make it keep quarter, and sever it wholly
from their serious affairs and actions of life; for if it
check once with business, it troubleth men's fortunes,
and maketh men that they can nowise be true to their
own ends. I know not how, but martial men are given
to love; I think it is, but as they are given to wine,
for perils commonly ask to be paid in pleasures. There
is in man's nature a secret inclination and motion towards love of others, which, if it be not spent upon
some one or a few, doth naturally spread itself towards many, and maketh men become humane and
charitable, as it is seen sometimes in friars. Nuptial
love maketh mankind, friendly love perfecteth it, but
wanton love corrupteth and embaseth it.

XI.—OF GREAT PLACE.[1]

MEN in great place are thrice servants—servants
of the sovereign or state, servants of fame, and servants of business; so as they have no freedom neither

[5] He refers here to the judgment of Paris, mentioned by Ovid
in his Epistles, of the Heroines.
[1] Montaigne has treated this subject before Bacon, under the
title of *De l'incommodité de la Grandeur* (B. iii. ch. vii.).

in their persons, nor in their actions, nor in their times. It is a strange desire to seek power and to lose liberty; or to seek power over others, and to lose power over a man's self. The rising unto place is laborious, and by pains men come to greater pains: and it is sometimes base, and by indignities men come to dignities. The standing is slippery, and the regress is either a downfall, or at least an eclipse, which is a melancholy thing: "Cum non sis qui fueris, non esse cur velis vivere."[2] Nay, retire men cannot when they would, neither will they when it were reason; but are impatient of privateness even in age and sickness, which require the shadow; like old townsmen, that will be still sitting at their street door, though thereby they offer age to scorn. Certainly, great persons had need to borrow other men's opinions to think themselves happy; for if they judge by their own feeling, they cannot find it; but if they think with themselves what other men think of them, and that other men would fain be as they are, then they are happy as it were by report, when, perhaps, they find the contrary within; for they are the first that find their own griefs, though they be the last that find their own faults. Certainly, men in great fortunes are strangers to themselves, and while they are in the puzzle of business, they have no time to tend their health either of body or mind.

"Illi mors gravis incubat,
Qui notus nimis omnibus,
Ignotus moritur."[3]

[2] "Since you are not what you were, there is no reason why you should wish to live."

[3] "Death presses heavily upon him, who, well known to all others, dies unknown to himself."—*Sen. Thyest.* ii. 401.

In place, there is license to do good and evil, whereof the latter is a curse; for in evil, the best condition is not to will, the second not to can. But power to do good is the true and lawful end of aspiring; for good thoughts, though God accept them, yet towards men are little better than good dreams, except they be put in act; and that cannot be without power and place, as the vantage and commanding ground. Merit and good works are the end of man's motion and conscience of same is the accomplishment of man's rest; if a man can be partaker of God's theatre, he shall likewise be partaker of God's rest. "Et conversus Deus, ut aspiceret opera, quæ fecerunt manus suæ, vidit quod omnia essent bona nimis;"[4] and then the Sabbath.

In the discharge of thy place, set before thee the best examples; for imitation is a globe of precepts, and after a time set before thee thine own example; and examine thyself strictly whether thou didst not best at first. Neglect not also the examples of those that have carried themselves ill in the same place; not to set off thyself by taxing their memory, but to direct thyself what to avoid. Reform, therefore, without bravery or scandal of former times and persons; but yet set it down to thyself, as well to create good precedents as to follow them. Reduce things to the first institution, and observe wherein and how they have degenerated; but yet ask counsel of both times— of the ancient time what is best, and of the latter time what is fittest. Seek to make thy course regular, that men may know beforehand what they may expect; but be not too positive and peremptory, and express

---

[4] "And God turned to behold the works which his hands had made, and he saw that everything was very good."—See *Gen* i. 31.

thyself well when thou digressest from thy rule. **Pre-serve** the right of thy place, but stir not questions of jurisdiction; and rather assume thy right in silence and *de facto*,[5] than voice it with claims and challenges. Preserve likewise the rights of inferior places; and think it more honor to direct in chief than to be busy in all. Embrace and invite helps and advices touch-ing the execution of thy place; and do not drive away such as bring thee information, as meddlers, but ac-cept of them in good part. The vices of authority are chiefly four: delays, corruption, roughness, and fa-cility. For delays, give easy access, keep times appointed, go through with that which is in hand, and interlace not business but of necessity. For corrup-tion, do not only bind thine own hands or thy servant's hands from taking, but bind the hands of suitors also from offering; for integrity used doth the one, but integrity professed, and with a manifest detestation of bribery, doth the other; and avoid not only the fault, but the suspicion. Whosoever is found variable, and changeth manifestly without manifest cause, giv-eth suspicion of corruption; therefore, always when thou changest thine opinion or course, profess it plain-ly, and declare it, together with the reasons that move thee to change, and do not think to steal it. A ser-vant or a favorite, if he be inward, and no other ap-parent cause of esteem, is commonly thought a by-way to close corruption. For roughness is a needless cause of discontent: severity breedeth fear; roughness breed-eth hate. Even reproofs from authority ought to be grave, not taunting. Facility[6] is worse than bribery, for bribes come but now and then; if importunity or idle

[5] "As a matter of course."
[6] Too great easiness of access.

respects[7] lead a man, he shall never be without; as Solomon saith, "To respect persons is not good; for such a
man will transgress for a piece of bread." [8]

It is most true that was anciently spoken: "A place
showeth the man; and it showeth some to the better,
and some to the worse:" "Omnium consensu capax
imperii, nisi imperasset," [9] saith Tacitus of Galba;
but of Vespasian he saith, "Solus imperantium, Vespasianus mutatus in melius;" [10] though the one was
meant of sufficiency, the other of manners and affection. It is an assured sign of a worthy and generous
spirit, whom honor amends; for honor is, or should be,
the place of virtue; and as in nature things move violently to their place, and calmly in their place, so
virtue in ambition is violent, in authority settled and
calm. All rising to great place is by a winding stair;
and if there be factions, it is good to side a man's self
whilst he is in the rising, and to balance himself when
he is placed. Use the memory of thy predecessor
fairly and tenderly; for if thou dost not, it is a debt
will sure be paid when thou art gone. If thou have
colleagues, respect them; and rather call them when
they look not for it, than exclude them when they
have reason to look to be called. Be not too sensible
or too remembering of thy place in conversation and
private answers to suitors; but let it rather be said,
"When he sits in place, he is another man."

[7] Predilections that are undeserved.

[8] Proverbs xxviii. 21. The whole passage stands thus in our
version: "He that maketh haste to be rich shall not be innocent. To have respect of persons is not good; for, for a piece
of bread, that man will transgress."

[9] "By the consent of all he was fit to govern, if he had not
governed."

[10] "Of the emperors, Vespasian alone changed for the better
after his accession."—Tac. Hist. i. 49, 50 (A. L. ii. xxi. 5).

XII.—OF BOLDNESS.

It is a trivial grammar-school text, but yet worthy a wise man's consideration. Question was asked of Demosthenes, what was the chief part of an orator? He answered, Action. What next?—Action. What next again?—Action.[1] He said it that knew it best, and had, by nature, himself no advantage in that he commended. A strange thing, that that part of an orator which is but superficial, and rather the virtue of a player, should be placed so high above those other noble parts of invention, elocution, and the rest; nay, almost alone, as if it were all in all. But the reason is plain. There is in human nature generally more of the fool than of the wise; and therefore, those faculties by which the foolish part of men's minds is taken are most potent. Wonderful like is the case of boldness in civil business. What first?—Boldness: what second and third?—Boldness. And yet boldness is a child of ignorance and baseness, far inferior to other parts; but, nevertheless, it doth fascinate, and bind hand and foot those that are either shallow in judgment or weak in courage, which are the greatest part, yea, and prevaileth with wise man at weak times; therefore, we see it hath done wonders in popular states, but with senates and princes less, and more, ever upon the first entrance of bold persons into action than soon after; for boldness is an ill keeper of promise. Surely, as there are mountebanks for the natural body, so are there mountebanks for the politic body; men that undertake great cures, and perhaps have been lucky in two or three experiments, but want the

[1] Plut. vit. Demosth. 17. 18.

grounds of science, and therefore cannot hold out; nay, you shall see a bold fellow many times do Mahomet's miracle. Mahomet made the people believe that he would call a hill to him, and from the top of it offer up his prayers for the observers of his law. The people assembled; Mahomet called the hill to come to him again and again; and when the hill stood still, he was never a whit abashed, but said, "If the hill will not come to Mahomet, Mahomet will go to the hill." So these men, when they have promised great matters and failed most shamefully, yet if they have the perfection of boldness, they will but slight it over, and make a turn, and no more ado. Certainly, to men of great judgment, bold persons are a sport to behold; nay, and to the vulgar also boldness hath somewhat of the ridiculous; for if absurdity be the subject of laughter, doubt you not but great boldness is seldom without some absurdity; especially it is a sport to see when a bold fellow is out of countenance, for that puts his face into a most shrunken and wooden posture, as needs it must; for in bashfulness the spirits do a little go and come, but with bold men, upon like occasion, they stand at a stay; like a stale at chess, where it is no mate, but yet the game cannot stir; but this last were fitter for a satire than for a serious observation. This is well to be weighed, that boldness is ever blind, for it seeth not dangers and inconveniences; therefore, it is ill in counsel, good in execution; so that the right use of bold persons is, that they never command in chief, but be seconds and under the direction of others; for in counsel it is good to see dangers; and in execution not to see them except they be very great.

XIII.—OF GOODNESS, AND GOODNESS OF NATURE.

I TAKE goodness in this sense, the affecting of the weal of men, which is what the Grecians call *philanthropia;* and the word humanity, as it is used, is a little too light to express it. Goodness I call the habit, and goodness of nature the inclination. This, of all virtues and dignities of the mind, is the greatest, being the character of the Deity; and without it man is a busy, mischievous, wretched thing, no better than a kind of vermin. Goodness answers to the theological virtue charity, and admits no excess but error. The desire of power in excess caused the angels to fall;[1] the desire of knowledge in excess caused man to fall; but in charity there is no excess, neither can angel or man come in danger by it. The inclination to goodness is imprinted deeply in the nature of man, insomuch that if it issue not towards men, it will take unto other living creatures; as it is seen in the Turks, a cruel people, who nevertheless are kind to beasts, and give alms to dogs and birds; insomuch, as Busbechius[2] reporteth, a Christian boy in Constantinople

[1] It is not improbable that this passage suggested Pope's beautiful lines in the *Essay on Man,* Ep. i. 125-28.
"Pride still is aiming at the blest abodes,
Men would be angels, angels would be gods.
Aspiring to be gods, if angels fell,
Aspiring to be angels, men rebel."
[2] Auger Gislen Busbec, or Busbequius, a learned traveller, born at Comines, in Flanders, in 1522. He was employed by the Emperor Ferdinand as ambassador to the Sultan Solyman II. He was afterwards ambassador to France, where he died, in 1592. His "Letters" relative to his travels in the East, which are written in Latin, contain much interesting information. They were the pocket companion of Gibbon, and are highly praised by him.

had like to have been stoned for gagging in a wag-
gishness a long-billed fowl.[3] Errors, indeed, in this
virtue, of goodness or charity, may be committed.
The Italians have an ungracious proverb: "Tanto
buon che val niente;" "So good, that he is good for
nothing;" and one of the doctors of Italy, Nicholas
Machiavel,[4] had the confidence to put in writing, almost in plain terms, "That the Christian faith had
given up good men in prey to those that are tyran-

[3] In this instance the stork or crane was probably protected,
not on the abstract grounds mentioned in the text, but for
reasons of state policy and gratitude combined. In Eastern cli-
mates the cranes and dogs are far more efficacious than human
agency in removing filth and offal, and thereby diminishing the
chances of pestilence. Superstition, also, may have formed another motive, as we learn from a letter written from Adrianople,
by Lady Montagu, in 1718, that storks were "held there in a
sort of religious reverence, because they are supposed to make
every winter the pilgrimage to Mecca. To say truth, they are
the happiest subjects under the Turkish government, and are so
sensible of their privileges, that they walk the streets without
fear, and generally build their nests in the lower parts of the
houses. Happy are those whose houses are so distinguished, as
the vulgar Turks are perfectly persuaded that they will not be
that year attacked either by fire or pestilence." Storks are still
protected, by municipal law, in Holland, and roam unmolested
about the market-places.

[4] Nicolo Machiavelli, a Florentine statesman. He wrote "Discourses on the first Decade of Livy," which were conspicuous
for their liberality of sentiment, and just and profound reflec-
tions. This work was succeeded by his famous treatise, "Il
Principe," "The Prince;" his patrón, Cæsar Borgia, being the
model of the perfect prince there described by him. The whole
scope of this work is directed to one subject—the maintenance
of power, however acquired. Though its precepts are no doubt
based upon the actual practice of the Italian politicians of that
day, it has been suggested by some writers that the work was
a covert exposure of the deformity of the shocking maxims that
it professes to inculcate. The question of his motives has been
much discussed, and is still considered open. The word "Machi-
avellism" has, however, been adopted to denote all that is
deformed, insincere, and perfidious in politics. He died in great
poverty, in the year 1527.

nical and unjust;" [5] which he spake, because, indeed,
there was never law, or sect, or opinion did so much
magnify goodness as the Christian religion doth;
therefore, to avoid the scandal and the danger both,
it is good to take knowledge of the errors of a habit
so excellent. Seek the good of other men, but be not
in bondage to their faces or fancies; for that is but
facility or softness, which taketh an honest mind
prisoner. Neither give thou Æsop's cock a gem, who
would be better pleased and happier if he had had a
barley-corn. The example of God teacheth the lesson
truly: "He sendeth his rain, and maketh his sun to
shine upon the just and the unjust;" [6] but he doth not
rain wealth, nor shine honor and virtues upon men
equally; common benefits are to be communicate with
all, but peculiar benefits with choice. And beware
how, in making the portraiture, thou breakest the
pattern; for divinity maketh the love of ourselves the
pattern, the love of our neighbors but the portraiture:
"Sell all thou hast, and give it to the poor, and follow
me;" [7] but sell not all thou hast, except thou come and
follow me; that is, except thou have a vocation wherein thou mayest do as much good with little means as
with great; for otherwise, in feeding the streams thou
driest the fountain. Neither is there only a habit of
goodness directed by right reason, but there is in some
men, even in nature, a disposition towards it; as, on

[5] *Vide* Disc. Sop. Liv. ii. 2.
[6] St. Matthew v. 45. "For he maketh his sun rise on the evil
and on the good, and sendeth rain on the just and on the unjust."
[7] This is a portion of our Saviour's reply to the rich man who
asked him what he should do to inherit eternal life: "Then Jesus
beholding him, loved him, and said unto him, One thing thou
lackest: go thy way, sell whatsoever thou hast, and give to the
poor, and thou shalt have treasure in heaven; and come, take up
the cross, and follow me."—*St. Mark* x. 21.

the other side, there is a natural malignity, for there
be that in their nature do not affect the good of others.
The lighter sort of malignity turneth but to a cross-
ness, or forwardness, or aptness to oppose, or difficile-
ness, or the like; but the deeper sort to envy, and mere
mischief. Such men in other men's calamities are, as
it were, in season, and are ever on the loading part;
not so good as the dogs that licked Lazarus's sores,[8]
but like flies that are still buzzing upon any thing
that is raw; misanthropi, that make it their practice
to bring men to the bough, and yet have never a tree
for the purpose in their gardens, as Timon[9] had. Such
dispositions are the very errors of human nature, and
yet they are the fittest timber to make great politics
of; like to knee timber,[10] that is good for ships that
are ordained to be tossed, but not for building houses
that shall stand firm. The parts and signs of goodness
are many. If a man be gracious and courteous to
strangers, it shows he is a citzen of the world, and
that his heart is no island cut off from other lands,
but a continent that joins to them; if he be compas-
sionate towards the afflictions of others, it shows that

---

[8] See St. Luke xvi. 21.

[9] Timon of Athens, as he is generally called (being so styled
by Shakespeare in the play which he has founded on his story),
was surnamed the "Misanthrope," from the hatred which he bore
to his fellow-men. He was attached to Apemantus, another
Athenian of similar character to himself, and he professed to
esteem Alcibiades, because he foresaw that he would one day
bring ruin on his country. Going to the public assembly on one
occasion, he mounted the rostrum, and stated that he had a
fig-tree, on which many worthy citizens had ended their days by
the halter; that he was going to cut it down for the purpose
of building on the spot, and therefore recommended all such as
were inclined, to avail themselves of it before it was too late.

[10] A piece of timber that has grown crooked, and has been so
cut that the trunk and branch form an angle.

his heart is like the noble tree that is wounded itself
when it gives the balm;[11] if he easily pardons and re-
mits offences, it shows that his mind is planted above
injuries, so that he cannot be shot; if he be thankful
for small benefits, it shows that he weighs men's
minds, and not their trash; but, above all, if he have
St. Paul's perfection, that he would wish to be an
anathema[12] from Christ for the salvation of his breth-
ren, it shows much of a divine nature, and a kind of
conformity with Christ himself.

XIV.—OF NOBILITY.

WE will speak of nobility, first, as a portion of an
estate, then as a condition of particular persons. A
monarchy, where there is no nobility at all, is ever a
pure and absolute tyranny as that of the Turks; for
nobility attempers sovereignty, and draws the eyes
of the people somewhat aside from the line royal:
but for democracies they need it not; and they are
commonly more quiet and less subject to sedition
than where there are stirps of nobles; for men's eyes
are upon the business, and not upon the persons; or
if upon the persons, it is for the business sake, as fittest, and not for flags and pedigree. We see the
Switzers last well, notwithstanding their diversity of

[11] He probably here refers to the myrrh-tree. Incision is the
method usually adopted for extracting the resinous juices of
trees; as in the India-rubber and gutta-percha trees.

[12] "A votive," and, in the present instance, a "vicarious offering." He alludes to the words of St. Paul in his Second Epistle
to Timothy ii. 10: "Therefore I endure all things for the elect's
sake, that they may also obtain the salvation which is in Christ
Jesus with eternal glory."

religion and of cantons; for utility is their bond, and not respects.[1] The United Provinces of the Low Countries[2] in their government excel; for where there is an equality the consultations are more indifferent, and the payments and tributes more cheerful. A great and potent nobility addeth majesty to a monarch, but diminisheth power, and putteth life and spirit into the people, but presseth their fortune. It is well when nobles are not too great for sovereignty nor for justice; and yet maintained in that height, as the insolency of inferiors may be broken upon them, before it come on too fast upon the majesty of kings. A numerous nobility causeth poverty and inconvenience in a state, for it is a surcharge of expense; and besides, it being of necessity that many of the nobility fall in time to be weak in fortune, it maketh a kind of disproportion between honor and means.

As for nobility in particular persons, it is a reverend thing to see an ancient castle or building not in decay, or to see a fair timber-tree sound and perfect; how much more to behold an ancient noble family, which hath stood against the waves and weathers of time! For new nobility is but the act of power, but ancient nobility is the act of time. Those that are first raised to nobility are commonly more virtuous,[3] but less innocent than their descendants; for there is rarely any rising but by a commixture of good and

[1] Consideration of, or predilection for, particular persons.

[2] The Low Countries had then recently emancipated themselves from the galling yoke of Spain. They were called the Seven United Provinces of the Netherlands.

[3] This passage may at first sight appear somewhat contradictory; but he means to say, that those who are first ennobled will commonly be found more conspicuous for the prominence of their qualities, both good and bad.

evil arts; but it is reason the memory of their virtues
remain to their posterity, and their faults die with
themselves. Nobility of birth commonly abateth industry, and he that is not industrious, envieth him
that is; besides, noble persons cannot go much higher;
and he that standeth at a stay when others rise, can
hardly avoid motions of envy. On the other side, nobility extinguisheth the passive envy from others towards them, because they are in possession of honor.
Certainly, kings that have able men of their nobility
shall find ease in employing them, and a better slide
into their business; for people naturally bend to them,
as born in some sort to command.

XV.—OF SEDITIONS AND TROUBLES.

SHEPHERDS of people had need know the calendars
of tempests in state, which are commonly greatest
when things grow to equality; as natural tempests
are greatest about the equinoctia,[1] and as there are
certain hollow blasts of wind and secret swellings of
seas before a tempest, so are there in states:—

> "Ille etiam cæcos instare tumultus
> Sæpe monet, fraudesque et operta tumescere bella."[2]

Libels and licentious discourses against the state,
when they are frequent and open; and in like sort
false news, often running up and down, to the disadvantage of the state, and hastily embraced, are

[1] The periods of the Equinoxes.
[2] "He often warns, too, that secret revolt is impending, that
treachery and open warfare are ready to burst forth."—*Virg.
Georg.* i. 465.

amongst the signs of troubles. Virgil, giving the pedigree of Fame, saith she was sister to the giants:—

"Illam Terra parens, irâ irritata Deorum,
    Extremam (ut perhibent) Cœo Enceladoque sororem
    Progenuit." [3]

As if fames were the relics of seditions past; but
they are no less indeed the preludes of seditions to
come. Howsoever, he noteth it right, that seditious
tumults and seditious fames differ no more but
as brother and sister, masculine and feminine;
especially if it come to that, that the best actions of a state, and the most plausible, and which
ought to give greatest contentment, are taken in ill
sense, and traduced; for that shows the envy great,
as Tacitus saith, "Conflatâ magnâ invidiâ, seu bene,
seu male, gesta premunt." [4] Neither doth it follow,
that because these fames are a sign of troubles, that
the suppressing of them with too much severity should
be a remedy of troubles; for the despising of them
many times checks them best, and the going about to
stop them doth but make a wonder long-lived. Also
that kind of obedience, which Tacitus speaketh of, is
to be held suspected: "Erant in officio, sed tamen qui
mallent imperantium mandata interpretari, quam
exsequi;" [5] disputing, excusing, cavilling upon man-

[3] "Mother Earth, exasperated at the wrath of the Deities, produced her, as they tell, a last birth, a sister to the giants Cœus,
and Enceladus."—*Virg. Æn.* iv. 179.

[4] "Great public odium once excited, his deeds, whether good
or whether bad, cause his downfall." Bacon has here quoted
incorrectly, probably from memory. The words of Tacitus are
(*Hist.* B. i. C. 7): "Inviso semel principe, seu bene, seu male,
facta premunt,"—"The ruler once detested, his actions, whether
good or whether bad, cause his downfall."

[5] "They attended to their duties; but still, as preferring rather
to discuss the commands of their rulers, than to obey them."—
Tac. Hist. i.. 39.

dates and directions, is a kind of shaking off the yoke, and assay of disobedience; especially if, in those disputings, they which are for the direction speak fearfully and tenderly, and those that are against it audaciously.

Also, as Machiavel noteth well, when princes, that ought to be common parents, make themselves as a party, and lean to a side; it is as a boat that is overthrown by uneven weight on the one side, as was well seen in the time of Henry the Third of France; for first himself entered league[6] for the extirpation of the Protestants, and presently after the same league was turned upon himself; for when the authority of princes is made but an accessory to a cause, and that there be other bands that tie faster than the band of sovereignty, kings begin to be put almost out of possession.

Also, when discords, and quarrels, and factions are carried openly and audaciously, it is a sign the reverence of government is lost; for the motions of the greatest persons in a government ought to be as the motions of the planets under "primum mobile," [7] according to the old opinion, which is, that everyone of them is carried swiftly by the highest motion, and softly in their own motion; and therefore, when great ones in their own particular motion move violently,

[6] He alludes to the bad policy of Henry the Third of France, who espoused the part of "The League," which was formed by the Duke of Guise and other Catholics for the extirpation of the Protestant faith. When too late he discovered his error, and finding his own authority entirely superseded, he caused the Duke of Guise and the Cardinal De Lorraine, his brother, to be assassinated.

[7] "The primary motive power." He alludes to an imaginary centre of gravitation, or central body, which was supposed to set all the other heavenly bodies in motion.

and as Tacitus expresseth it well, "liberius quam ut imperantium meminissent,"[8] it is a sign the orbs are out of frame; for reverence is that wherewith princes are girt from God, who threateneth the dissolving thereof: "Solvam cingula regum."[9]

So when one of the four pillars of government are mainly shaken or weakened (which are religion, justice, counsel, and treasure), men had need to pray for fair weather. But let us pass from this part of predictions (concerning which, nevertheless, more light may be taken from that which followeth), and let us speak first of the materials of seditions: then of the motives of them; and thirdly of the remedies.

Concerning the materials of seditions, it is a thing well to be considered, for the surest way to prevent seditions (if the times do bear it), is to take away the matter of them; for if there be fuel prepared, it is hard to tell whence the spark shall come that shall set it on fire. The matter of seditions is of two kinds, much poverty and much discontentment. It is certain, so many overthrown estates, so many votes for troubles. Lucan noteth well the state of Rome before the civil war:—

> "Hinc usura vorax, rapidumque in tempore fœnus,
> Hinc concussa fides, et multis utile bellum."[10]

This same "multis utile bellum,"[11] is an assured and

---

[8] "Too freely to remember their own rulers."

[9] "I will unloose the girdles of kings." He probably alludes here to the first verse of the 45th chapter of Isaiah: "Thus saith the Lord to his anointed, to Cyrus, whose right hand I have holden, to subdue nations before him; and I will loose the loins of kings, to open before him the two-leaved gates."

[10] "Hence devouring usury, and interest accumulating in lapse of time; hence shaken credit, and warfare, profitable to the many."—*Lucan. Phars.* i. 181.

[11] "Warfare profitable to the many."

infallible sign of a state disposed to seditions and troubles; and if this poverty and broken estate in the better sort be joined with a want and necessity in the mean people, the danger is imminent and great; for the rebellions of the belly are the worst. As for discontentments, they are in the politic body like to humors in the natural, which are apt to gather a preternatural heat and to inflame; and let no prince measure the danger of them by this, whether they be just or unjust; for that were to imagine people to be too reasonable, who do often spurn at their own good; nor yet by this, whether the griefs whereupon they rise be in fact great or small; for they are the most dangerous discontentments where the fear is greater than the feeling: "Dolendi modus, timendi non item." [12] Besides, in great oppressions, the same things that provoke the patience, do withal mate[13] the courage; but in fears it is not so; neither let any prince or state be secure concerning discontentments, because they have been often or have been long, and yet no peril hath ensued; for as it is true that every vapor or fume doth not turn into a storm, so it is nevertheless true that storms, though they blow over divers times, yet may fall at last; and, as the Spanish proverb noteth well, "The cord breaketh at the last by the weakest pull." [14]

The causes and motives of seditions are, innovation in religion, taxes, alteration of laws and customs, breaking of privileges, general oppression, advancement of unworthy persons, strangers, dearths, disbanded soldiers, factions grown desperate, and what-

---

[12] "To grief there is a limit, not so to fear."
[13] "Check," or "daunt."
[14] This is similar to the proverb now in common use: " 'Tis the last feather that breaks the back of the camel."

soever in offending people joineth and knitteth them in a common cause.

For the remedies, there may be some general preservatives, whereof we will speak; as for the just cure, it must answer to the particular disease, and so be left to counsel rather than rule.

The first remedy, or prevention, is to remove, by all means possible, that material cause of sedition whereof we spake, which is, want and poverty in the estate;[15] to which purpose serveth the opening and well-balancing of trade; the cherishing of manufactures; the banishing of idleness; the repressing of waste and excess by sumptuary laws;[16] the improvement and husbanding of the soil; the regulating of prices of things vendible; the moderating of taxes and tributes, and the like. Generally, it is to be foreseen that the population of a kingdom (especially if it be not mown down by wars) do not exceed the stock of the kingdom which should maintain them; neither is the population to be reckoned only by number; for a smaller number, that spend more and earn less, do wear out an estate sooner than a greater number that live lower and gather more. Therefore the multiplying of nobility and other degrees of quality, in an overproportion to the common people, doth speedily bring a state to necessity; and so doth likewise an over-

[15] The state.

[16] Though sumptuary laws are probably just in theory, they have been found impracticable in any other than infant states. Their principle, however, is certainly recognized in such countries as by statutory enactment discountenance gaming. Those who are opposed to such laws upon principle, would do well to look into Bernard Mandeville's "Fable of the Bees," or "Private Vices Public Benefits." The Romans had numerous sumptuary laws, and in the Middle Ages there were many enactments in this country against excess of expenditure upon wearing apparel and the pleasures of the table.

grown clergy, for they bring nothing to the stock;[17] and in like manner, when more are bred scholars than preferments can take off.

It is likewise to be remembered, that, forasmuch as the increase of any estate must be upon the foreigner[18] (for whatsoever is somewhere gotten is somewhere lost), there be but three things which one nation selleth unto another; the commodity, as nature yieldeth it; the manufacture; and the vecture, or carriage; so that, if these three wheels go, wealth will flow as in a spring tide. And it cometh many times to pass, that, "materiam superabit opus," [19] that the work and carriage is more worth than the material, and enricheth a state more; as is notably seen in the Low Countrymen, who have the best mines[20] above ground in the world.

Above all things, good policy is to be used, that the treasure and moneys in a state be not gathered into few hands; for, otherwise, a state may have a great stock, and yet starve. And money is like muck,[21] not good except it be spread. This is done chiefly by suppressing, or, at the least, keeping a strait hand upon the devouring trades of usury, engrossing[22] great pasturages, and the like.

[17] He means that they do not add to the capital of the country.
[18] At the expense of foreign countries.
[19] "The workmanship will surpass the material."—*Ovid, Met.* B. ii. l. 5.
[20] He alludes to the manufactures of the Low Countries.
[21] Like manure.
[22] Sometimes printed *engrossing, great pasturages.* By *engrossing,* is meant the trade of *engrossers*—men who buy up all that can be got of a particular commodity, then raise the price. By *great pasturages* is meant turning corn land into pasture. Of this practice great complaints had been made for near a century before Bacon's time, and a law passed to prevent it.—See *Lord Herbert of Cherbury's History of Henry VIII.*

For removing discontentments, or, at least, the danger of them, there is in every state (as we know) two portions of subjects, the nobles and the commonalty. When one of these is discontent, the danger is not great; for common people are of slow motion, if they be not excited by the greater sort; and the greater sort are of small strength, except the multitude be apt and ready to move of themselves; then is the danger, when the greater sort do but wait for the troubling of the waters amongst the meaner, that then they may declare themselves. The poets feign that the rest of the gods would have bound Jupiter, which he hearing of, by the counsel of Pallas, sent for Briareus, with his hundred hands, to come in to his aid; an emblem, no doubt, to show how safe it is for monarchs to make sure of the good-will of common people.

To give moderate liberty for griefs and discontentments to evaporate (so it be without too great insolency or bravery), is a safe way; for he that turneth the humors back, and maketh the wound bleed inwards, endangereth malign ulcers and pernicious imposthumations.

The part of Epimetheus[23] might well become Prometheus, in the case of discontentments, for there is not a better provision against them. Epimetheus,

[23] The myth of Pandora's box, which is here referred to, is related in the *Works and Days* of Hesiod. Epimetheus was the personification of "Afterthought," while his brother Prometheus represented "Forethought," or prudence. It was not Epimetheus that opened the box, but Pandora—"All-gift," whom, contrary to the advice of his brother, he had received at the hands of Mercury, and had made his wife. In their house stood a closed jar, which they were forbidden to open. Till her arrival, this had been kept untouched; but her curiosity prompting her to open the lid, all the evils hitherto unknown to man flew out and spread over the earth, and she only shut it down in time to prevent the escape of Hope.

when griefs and evils flew abroad, at last shut the lid, and kept Hope in the bottom of the vessel. Certainly, the politic and artificial nourishing and entertaining of hopes, and carrying men from hopes to hopes, is one of the best antidotes against the poison of discontentments; and it is a certain sign of a wise government and proceeding, when it can hold men's hearts by hopes, when it cannot by satisfaction; and when it can handle things in such manner as no evil shall appear so peremptory, but that it hath some outlet of hope; which is the less hard to do, because both particular persons and factions are apt enough to flatter themselves, or at least to brave that which they believe not.

Also the foresight and prevention, that there be no likely or fit head whereunto discontented persons may resort, and under whom they may join, is a known but an excellent point of caution. I understand a fit head to be one that hath greatness and reputation, that hath confidence with the discontented party, and upon whom they turn their eyes, and that is thought discontented in his own particular: which kind of persons are either to be won and reconciled to the state, and that in a fast and true manner; or to be fronted with some other of the same party that may oppose them, and so divide the reputation. Generally, the dividing and breaking of all factions and combinations that are adverse to the state, and setting them at distance, or, at least, distrust amongst themselves, is not one of the worst remedies; for it is a desperate case, if those that hold with the proceeding of the state be full of discord and faction, and those that are against it be entire and united.

I have noted, that some witty and sharp speeches,

which have fallen from princes, have given fire to
seditions. Cæsar did himself infinite hurt in that
speech—"Sylla nescivit literas, non potuit dictare," [24]
for it did utterly cut off that hope which men had entertained, that he would, at one time or other, give
over his dictatorship. Galba undid himself by that
speech, "Legi a se militem, non emi;" [25] for it put the
soldiers out of hope of the donative. Probus, likewise,
by that speech, "Si vixero, non opus erit amplius Ro-
mano imperio militibus;" [26] a speech of great despair
for the soldiers, and many the like. Surely princes
had need, in tender matters and ticklish times, to beware what they say, especially in these short speeches,
which fly abroad like darts, and are thought to be
shot out of their secret intentions; for as for large
discourses, they are flat things, and not so much noted.

Lastly, let princes, against all events, not be without some great person, one or rather more, of military valor, near unto them, for the repressing of seditions in their beginnings; for without that, there useth
to be more trepidation in court upon the first breaking out of troubles than were fit, and the state runneth the danger of that which Tacitus saith: "Atque

[24] "Sylla did not know his letters, *and so* he could not dictate."
This saying is attributed by Suetonius to Julius Cæsar. It is a
play on the Latin verb *dictare,* which means either "to dictate,"
or "to act the part of Dictator," according to the context. As
this saying was presumed to be a reflection on Sylla's ignorance,
and to imply that by reason thereof he was unable to maintain
his power, it was concluded by the Roman people that Cæsar,
who was an elegant scholar, feeling himself subject to no such
inability, did not intend speedily to yield the reins of power.—
Suet. Vit. C. Jul. Cæs. 77, i. and *Cf. A. L.* i. vii. 12.

[25] "That soldiers were levied by him, not bought."—*Tac. Hist.*
i. 5.

[26] "If I live, there shall no longer be need of soldiers in the
Roman empire."—*Flav. Vop. Vit. Prob.* 20.

is habitus animorum fuit, ut pessimum facinus auder-
ent pauci, plures vellent, omnes paterentur:"[27] but
let such military persons be assured, and well reputed
of, rather than factious and popular; holding also good
correspondence with the other great men in the state,
or else the remedy is worse than the disease.

XVI.—OF ATHEISM.

I HAD rather believe all the fables in the legends,[1]
and the Talmud,[2] and the Alcoran, than that this universal frame is without a mind; and, therefore, God
never wrought miracle to convince atheism, because
his ordinary works convince it. It is true that a little
philosophy[3] inclineth man's mind to atheism, but depth
in philosophy bringeth men's minds about to religion;
for while the mind of man looketh upon second causes
scattered, it may sometimes rest in them, and go no
further; but when it beholdeth the chain of them confederate, and linked together, it must needs fly to
Providence and Deity. Nay, even that school which
is most accused of atheism, doth most demonstrate

[27] "And such was the state of feeling, that a few dared to per-
petrate the worst of crimes; more wished to do so; all submitted
to it."—*Hist.* i. 28.
  [1] He probably alludes to the legends or miraculous stories of
the saints; such as walking with their heads off, preaching to
the fishes, sailing over the sea on a cloak, &c. &c.
  [2] This is a book that contains the Jewish traditions, and the
rabbinical explanations of the law. It is replete with wonderful
narratives.
  [3] This passage not improbably contains the germ of Pope's
famous lines:—

        "A little learning is a dangerous thing;
        Drink deep, or taste not the Pierian spring."

religion: that is, the school of Leucippus,[4] and Democritus,[5] and Epicurus; for it is a thousand times more credible that four mutable elements, and one immutable fifth essence,[6] duly and eternally placed, need no God, than that an army of infinite small portions, or seeds unplaced, should have produced this order and beauty without a divine marshal. The Scripture saith, "The fool hath said in his heart, there is no God;"[7] it is not said, "The fool hath thought in his heart;" so as he rather saith it by rote to himself, as that he would have, than that he can thoroughly believe it, or be persuaded of it; for none deny there is a God, but those for whom it maketh[8] that there were no God. It appeareth in nothing more, that atheism is rather in the lip than in the heart of man, than by this, that atheists will ever be talking of that their opinion, as if they fainted in it within themselves, and would be glad to be strengthened by the consent of others; nay more, you shall have atheists strive to get disciples, as it fareth with other sects; and, which is most of all, you shall have of them that will suffer for atheism, and not recant; whereas, if they did truly think that there were no such thing as God, why should they trouble themselves? Epicurus is charged,

[4] A philosopher of Abdera; the first who taught the system of atoms, which was afterwards more fully developed by Democritus and Epicurus.

[5] He was a disciple of the last-named philosopher, and held the same principles; he also denied the existence of the soul after death. He is considered to have been the parent of experimental philosophy, and was the first to teach, what is now confirmed by science, that the Milky Way is an accumulation of stars.

[6] Spirit.

[7] Psalm xiv. 1, and liii. 1.

[8] To whose (seeming) advantage it is; the wish being father to the thought.

that he did but dissemble for his credit's sake, when he affirmed there were blessed natures, but such as enjoyed themselves without having respect to the government of the world. Wherein they say he did temporize, though in secret he thought there was no God; but certainly he is traduced, for his words are noble and divine: "Non Deos vulgi negare profanum; sed vulgi opiniones Diis applicare profanum." [9] Plato could have said no more; and, although he had the confidence to deny the administration, he had not the power to deny the nature. The Indians[10] of the west have names for their particular gods, though they have no name for God; as if the heathens should have had the names Jupiter, Apollo, Mars, &c., but not the word Deus, which shows that even those barbarous people have the notion, though they have not the latitude and extent of it; so that against atheists the very savages take part with the very subtlest philosophers. The contemplative atheist is rare; a Diagoras,[11] a Bion,[12] a Lucian,[13] perhaps, and some others, and yet they seem to be more than they are; for that all that

[9] "It is not profane to deny *the existence of* the deities of the vulgar; but, to apply to the divinities the received notions of the vulgar is profane."—*Diog. Laert.* x. 123.

[10] He alludes to the native tribes of the continent of America and the West Indies.

[11] He was an Athenian philosopher, who, from the greatest superstition, became an avowed atheist. He was proscribed by the Areiopagus for speaking against the gods with ridicule and contempt, and is supposed to have died at Corinth.

[12] A Greek philosopher, a disciple of Theodorus the atheist, to whose opinions he adhered. His life was said to have been profligate, and his death superstitious.

[13] Lucian ridiculed the follies and pretensions of some of the ancient philosophers; but though the freedom of his style was such as to cause him to be censured for impiety, he hardly deserves the stigma of atheism here cast upon him by the learned author.

impugn a received religion, or superstition, are, by the
adverse part, branded with the name of atheists. But
the great atheists indeed are hypocrites, which are
ever handling holy things, but without feeling, so as
they must needs be cauterized in the end. The causes
of atheism are: divisions in religion, if they be many;
for any one main division addeth zeal to both sides,
but many divisions introduce atheism. Another is,
scandal of priests, when it is come to that which St.
Bernard saith: "Non est jam dicere, ut populus, sic
sacerdos; quia nec sic populus, ut sacerdos."[14]   A
third is, custom of profane scoffing in holy matters,
which doth by little and little deface the reverence of
religion: and lastly, learned times, specially with
peace and prosperity; for troubles and adversities do
more bow men's minds to religion. They that deny
a God destroy a man's nobility, for certainly man is
of kin to the beasts by his body; and if he be not of
kin to God by his spirit, he is a base and ignoble creature. It destroys likewise magnanimity, and the raising of human nature; for, take an example of a dog,
and mark what a generosity and courage he will put
on when he finds himself maintained by a man, who,
to him, is instead of a God, or "melior natura;"[15]
which courage is manifestly such as that creature,
without that confidence of a better nature than his
own, could never attain. So man, when he resteth and
assureth himself upon divine protection and favor,

[14] "It is not for us now to say, 'Like priest like people,' for
the people are not even so *bad* as the priest." St. Bernard,
abbot of Clairvaux, preached the second Crusade against the
Saracens, and was unsparing in his censures of the sins then
prevalent among the Christian priesthood. His writings are
voluminous, and by some he has been considered as the latest
of the fathers of the Church.

[15] "A superior nature."

gathereth a force and faith, which human nature in itself could not obtain; therefore, as atheism is in all respects hateful, so in this, that it depriveth human nature of the means to exalt itself above human frailty. As it is in particular persons, so it is in nations: never was there such a state for magnanimity as Rome. Of this state hear what Cicero saith: "Quam volumus, licet, Patres conscripti, nos amemus, tamen nec numero Hispanos, nec robore Gallos, nec calliditate Pœnos, nec artibus Græcos, nec denique hoc ipso hujus gentis et terræ domestico nativoque sensu Italos ipsos et Latinos; sed pietate, ac religione, atque hâc unâ sapientiâ, quod Deorum immortalium numine omnia regi, gubernarique perspeximus, omnes gentes, nationesque superavimus." [16]

XVII.—OF SUPERSTITION.

IT were better to have no opinion of God at all, than such an opinion as is unworthy of him; for the one is unbelief, the other is contumely,[1] and certainly superstition is the reproach of the Deity. Plutarch

[16] "We may admire ourselves, conscript fathers, as much as we please; still, neither by numbers *did we vanquish* the Spaniards, nor by bodily strength the Gauls, nor by cunning the Carthaginians, nor through the arts the Greeks, nor, in fine, by the inborn and native good sense of this *our* nation, and this *our* race and soil, the Italians and Latins themselves; but through our devotion and our religious feeling, and this, the sole *true* wisdom, the having perceived that all things are regulated and governed by the providence of the immortal Gods, have we subdued all races and nations."—*Cic. de. Harus. Respon.* 9.

[1] The justice of this position is, perhaps, somewhat doubtful. The superstitious man *must* have *some* scruples, while he who believes not in a God (if there is such a person), *needs have none.*

saith well to that purpose: "Surely," saith he, "I had rather a great deal men should say there was no such man at all as Plutarch, than that they should say that there was one Plutarch that would eat his children[2] as soon as they were born," as the poets speak of Saturn; and, as the contumely is greater towards God, so the danger is greater towards men. Atheism leaves a man to sense, to philosophy, to natural piety, to laws, to reputation, all which may be guides to an outward moral virtue, though religion were not; but superstition dismounts all these, and erecteth an absolute monarchy in the minds of men. Therefore atheism did never perturb states; for it makes men wary of themselves, as looking no further, and we see the times inclined to atheism (as the time of Augustus Cæsar) were civil times; but superstition hath been the confusion of many states, and bringeth in a new *primum mobile*,[3] that ravisheth all the spheres of government. The master of superstition is the people, and in all superstition wise men follow fools; and arguments are fitted to practice in a reversed order. It was gravely said by some of the prelates in the Council of Trent,[4] where the doctrine of the schoolmen bare great sway, that the schoolmen were like astronomers, which did feign eccentrics[5] and epicycles,[6]

[2] Time was personified in Saturn, and by this story was meant its tendency to destroy whatever it has brought into existence. —*Plut. de Superstit.* x.

[3] The primary motive power.

[4] This Council commenced in 1545, and lasted eighteen years. It was convened for the purpose of opposing the rising spirit of Protestantism, and of discussing and settling the disputed points of the Catholic faith.

[5] Irregular or anomalous movements.

[6] An epicycle is a smaller circle, whose centre is in the circumference of a greater one.

and such engines of orbs to save[7] the phenomena,
though they knew there were no such things; and, in
like manner, that the schoolmen had framed a number of subtle and intricate axioms and theorems, to
save the practice of the Church. The causes of superstition are, pleasing and sensual rites and ceremonies;
excess of outward and pharisaical holiness; over-great
reverence of traditions, which cannot but load the
Church; the stratagems of prelates for their own ambition and lucre; the favoring too much of good intentions, which openeth the gate to conceits and novelties; the taking an aim at divine matters by human,
which cannot but breed mixture of imaginations; and,
lastly, barbarous times, especially joined with calamities and disasters. Superstition, without a veil, is a
deformed thing; for, as it addeth deformity to an ape
to be so like a man, so the similitude of superstition to
religion makes it the more deformed; and as wholesome meat corrupeteth to little worms, so good forms
and orders corrupt into a number of petty observances.
There is a superstition in avoiding superstition, when
men think to do best if they go furthest from the superstition formerly received; therefore care would be
had that (as it fareth in ill purgings) the good be
not taken away with the bad, which commonly is done
when the people is the reformer.

XVIII.—OF TRAVEL.

TRAVEL, in the younger sort, is a part of education;
in the elder, a part of experience. He that travelleth
into a country before he hath some entrance into the

[7] To account for.

language, goeth to school, and not to travel. That young men travel under some tutor or grave servant, I allow well, so that he be such a one that hath the language, and hath been in the country before; whereby he may be able to tell them what things are worthy to be seen in the country where they go, what acquaintances they are to seek, what exercises or discipline the place yieldeth; for else young men shall go hooded, and look abroad little. It is a strange thing that, in sea voyages, where there is nothing to be seen but sky and sea, men should make diaries; but in land travel, wherein so much is to be observed, for the most part they omit it, as if chance were fitter to be registered than observation. Let diaries, therefore, be brought in use. The things to be seen and observed are, the courts of princes, especially when they give audience to ambassadors; the courts of justice, while they sit and hear causes; and so of consistories[1] ecclesiastic; the churches and monasteries, with the monuments which are therein extant; the walls and fortifications of cities and towns; and so the havens and harbors, antiquities and ruins, libraries, colleges, disputations, and lectures, where any are; shipping and navies; houses and gardens of state and pleasure, near great cities; armories, arsenals, magazines, exchanges, burses, warehouses, exercises of horsemanship, fencing, training of soldiers, and the like; comedies, such whereunto the better sort of persons do resort; treasuries of jewels and robes; cabinets and rarities; and, to conclude, whatsoever is memorable in the places where they go, after all which the tutors or servants ought to make diligent inquiry. As for triumphs, masks, feasts, weddings, funerals, capital executions,

[1] Synods, or councils.

and such shows, men need not to be put in mind of them; yet they are not to be neglected. If you will have a young man to put his travel into a little room, and in short time to gather much, this you must do: first, as was said, he must have some entrance into the language before he goeth; then he must have such a servant, or tutor, as knoweth the country, as was likewise said; let him carry with him also some card or book, describing the country where he travelleth, which will be a good key to his inquiry; let him keep also a diary; let him not stay long in one city or town, more or less, as the place deserveth, but not long; nay, when he stayeth in one city or town, let him change his lodging from one end and part of the town to another, which is a great adamant of acquaintance; let him sequester himself from the company of his countrymen, and diet in such places where there is good company of the nation where he travelleth; let him, upon his removes from one place to another, procure recommendation to some person of quality residing in the place whither he removeth, that he may use his favor in those things he desireth to see or know: thus he may abridge his travel with much profit. As for the acquaintance which is to be sought in travel, that which is most of all profitable, is acquaintance with the secretaries and employed men[2] of ambassadors, for so in travelling in one country he shall suck the experience of many; let him also see and visit eminent persons in all kinds which are of great name abroad, that he may be able to tell how the life agreeth with the fame. For quarrels, they are with care and discretion to be avoided; they are commonly for mis-

[2] At the present day called *attachés.*

tresses, healths,[3] place, and words; and let a man beware how he keepeth company with choleric and quarrelsome persons, for they will engage him into their own quarrels. When a traveller returneth home, let him not leave the countries where he hath travelled altogether behind him, but maintain a correspondence by letters with those of his acquaintance which are of most worth; and let his travel appear rather in his discourse than in his apparel or gesture, and in his discourse let him be rather advised in his answers, than forward to tell stories; and let it appear that he doth not change his country manners for those of foreign parts, but only prick in some flowers of that he hath learned abroad into the customs of his own country.

XIX.—OF EMPIRE.

It is a miserable state of mind to have few things to desire, and many things to fear; and yet that commonly is the case of kings, who, being, at the highest, want matter of desire,[1] which makes their minds more languishing; and have many representations of perils and shadows, which makes their minds the less clear; and this is one reason, also, of that effect which the Scripture speaketh of, "that the king's heart is inscrutable;"[2] for multitude of jealousies, and lack of some predominant desire, that should marshal and put in order all the rest, maketh any man's heart hard

[3] He probably means the refusing to join on the occasion of drinking healths when taking wine.
[1] Something to create excitement.
[2] "The heart of kings is unsearchable."—*Prov.* v. 3.

to find or sound. Hence it comes, likewise, that
princes many times make themselves desires, and set
their hearts upon toys: sometimes upon a building;
sometimes upon erecting of an order; sometimes upon
the advancing of a person; sometimes upon obtaining
excellency in some art or feat of the hand,—as Nero
for playing on the harp; Domitian for certainty of
the hand with the arrow; Commodus for playing at
fence;[3] Caracalla for driving chariots, and the like.
This seemeth incredible unto those that know not the
principle, that the mind of man is more cheered and
refreshed by profiting in small things than by standing at a stay[4] in great. We see, also, that kings that
have been fortunate conquerors in their first years, it
being not possible for them to go forward infinitely,
but that they must have some check or arrest in their
fortunes, turn in their latter years to be superstitious
and melancholy; as did Alexander the Great, Diocletian,[5] and, in our memory, Charles the Fifth,[6] and
others; for he that is used to go forward, and findeth
a stop, falleth out of his own favor, and is not the
thing he was.

To speak now of the true temper of empire, it is
a thing rare and hard to keep, for both temper and
distemper consist of contraries; but it is one thing to
mingle contraries, another to interchange them. The
answer of Apollonius to Vespasian is full of excellent

[3] Commodus fought naked in public as a gladiator, and prided
himself on his skill as a swordsman.
[4] Making a stop at, or dwelling too long upon.
[5] After a prosperous reign of twenty-one years, Diocletian
abdicated the throne, and retired to a private station.
[6] After having reigned thirty-five years, he abdicated the
thrones of Spain and Germany, and passed the last two years
of his life in retirement at St. Just, a convent in Estremadura.

instruction. Vespasian asked him, "What was Nero's overthrow?" He answered, "Nero could touch and tune the harp well; but in government sometimes he used to wind the pins too high, sometimes to let them down too low." [7] And certain it is, that nothing destroyeth authority so much as the unequal and untimely interchange of power pressed too far, and relaxed too much.

This is true, that the wisdom of all these latter times in princes' affairs is rather fine deliveries, and shiftings of dangers and mischiefs, when they are near, than solid and grounded courses to keep them aloof; but this is but to try masteries with fortune, and let men beware how they neglect and suffer matter of trouble to be prepared. For no man can forbid the spark, nor tell whence it may come. The difficulties in princes' business are many and great; but the greatest difficulty is often in their own mind. For it is common with princes (saith Tacitus) to will contradictories: "Sunt plerumque regum voluntates vehementes, et inter se contrariæ;" [8] for it is the solecism of power to think to command the end, and yet not to endure the mean.

Kings have to deal with their neighbors, their wives, their children, their prelates or clergy, their nobles, their second nobles or gentlemen, their merchants, their commons, and their men of war; and from all these arise dangers, if care and circumspection be not used.

First, for their neighbors, there can no general rule

[7] Philost. vit. Apoll. Tyan. v. 28.

[8] "The desires of monarchs are generally impetuous and conflicting among themselves."—Quoted rightly, *A. L.* ii. xxii. 5, from *Sallust* (B. J. 113).

be given (the occasions are so variable), save one which ever holdeth; which is, that princes do keep due sentinel, that none of their neighbors do overgrow so (by increase of territory, by embracing of trade, by approaches, or the like), as they become more able to annoy them than they were; and this is generally the work of standing counsels to foresee and to hinder it. During that triumvirate of kings, King Henry the Eighth of England, Francis the First, King of France,[9] and Charles the Fifth, Emperor, there was such a watch kept that none of the three could win a palm of ground, but the other two would straightways balance it, either by confederation, or, if need were, by a war; and would not, in any wise, take up peace at interest; and the like was done by that league (which Guicciardini[10] saith was the security of Italy) made between Ferdinando, King of Naples, Lorenzius Medicis, and Ludovicus Sforza, potentates, the one of Florence, the other of Milan. Neither is the opinion of some of the schoolmen to be received, that a war cannot justly be made, but upon a precedent injury or provocation; for there is no question, but a just fear of an imminent danger, though there be no blow given, is a lawful cause of a war.

For their wives, there are cruel examples of them. Livia is infamed[11] for the poisoning of her husband;

[9] He was especially the rival of the Emperor Charles the Fifth, and was one of the most distinguished sovereigns that ever ruled over France.

[10] An eminent historian of Florence. His great work, which is here alluded to, is, "The History of Italy during his own Time," which is considered one of the most valuable productions of that age.

[11] Spoken badly of. Livia was said to have hastened the death of Augustus, to prepare the accession of her son Tiberius to the throne.

Roxolana, Solyman's wife,[12] was the destruction of that renowned prince, Sultan Mustapha, and otherwise troubled his house and succession; Edward the Second of England's Queen[13] had the principal hand in the deposing and murder of her husband.

This kind of danger is then to be feared chiefly when the wives have plots for the raising of their own children, or else that they be advoutresses.[14]

For their children, the tragedies likewise of dangers from them have been many; and generally the entering of fathers into suspicion of their children hath been ever unfortunate. The destruction of Mustapha (that we named before) was so fatal to Solyman's line, as the succession of the Turks from Solyman until this day is suspected to be untrue, and of strange blood; for that Selymus the Second was thought to be supposititious.[15] The destruction of Crispus, a young prince of rare towardness, by Constantinus the Great, his father, was in like manner fatal to his house; for both Constantinus and Constance, his sons, died violent deaths; and Constantius, his other son, did little better, who died indeed of sickness, but after that Julianus had taken arms against him. The de-

[12] Solyman the Magnificent was one of the most celebrated of the Ottoman monarchs. He took the Isle of Rhodes from the Knights of St. John. He also subdued Moldavia, Wallachia, and the greatest part of Hungary, and took from the Persians Georgia and Bagdad. He died A. D. 1566. His wife Roxolana (who was originally a slave called Rosa or Hazathya), with the Pasha Rustan, conspired against the life of his son Mustapha, and by their instigation this distinguished prince was strangled in his father's presence.

[13] The infamous Isabella of Anjou.

[14] Adulteresses.

[15] He, however, distinguished himself by taking Cyprus from the Venetians in the year 1571.

struction of Demetrius,[16] son to Philip the Second of Macedon, turned upon the father, who died of repentance. And many like examples there are; but few or none where the fathers had good by such distrust, except it were where the sons were up in open arms against them; as was Selymus the First against Bajazet, and the three sons of Henry the Second, King of England.

For their prelates, when they are proud and great, there is also danger from them; as it was in the times of Anselmus[17] and Thomas Becket, Archbishops of Canterbury, who, with their crosiers, did almost try it with the king's sword; and yet they had to deal with stout and haughty kings; William Rufus, Henry the First, and Henry the Second. The danger is not from that state, but where it hath a dependence of foreign authority; or where the churchmen come in and are elected, not by the collation of the King, or particular patrons, but by the people.

For their nobles, to keep them at a distance it is not amiss; but to depress them may make a king more absolute, but less safe, and less able to perform anything that he desires. I have noted it in my History of King Henry the Seventh of England, who depressed his nobility, whereupon it came to pass that his times were full of difficulties and troubles; for the nobility, though they continued loyal unto him, yet did they not

[16] He was falsely accused by his brother Perseus of attempting to dethrone his father, on which he was put to death by the order of Philip, B. C. 180.

[17] Anselm was Archbishop of Canterbury in the time of William Rufus and Henry the First. Though his private life was pious and exemplary, through his rigid assertion of the rights of the clergy he was continually embroiled with his sovereign. Thomas à Becket pursued a similar course, but with still greater violence.

coöperate with him in his business; so that, in effect, he was fain to do all things himself.

For their second nobles, there is not much danger from them, being a body dispersed. They may sometimes discourse high, but that doth little hurt; besides, they are a counterpoise to the higher nobility, that they grow not too potent; and, lastly, being the most immediate in authority with the common people, they do best temper popular commotions.

For their merchants, they are "vena porta:" [18] and if they flourish not, a kingdom may have good limbs, but will have empty veins, and nourish little. Taxes and imposts upon them do seldom good to the king's revenue, for that which he wins[19] in the hundred[20] he loseth in the shire; the particular rates being increased, but the total bulk of trading rather decreased.

For their commons, there is little danger from them, except it be where they have great and potent heads; or where you meddle with the point of religion, or their customs, or means of life.

For their men of war, it is a dangerous state where they live and remain in a body, and are used to donatives; whereof we see examples in the Janizaries[21] and Prætorian bands of Rome; but trainings of men, and arming them in several places, and under several com-

[18] The great vessel that conveys the blood to the liver, after it has been enriched by the absorption of nutriment from the intestines.

[19] This is an expression similar to our proverb, "Penny-wise and pound-foolish."

[20] A subdivision of the shire.

[21] The Janizaries were the body-guards of the Turkish sultans, and enacted the same disgraceful part in making and unmaking monarchs, as the mercenary Prætorian guards of the Roman Empire.

manders, and without donatives, are things of defence and no danger.

Princes are like to heavenly bodies, which cause good or evil times; and which have much veneration, but no rest. All precepts concerning kings are in effect comprehended in those two remembrances, "Memento quod es homo;" [22] and "Memento quod es Deus," [23] or "vice Dei;" [24] the one bridleth their power and the other their will.

XX.—OF COUNSEL.

THE greatest trust between man and man is the trust of giving counsel; for in other confidences men commit the parts of life, their lands, their goods, their children, their credit, some particular affair; but to such as they make their counsellors they commit the whole; by how much the more they are obliged to all faith and integrity. The wises' princes need not think it any diminution to their greatness, or derogation to their sufficiency to rely upon counsel. God himself is not without, but hath made it one of the great names of his blessed Son, "The Counsellor." [1] Solomon hath pronounced that, "in counsel is stability." [2] Things will have their first or second agitation: if they be not tossed upon the arguments of counsel, they will

[22] "Remember that thou art a man."

[23] "Remember that thou art a God."

[24] "The representative of God."

[1] Isaiah ix. 6: "His name shall be called, Wonderful, Counsellor, The mighty God, The everlasting Father, The Prince of Peace."

[2] Prov. xx. 18: "Every purpose is established by counsel; and with good advice make war."

be tossed upon the waves of fortune, and be full of inconstancy, doing and undoing, like the reeling of a drunken man. Solomon's son[3] found the force of counsel, as his father saw the necessity of it; for the beloved kingdom of God was first rent and broken by ill counsel; upon which counsel there are set for our instruction the two marks whereby bad counsel is forever best discerned, that it was young counsel for the persons, and violent counsel for the matter.

The ancient times do set forth in figure both the incorporation and inseparable conjunction of counsel with kings, and the wise and politic use of counsel by kings; the one, in that they say Jupiter did marry Metis, which signifieth counsel; whereby they intend that sovereignty is married to counsel; the other in that which followeth, which was thus: they say, after Jupiter was married to Metis, she conceived by him and was with child; but Jupiter suffered her not to stay till she brought forth, but eat her up; whereby he became himself with child, and was delivered of Pallas armed, out of his head.[4] Which monstrous fable containeth a secret of empire, how kings are to make use of their council of state; that first, they ought to refer matters unto them, which is the first begetting or impregnation; but when they are elaborate, moulded, and shaped in the womb of their counsel, and grow ripe and ready to be brought forth, that then they suffer not their council to go through with the resolution and direction, as if it depended on them; but take the matter back into their own hands, and make it appear to the world, that the decrees and

[3] The wicked Rehoboam, from whom the ten tribes of Israel revolted, and elected Jeroboam their king.—See 1 *Kings* xii.
[4] Hesiod. Theog. 886.

final directions (which, because they come forth with prudence and power, are resembled to Pallas armed), proceeded from themselves; and not only from their authority, but (the more to add reputation to themselves) from their head and device.

Let us now speak of the inconveniences of counsel, and of the remedies. The inconveniences that have been noted in calling and using counsel are three: first, the revealing of affairs, whereby they become less secret; secondly, the weakening of the authority of princes, as if they were less of themselves; thirdly, the danger of being unfaithfully counselled, and more for the good of them that counsel than of him that is counselled; for which inconveniences, the doctrine of Italy, and practice of France, in some kings' times, hath introduced cabinet councils; a remedy worse than the disease.[5]

As to secrecy, princes are not bound to communicate all matters with all counsellors, but may extract and select; neither is it necessary that he that consulteth what he should do, should declare what he will do; but let princes beware that the unsecreting of their affairs comes not from themselves; and, as for cabinet councils, it may be their motto, "Plenus rimarum sum:"[6] one futile person, that maketh it his glory to tell, will do more hurt than many that know it their duty to conceal. It is true, there be some affairs which require extreme secrecy, which will hardly go beyond one or two persons besides the king. Neither are those counsels unprosperous; for, besides the se-

---

[5] The political world has not been convinced of the truth of this doctrine of Lord Bacon; as cabinet councils are now held probably by every sovereign in Europe.

[6] "I am full of outlets."—*Ter. Eun.* I. ii. 25.

trecy, they commonly go on constantly in one spirit of direction without distraction; but then it must be a prudent king, such as is able to grind with a hand-mill;[7] and those inward counsellors had need also to be wise men, and especially true and trusty to the king's ends; as it was with King Henry the Seventh of England, who, in his greatest business, imparted himself to none, except it were to Morton[8] and Fox.[9]

For weakening of authority, the fable[10] showeth the remedy; nay, the majesty of kings is rather exalted than diminished when they are in the chair of council; neither was there ever prince bereaved of his dependencies by his council, except where there hath been either an over-greatness in one counsellor, or an over-strict combination in divers, which are things soon found and holpen.[11]

For the last inconvenience, that men will counsel with an eye to themselves; certainly, "non inveniet fidem super terram,"[12] is meant of the nature of

[7] That is, without a complicated machinery of government.

[8] Master of the Rolls and Privy Councillor under Henry VI., to whose cause he faithfully adhered. Edward IV. promoted him to the See of Ely, and made him Lord Chancellor. He was elevated to the See of Canterbury by Henry VII., and in 1493 received the Cardinal's hat.

[9] Privy Councillor and Keeper of the Privy Seal to Henry VII., and, after enjoying several bishoprics in succession, translated to the See of Winchester. He was an able statesman, and highly valued by Henry VII. On the accession of Henry VIII. his political influence was counteracted by Wolsey; on which he retired to his diocese, and devoted the rest of his life to acts of piety and munificence.

[10] Before mentioned, relative to Jupiter and Metis.

[11] Remedied.

[12] "He shall not find faith upon the earth." Lord Bacon probably alludes to the words of our Saviour, St. Luke xviii. 8: "When the Son of man cometh, shall he find faith upon the earth?"

times,[13] and not of all particular persons. There be
that are in nature faithful and sincere, and plain and
direct, not crafty and involved: let princes, above all,
draw to themselves such natures. Besides, counsellors are not commonly so united, but that one counsellor keepeth sentinel over another; so that if any do
counsel out of faction or private ends, it commonly
comes to the king's ear; but the best remedy is, if
princes know their counsellors, as well as their counsellors know them:—

"Principis est virtus maxima nosse suos."[14]

And on the other side, counsellors should not be too
speculative into their sovereign's person. The true
composition of a counsellor is, rather to be skilful in
their master's business than in his nature;[15] for then
he is like to advise him, and not to feed his humor.
It is of singular use to princes, if they take the opinions of their council both separately and together;
for private opinion is more free, but opinion before
others is more reverend. In private, men are more
bold in their own humors; and in consort, men are
more obnoxious[16] to others' humors; therefore it is
good to take both; and of the inferior sort rather in
private, to preserve freedom; of the greater, rather in
consort, to preserve respect. It is in vain for princes
to take counsel concerning matters, if they take no
counsel likewise concerning persons; for all matters
are as dead images; and the life of the execution of
affairs resteth in the good choice of persons. Neither

[12] He means to say, that this remark was only applicable to a
particular time, namely, the coming of Christ. The period of
the destruction of Jerusalem was probably referred to.

[14] " 'Tis the especial virtue of a prince to know his own men."

[15] In his disposition, or inclination.

[16] Liable to opposition from.

is it enough to consult concerning persons, "secundum genera," [17] as in an idea or mathematical description, what the kind and character of the person should be; for the greatest errors are committed, and the most judgment is shown, in the choice of individuals. It was truly said, "Optimi consiliarii mortui:" [18] "books will speak plain when counsellors blanch;" [19] therefore it is good to be conversant in them, specially the books of such as themselves have been actors upon the stage.

The councils at this day in most places are but familiar meetings, where matters are rather talked on than debated; and they run too swift to the order or act of council. It were better that in causes of weight, the matter were propounded one day and not spoken to till the next day; "In nocte consilium;" [20] so was it done in the commission of union[21] between England and Scotland, which was a grave and orderly assembly. I commend set days for petitions; for both it gives the suitors more certainty for their attendance, and it frees the meetings for matters of estate, that they may "hoc agere." [22] In choice of committees for ripening business for the council, it is better to choose

[17] "According to classes," or, as we vulgarly say, "in the lump." Lord Bacon means that princes are not, as a matter of course, to take counsellors merely on the presumption of talent, from their rank and station; but that, on the contrary, they are to select such as are tried men, and with regard to whom there can be no mistake.

[18] "The best counsellors are the dead."

[19] "Are afraid" to open their mouths.

[20] "Night-time for counsel."—ἐν νυκτὶ βουλή Gaisf. Par. Gr. B. 359.

[21] On the accession of James the Sixth of Scotland to the throne of England in 1603.

[22] A phrase much in use with the Romans, signifying, "to attend to the business in hand."

indifferent persons, than to make an indifferency by
putting in those that are strong on both sides. I commend, also, standing commissions; as for trade, for
treasure, for war, for suits, for some provinces; for
where there be divers particular councils, and but
one council of estate (as it is in Spain), they are in
effect no more than standing commissions, save that
they have greater authority. Let such as are to inform councils out of their particular professions (as
lawyers, seamen, mintmen, and the like) be first
heard before committees; and then, as occasion serves,
before the council; and let them not come in multi-
tudes, or in a tribunitious[23] manner; for that is to
clamor councils, not to inform them. A long table and
a square table, or seats about the walls, seem things of
form, but are things of substance; for at a long table
a few at the upper end, in effect, sway all the business; but in the other form there is more use of the
counsellors' opinions that sit lower. A king, when he
presides in council, let him beware how he opens his
own inclination too much in that which he propound-
eth; for else counsellors will but take the wind of
him, and, instead of giving free counsel, will sing him
a song of "placebo." [24]

XXI.—OF DELAYS.

FORTUNE is like the market, where, many times, if
you can stay a little, the price will fall; and again, it
is sometimes like Sibylla's offer,[1] which at first offer-

[23] A tribunitial or declamatory manner.
[24] "I'll follow the bent of your humor."
[1] The Sibyl alluded to here is the Cumæan, the most celebrated,
who offered the Sibylline Books for sale to Tarquin the Proud,

eth the commodity at full, then consumeth part and part, and still holdeth up the price; for occasion (as it is in the common verse) "turneth a bald noddle,[2] after she hath presented her locks in front, and no hold taken;" or, at least, turneth the handle of the bottle first to be received, and after the belly, which is hard to clasp.[3] There is surely no greater wisdom than well to time the beginnings and onsets of things. Dangers are no more light, if they once seem light; and more dangers have deceived men than forced them; nay, it were better to meet some dangers half-way, though they come nothing near, than to keep too long a watch upon their approaches; for if a man watch too long, it is odds he will fall asleep. On the other side, to be deceived with too long shadows (as some have been when the moon was low, and shone on their enemies' back), and so to shoot off before the time; or to teach dangers to come on by over early buckling towards them, is another extreme. The

[2] Bald head. He alludes to the common saying: "Take time by the forelock."
[3] Phæd. viii.

"At this time, an unknown woman appeared at court, loaded with nine volumes, which she offered to sell, but at a very considerable price. Tarquin refusing to give it, she withdrew and burnt three of the nine. Some time after she returned to court, and demanded the same price for the remaining six. This made her looked upon as a mad woman, and she was driven away with scorn. Nevertheless, having burnt the half of what were left, she came a third time, and demanded for the remaining three the same price which she had asked for the whole nine. The novelty of such a proceeding, made Tarquin curious to have the books examined. They were put, therefore, into the hands of the augurs, who, finding them to be the oracles of the Sybil of Cumæ, declared them to be an invaluable treasure. Upon this the woman was paid the sum she demanded, and she soon after disappeared, having first exhorted the Romans to preserve her books with care."—*Hooke's Roman History.*

ripeness or unripeness of the occasion (as we said)
must ever be well weighed; and generally it is good
to commit the beginnings of all great actions to Argus
with his hundred eyes, and the ends to Briareus with
his hundred hands, first to watch and then to speed;
for the helmet of Pluto,[4] which maketh the politic
man go invisible, is secrecy in the council, and celerity
in the execution; for when things are once come to the
execution, there is no secrecy comparable to celerity;
like the motion of a bullet in the air, which flieth so
swift as it outruns the eye.

XXII.—OF CUNNING.

WE take cunning for a sinister, or crooked wisdom;
and, certainly, there is great difference between a cunning man and a wise man, not only in point of hon-
esty, but in point of ability. There be that can pack
the cards,[1] and yet cannot play well; so there are
some that are good in canvasses and factions, that are
otherwise weak men. Again, it is one thing to understand persons, and another thing to understand matters; for many are perfect in men's humors that are
not greatly capable of the real part of business, which
is the constitution of one that hath studied men more
than books. Such men are fitter for practice than for
counsel, and they are good but in their own alley.
Turn them to new men, and they have lost their aim;

[4] Hom. Il. v. 845.
[1] Packing the cards is an admirable illustration of the author's
meaning. It is a cheating exploit, by which knaves, who, perhaps, are inferior players, insure to themselves the certainty of
good hands.

so as the old rule, to know a fool from a wise man, "Mitte ambos nudos ad ignotos, et videbis,"[2] doth scarce hold for them; and, because these cunning men are like haberdashers[3] of small wares, it is not amiss to set forth their shop.

It is a point of cunning to wait upon[4] him with whom you speak with your eye, as the Jesuits give it in precept; for there be many wise men that have secret hearts and transparent countenances; yet this would be done with a demure abasing of your eye sometimes, as the Jesuits also do use.

Another is, that when you have any thing to obtain of present dispatch, you entertain and amuse the party with whom you deal with some other discourse, that he be not too much awake to make objections. I knew a counsellor and secretary that never came to Queen Elizabeth of England, with bills to sign, but he would always first put her into some discourse of estate,[5] that she might the less mind the bills.

The like surprise may be made by moving things[6] when the party is in haste, and cannot stay to consider advisedly of that is moved.

If a man would cross a business that he doubts some other would handsomely and effectually move, let him pretend to wish it well, and move it himself, in such sort as may foil it.

[2] "Send them both naked among strangers, and *then* you will see."

[3] This word is used here in its primitive sense of "retail dealers." It is said to have been derived from a custom of the Flemings, who first settled in this country in the fourteenth century, stopping the passengers as they passed their shops, and saying to them, "Haber das, herr?"—"Will you take this, sir?" The word is now generally used as synonymous with linen-draper.

[4] To watch.

[5] State.

[6] Discussing matters.

The breaking off in the midst of that one was about to say, as if he took himself up, breeds a greater appetite in him with whom you confer to know more.

And because it works better when any thing seemeth to be gotten from you by question than if you offer it of yourself, you may lay a bait for a question, by showing another visage and countenance than you are wont; to the end, to give occasion for the party to ask what the matter is of the change, as Nehemiah[7] did: "And I had not, before that time, been sad before the king."

In things that are tender and unpleasing, it is good to break the ice by some whose words are of less weight, and to reserve the more weighty voice to come in as by chance, so that he may be asked the question upon the other's speech; as Narcissus did, in relating to Claudius the marriage[8] of Messalina and Silius.

In things that a man would not be seen in himself, it is a point of cunning to borrow the name of the world; as to say, "The world says," or "There is a speech abroad."

I knew one, that when he wrote a letter, he would put that which was most material in a postscript, as if it had been a by-matter.

I knew another, that when he came to have speech,[9]

[7] He refers to the occasion when Nehemiah, on presenting the wine, as cup-bearer to King Artaxerxes, appeared sorrowful, and, on being asked the reason of it, entreated the king to allow Jerusalem to be rebuilt.—*Nehemiah* ii. 1.

[8] This can hardly be called a marriage, as, at the time of the intrigue, Messalina was the wife of Claudius; but she forced Caius Silius, of whom she was deeply enamored, to divorce his own wife, that she herself might enjoy his society. The intrigue was disclosed to Claudius by Narcissus, who was his freedman, and the pander to his infamous vices; on which Silius was put to death. Vide *Tac. Ann.* xi. 29, *seq.*

[9] To speak in his turn.

he would pass over that that he intended most; and go forth and come back again, and speak of it as a thing that he had almost forgot.

Some procure themselves to be surprised at such times as it is like the party that they work upon will suddenly come upon them, and to be found with a letter in their hand, or doing somewhat which they are not accustomed, to the end they may be apposed of[10] those things which of themselves they are desirous to utter.

It is a point of cunning to let fall those words in a man's own name, which he would have another man learn and use, and thereupon take advantage. I knew two that were competitors for the secretary's place in Queen Elizabeth's time, and yet kept good quarter[11] between themselves, and would confer one with another upon the business; and the one of them said, that to be a secretary in the declination of a monarchy was a ticklish thing, and that he did not affect it;[12] the other straight caught up those words, and discoursed with divers of his friends, that he had no reason to desire to be secretary in the declination of a monarchy. The first man took hold of it, and found means it was told the queen, who, hearing of a declination of a monarchy, took it so ill, as she would never after hear of the other's suit.

There is a cunning, which we in England call "the turning of the cat in the pan;" which is, when that which a man says to another, he lays it as if another had said it to him; and, to say truth, it is not easy, when such a matter passed between two, to make it

[10] Be questioned upon.
[11] Kept on good terms.
[12] Desire it.

appear from which of them it first moved and began.

It is a way that some men have, to glance and dart at others by justifying themselves by negatives; as to say, "This I do not;" as Tigellinus did towards Burrhus: "Se non diversas spes, sed incolumitatem imperatoris simpliciter spectare." [13]

Some have in readiness so many tales and stories, as there is nothing they would insinuate, but they can wrap it into a tale;[14] which serveth both to keep themselves more in guard, and to make others carry it with more pleasure.

It is a good point of cunning for a man to shape the answer he would have in his own words and propositions; for it makes the other party stick the less.

It is strange how long some men will lie in wait to speak somewhat they desire to say; and how far about they will fetch,[15] and how many other matters they will beat over to come near it. It is a thing of great patience, but yet of much use.

A sudden, bold, and unexpected question doth many times surprise a man, and lay him open. Like to him, that, having changed his name, and walking in Paul's,[16] another suddenly came behind him and called him by his true name, whereat straightways he looked back.

But these small wares and petty points of cunning are infinite, and it were a good deed to make a list of

[13] "That he did not have various hopes in view, but solely the safety of the emperor." Tigellinus was the profligate minister of Nero, and Africanus Burrhus was the chief of the Prætorian Guards.—*Tac. Ann.* xiv. 57.

[14] As Nathan did, when he reproved David for his criminality with Bathsheba.—2 *Samuel* xii.

[15] Use indirect stratagems.

[16] He alludes to the old Cathedral of St. Paul, in London, which, in the sixteenth century, was a common lounge for idlers.

them; for that nothing doth more hurt in a state than
that cunning men pass for wise.

But certainly, some there are that know the resorts[17]
and falls[18] of business that cannot sink into the main
of it;[19] like a house that hath convenient stairs and en-
tries, but never a fair room. Therefore you shall see
them find out pretty looses[20] in the conclusion, but are
noways able to examine or debate matters; and yet
commonly they take advantage of their inability, and
would be thought wits of direction. Some build rather
upon the abusing of others, and (as we now say) putting tricks upon them, than upon soundness of their
own proceedings; but Solomon saith: "Prudens ad-
vertit ad gressus suos; stultus divertit ad dolos." [21]

XXIII.—OF WISDOM FOR A MAN'S SELF.

AN ant is a wise creature for itself, but it is a
shrewd[1] thing in an orchard or garden; and certainly,
men that are great lovers of themselves waste the public. Divide with reason between self-love and society;
and be so true to thyself as thou be not false to others,
especially to thy king and country. It is a poor centre
of a man's actions, himself. It is right earth; for that
only stands fast upon his own centre;[2] whereas all

[17] Movements, or springs.   [18] Chances, or vicissitudes.
[19] Enter deeply into.   [20] Faults, or weak points.
[21] "The wise man gives heed to his own footsteps; the fool
turneth aside to the snare." No doubt he here alludes to Ecclesiastes xiv. 2, which passage is thus rendered in our version:
"The wise man's eyes are in his head; but the fool walketh in
darkness."
[1] Mischievous.

things that have affinity with the heavens, move upon the centre of another, which they benefit. The referring of all to a man's self is more tolerable in a sovereign prince, because themselves are not only themselves, but their good and evil is at the peril of the public fortune; but it is a desperate evil in a servant to a prince, or a citizen in a republic; for whatsoever affairs pass such a man's hands, he crooketh them to his own ends, which must needs be often eccentric to the ends of his master or state. Therefore, let princes or states choose such servants as have not this mark; except they mean their service should be made but the accessary. That which maketh the effect more pernicious is, that all proportion is lost. It were disproportion enough for the servant's good to be preferred before the master's; but yet it is a greater extreme, when a little good of the servant shall carry things against a great good of the master. And yet that is the case of bad officers, treasurers, ambassadors, generals, and other false and corrupt servants; which set a bias upon their bowl, of their own petty ends and envies, to the overthrow of their master's great and important affairs; and, for the most part, the good such servants receive is after the model of their own fortune; but the hurt they sell for that good is after the model of their master's fortune. And certainly, it is the nature of extreme self-lovers, as they will set a house on fire, an it were but to roast their eggs; and yet these men many times hold credit with their masters, because their study is but to please them, and profit themselves; and for either respect they will abandon the good of their affairs.

[2] It must be remembered that Bacon was not a favorer of the Copernican system.

Wisdom for a man's self is, in many branches thereof, a depraved thing. It is the wisdom of rats, that will be sure to leave a house somewhat before it fall; it is the wisdom of the fox, that thrusts out the badger who digged and made room for him; it is the wisdom of crocodiles, that shed tears when they would devour. But that which is specially to be noted is, that those which (as Cicero says of Pompey) are "sui amantes, sine rivali," [3] are many times unfortunate; and whereas they have all their times sacrificed to themselves, they become in the end themselves sacrifices to the inconstancy of fortune, whose wings they thought by their self-wisdom to have pinioned.

XXIV.—OF INNOVATIONS.

As the births of living creatures at first are ill-shapen, so are all innovations, which are the births of time; yet, notwithstanding, as those that first bring honor into their family are commonly more worthy than most that succeed, so the first precedent (if it be good) is seldom attained by imitation; for ill to man's nature as it stands perverted, hath a natural motion strongest in continuance, but good, as a forced motion, strongest at first. Surely, every medicine[1] is an innovation, and he that will not apply new remedies must expect new evils, for time is the greatest innovator; and if time, of course, alter things to the worse, and wisdom and counsel shall not altar them to the better, what shall be the end? It is true, that what is

[3] "Lovers of themselves without a rival."—*Ad. Qu. Fr.* iii. 8.
[1] Remedy.

settled by custom, though it be not good, yet, at least, it is fit; and those things which have long gone together, are, as it were, confederate within themselves;[2] whereas new things piece not so well; but, though they help by their utility, yet they trouble by their inconformity; besides, they are like strangers, more admired and less favored. All this is true, if time stood still, which, contrariwise, moveth so round, that a froward retention of custom is as turbulent a thing as an innovation; and they that reverence too much old times are but a scorn to the new. It were good, therefore, that men in their innovations would follow the example of time itself, which indeed innovateth greatly, but quietly, and by degrees scarce to be perceived; for, otherwise, whatsoever is new is unlooked for, and ever it mends some and pairs[3] other; and he that is holpen, takes it for a fortune, and thanks the time; and he that is hurt, for a wrong, and imputeth it to the author. It is good, also, not to try experiments in states, except the necessity be urgent, or the utility evident; and well to beware that it be the reformation that draweth on the change, and not the desired change that pretendeth the reformation; and lastly, that the novelty, though it be not rejected, yet be held for a suspect,[4] and, as the Scripture saith, "That we make a stand upon the ancient way, and then look about us, and discover what is the straight and right way, and so to walk in it.[5]

[2] Adapted to each other.

[3] Injures or impairs.

[4] A thing suspected.

[5] He probably alludes to Jeremiah vi. 16: "Thus saith the Lord, Stand ye in the ways, and see, and ask for the old paths, where is the good way, and walk therein, and ye shall find rest for your souls."

XXV.—OF DISPATCH.

AFFECTED dispatch is one of the most dangerous things to business that can be; it is like that which the physicians call predigestion, or hasty digestion, which is sure to fill the body full of crudities, and secret seeds of diseases. Therefore, measure not dispatch by the times of sitting, but by the advancement of the business; and as in races, it is not the large stride, or high lift, that makes the speed, so in business, the keeping close to the matter, and not taking of it too much at once, procureth dispatch. It is the care of some, only to come off speedily for the time, or to contrive some false periods of business, because they may seem men of dispatch; but it is one thing to abbreviate by contracting,[1] another by cutting off; and business so handled at several sittings, or meetings, goeth commonly backward and forward in an unsteady manner. I knew a wise man[2] that had it for a byword, when he saw men hasten to a conclusion, "Stay a little, that we may make an end the sooner."

On the other side, true dispatch is a rich thing; for time is the measure of business, as money is of wares; and business is bought at a dear hand where there is small dispatch. The Spartans and Spaniards have been noted to be of small dispatch: "Mi venga la muerte de Spagna;" "Let my death come from Spain;" for then it will be sure to be long in coming.

Give good hearing to those that give the first in,

[1] That is, by means of good management.
[2] It is supposed that he here alludes to Sir Amyas Paulet, a very able statesman, and the ambassador of Queen Elizabeth to the court of France

formation in business, and rather direct them in the beginning, than interrupt them in the continuance of their speeches; for he that is put out of his own order will go forward and backward, and be more tedious while he waits upon his memory, than he could have been if he had gone on in his own course; but sometimes it is seen that the moderator is more troublesome than the actor.

Iterations are commonly loss of time; but there is no such gain of time as to iterate often the state of the question; for it chaseth away many a frivolous speech as it is coming forth. Long and curious speeches are as fit for dispatch as a robe, or mantle, with a long train, is for a race. Prefaces, and passages,[3] and excusations,[4] and other speeches of reference to the person, are great wastes of time; and though they seem to proceed of modesty, they are bravery.[5] Yet beware of being too material when there is any impediment, or obstruction in men's wills; for preoccupation of mind[6] ever requireth preface of speech, like a fomentation to make the unguent enter.

Above all things, order and distribution, and singling out of parts, is the life of dispatch, so as the distribution be not too subtile; for he that doth not divide will never enter well into business; and he that divideth too much will never come out of it clearly. To choose time is to save time; and an unseasonable motion is but beating the air. There be three parts of business,—the preparation; the debate, or examination; and the perfection. Whereof, if you look for dispatch, let the middle only be the work of many, and the first and last the work of few. The proceed-

---

³ Quotations.   ⁵ Boasting.
ᵈ Apologies.   ⁶ Prejudice.

ing, upon somewhat conceived in writing, doth for the
most part facilitate dispatch; for though it should be
wholly rejected, yet that negative is more pregnant of
direction than an indefinite, as ashes are more gener-
ative than dust.

XXVI.—OF SEEMING WISE.

It hath been an opinion, that the French are wiser
than they seem, and the Spaniards seem wiser than
they are; but howsoever it be between nations, certainly it is so between man and man; for, as the
apostle saith of godliness, "Having a show of godliness, but denying the power thereof," [1] so certainly
there are, in points of wisdom and sufficiency, that do
nothing, or little very solemnly,—"magno conatu
nugas." [2] It is a ridiculous thing, and fit for a satire
to persons of judgment, to see what shifts these forma-
lists have, and what prospectives to make superficies
to seem body, that hath depth and bulk. Some are so
close and reserved, as they will not show their wares
but by a dark light, and seem always to keep back
somewhat; and when they know within themselves
they speak of that they do not well know, would nevertheless seem to others to know of that which they may
not well speak. Some help themselves with countenance and gesture, and are wise by signs; as Cicero
saith of Piso, that when he answered him, he fetched
one of his brows up to his forehead, and bent the other
down to his chin: "Respondes, altero ad frontem sub-
lato, altero ad mentum depresso supercilio; crudelita-

[1] 2 Tim. iii. 5.
[2] "Trifles with great effort."

tem tibi non placere." [3] Some think to bear it by
speaking a great word, and being peremptory; and go
on, and take by admittance that which they cannot
make good. Some, whatsoever is beyond their reach,
will seem to despise or make light of it as impertinent
or curious, and so would have their ignorance seem
judgment. Some are never without a difference, and
commonly by amusing men with a subtilty, blanch
the matter; of whom A. Gellius saith, "Hominem de-
lirum, qui verborum minutiis rerum frangit pondera." [4]
Of which kind also Plato, in his Protagoras, bringeth
in Prodicus in scorn, and maketh him make a speech
that consisteth of distinctions from the beginning to
the end.[5] Generally such men, in all deliberations,
find ease to be[6] of the negative side, and affect a credit
to object and foretell difficulties; for when propositions
are denied, there is an end of them, but if they be allowed, it requireth a new work; which false point of
wisdom is the bane of business. To conclude, there is
no decaying merchant, or inward beggar,[7] hath so
many tricks to uphold the credit of their wealth, as
these empty persons have to maintain the credit of
their sufficiency. Seeming wise men may make shift
to get opinion, but let no man choose them for employment; for certainly, you were better take for
business a man somewhat absurd than overformal.

[3] "With one brow raised to your forehead, the other bent
downward to your chin, you answer that cruelty delights you
not."—*In Pis.* 6.

[4] "A foolish man, who fritters away the weight of matters by
finespun trifling on words."—Vide *Quint.* x. 1.

[5] Plat. Protag. i. 337.

[6] Find it easier to make difficulties and objections than to
originate.

[7] One really in insolvent circumstances, though to the world he
does not appear so.

XXVII.—OF FRIENDSHIP.

IT had been hard for him that spake it, to have put more truth and untruth together in few words than in that speech: "Whosoever is delighted in solitude, is either a wild beast or a god:" [1] for it is most true, that a natural and secret hatred and aversion towards society in any man hath somewhat of the savage beast; but it is most untrue, that it should have any character at all of the divine nature, except it proceed, not out of a pleasure in solitude, but out of a love and desire to sequester a man's self for a higher conversation; such as is found to have been falsely and feignedly in some of the heathen; as Epimenides,[2] the Candian; Numa, the Roman; Empedocles, the Sicilian; and Apollonius, of Tyana; and truly and really in divers of the ancient hermits and holy fathers of the church. But little do men perceive what solitude is, and how far it extendeth; for a crowd is not

[1] He here quotes from a passage in the *Politica* of Aristotle, book i. "He who is unable to mingle in society, or who requires nothing, by reason of sufficing for himself, is no part of the state, so that he is either a wild beast or a divinity."

[2] Epimenides, a poet of Crete (of which Candia is the modern name), is said by Pliny to have fallen into a sleep which lasted 57 years. He was also said to have lived 299 years. Numa pretended that he was instructed in the art of legislation by the divine nymph Egeria, who dwelt in the Arician grove. Empedocles, the Sicilian philosopher, declared himself to be immortal, and to be able to cure all evils. He is said by some to have retired from society that his death might not be known, and to have thrown himself into the crater of Mount Ætna. Apollonius of Tyana, the Pythagorean philosopher, pretended to miraculous powers, and after his death a temple was erected to him at that place. His life is recorded by Philostratus; and some persons, among whom are Hierocles, Dr. More, in his Mystery of Godliness, and recently Strauss, have not hesitated to compare his miracles with those of our Saviour.

company, and faces are but a gallery of pictures, and talk but a tinkling cymbal, where there is no love. The Latin adage meeteth with it a little: "Magna civitas, magna solitudo:"[3] because in a great town friends are scattered, so that there is not that fellowship, for the most part, which is in less neighborhoods: but we may go further, and affirm most truly, that it is a mere and miserable solitude to want true friends, without which the world is but a wilderness; and even in this sense also of solitude, whosoever in the frame of his nature and affections is unfit for friendship, he taketh it of the beasts, and not from humanity.

A principal fruit of friendship is the ease and discharge of the fulness and swellings of the heart, which passions of all kinds do cause and induce. We know diseases of stoppings and suffocations are the most dangerous in the body, and it is not much otherwise in the mind. You may take sarza[4] to open the liver, steel to open the spleen, flower of sulphur for the lungs, castoreum[5] for the brain, but no receipt openeth the heart but a true friend, to whom you may impart griefs, joys, fears, hopes, suspicions, counsels, and whatsoever lieth upon the heart to oppress it, in a kind of civil shrift or confession.

It is a strange thing to observe how high a rate great kings and monarchs do set upon this fruit of friendship whereof we speak; so great, as they purchase it many times at the hazard of their own safety and greatness; for princes, in regard of the distance of their fortune from that of their subjects and ser-

---

[3] "A great city, a great desert."
[4] Sarsaparilla.
[5] A liquid matter of a pungent smell, extracted from a portion of the body of the beaver.

vants, cannot gather this fruit, except (to make themselves capable thereof) they raise some persons to be
as it were companions, and almost equals to themselves, which many times sorteth to inconvenience.
The modern languages give unto such persons the
name of favorites, or privadoes, as if it were matter
of grace or conversation; but the Roman name at-
taineth the true use and cause thereof, naming them
"participes curarum;"[6] for it is that which tieth the
knot. And we see plainly that this hath been done,
not by weak and passionate princes only, but by the
wisest and most politic that ever reigned, who have
oftentimes joined to themselves some of their servants, whom both themselves have called friends, and
allowed others likewise to call them in the same manner, using the word received between private men.

L. Sylla, when he commanded Rome, raised Pompey (after surnamed the Great) to that height, that
Pompey vaunted himself for Sylla's overmatch; for
when he had carried the consulship for a friend of his,
against the pursuit of Sylla, and that Sylla did a little
resent thereat, and began to speak great, Pompey
turned upon him again, and, in effect, bade him be
quiet; for that more men adored the sun rising than
the sun setting.[7] With Julius Cæsar, Decimus Brutus
had obtained that interest, as he set him down in his
testament for heir in remainder after his nephew;
and this was the man that had power with him to draw
him forth to his death; for when Cæsar would have
discharged the senate, in regard of some ill presages,
and specially a dream of Calphurnia, this man lifted

---

[6] "Partakers of cares."
[7] Plutarch (*Vit. Pomp.* 19) relates that Pompey said this upon
Sylla's refusal to give him a triumph.

him gently by the arm out of his chair, telling him he
hoped he would not dismiss the senate till his wife
had dreamt a better dream;[8] and it seemeth his favor
was so great, as Antonius, in a letter which is recited
verbatim in one of Cicero's Philippics, calleth him
venefica, "witch" as if he had enchanted Cæsar.[9]
Augustus raised Agrippa (though of mean birth) to
that height, as, when he consulted with Mæcenas
about the marriage of his daughter Julia, Mæcenas
took the liberty to tell him, that he must either marry
his daughter to Agrippa, or take away his life; there
was no third way, he had made him so great. With
Tiberius Cæsar, Sejanus had ascended to that height,
as they two were termed and reckoned as a pair of
friends. Tiberius, in a letter to him, saith, "Hæc pro
amicitiâ nostrâ non occultavi;"[10] and the whole senate dedicated an altar to Friendship, as to a goddess,
in respect of the great dearness of friendship between
them two. The like, or more, was between Septimius
Severus and Plautianus; for he forced his eldest son
to marry the daughter of Plautianus, and would often
maintain Plautianus in doing affronts to his son; and
did write, also, in a letter to the senate, by these
words: "I love the man so well, as I wish he may
over-live me."[11] Now, if these princes had been as a
Trajan, or a Marcus Aurelius, a man might have
thought that this had proceeded of an abundant goodness of nature; but being men so wise,[12] of such

[8] Plut. Vit. J. Cæs. 64.

[9] Cic. Philip. xiii. 11.

[10] "These things, by reason of our friendship, I have not concealed *from you*."—Vide *Tac. Ann.* iv. 40.

[11] Dio. Cass. lxxv.

[12] Such infamous men as Tiberius and Sejanus hardly deserv
this commendation.

strength and severity of mind, and so extreme lovers
of themselves, as all these were, it proveth most plainly that they found their own felicity (though as great
as ever happened to mortal men) but as an half-piece,
except they might have a friend to make it entire;
and yet, which is more, they were princes that had
wives, sons, nephews; and yet all these could not
supply the comfort of friendship.

It is not to be forgotten what Comineus[13] observeth
of his first master, Duke Charles the Hardy,[14] namely,
that he would communicate his secrets with none,
and, least of all, those secrets which troubled him
most. Whereupon he goeth on, and saith, that towards his latter time, that closeness did impair and
a little perish his understanding. Surely, Comineus
might have made the same judgment, also, if it had
pleased him, of his second master, Louis the Eleventh,
whose closeness was indeed his tormentor. The parable of Pythagoras is dark, but true: "Corne idito,"
"eat not the heart." [15] Certainly, if a man would
give it a hard phrase, those that want friends to open
themselves unto are cannibals of their own hearts; but
one thing is most admirable (wherewith I will con-

[13] Philip de Comines.
[14] Charles the Bold, Duke of Burgundy, the valiant antagonist
of Louis XI. of France. De Comines spent his early years at
his court, but afterwards passed into the service of Louis XI.
This monarch was notorious for his cruelty, treachery, and dissimulation, and had all the bad qualities of his contemporary,
Edward IV. of England, without any of his redeeming virtues.
[15] Pythagoras went still further than this, as he forbade his
disciples to eat flesh of any kind whatever. See the interesting
speech which Ovid attributes to him in the fifteenth book of
the Metamorphoses. Sir Thomas Browne, in his Pseudoxia
(Browne's Works, Bohn's Antiq. ed. vol. i. p. 27, et seq.), gives
some curious explanations of the doctrines of this philosopher.—
Plut. de Educat. Puer. 17.

clude this first fruit of friendship), which is, that this communicating of a man's self to his friend works two contrary effects, for it redoubleth joys, and cutteth griefs in halves; for there is no man that imparteth his joys to his friend, but he joyeth the more; and no man that imparteth his griefs to his friend, but he grieveth the less. So that it is, in truth, of operation upon a man's mind of like virtue as the alchemists used to attribute to their stone for man's body, that it worketh all contrary effects, but still to the good and benefit of nature. But yet, without praying in aid of alchemists, there is a manifest image of this in the ordinary course of nature; for, in bodies, union strengtheneth and cherisheth any natural action; and, on the other side, weakeneth and dulleth any violent impression; and even so it is of minds.

The second fruit of friendship is healthful and sovereign for the understanding, as the first is for the affections; for friendship maketh indeed a fair day in the affections from storm and tempests, but it maketh daylight in the understanding, out of darkness and confusion of thoughts. Neither is this to be understood only of faithful counsel, which a man receiveth from his friend; but before you come to that, certain it is, that whosoever hath his mind fraught with many thoughts, his wits and understanding do clarify and break up in the communicating and discoursing with another; he tosseth his thoughts more easily; he marshalleth them more orderly; he seeth how they look when they are turned into words; finally, he waxeth wiser than himself; and that more by an hour's discourse than by a day's meditation. It was well said by Themistocles to the king of Persia: "That speech was like cloth of Arras,[16] opened and put abroad, whereby the imagery doth appear in figure; whereas in thoughts they lie but as in packs." [17] Neither is this second fruit of friendship, in opening the understanding, restrained only to such friends as are able to give a man counsel (they indeed are best), but even without that a man learneth of himself, and bringeth his own thoughts to light, and whetteth his wits as against a stone, which itself cuts not. In a word, a man were better relate himself to a statue or picture, than to suffer his thoughts to pass in smother.

Add now, to make this second fruit of friendship complete, that other point which lieth more open, and falleth within vulgar observation; which is faithful counsel from a friend. Heraclitus saith well, in one of his enigmas, "Dry light is ever the best;" [18] and certain it is, that the light that a man receiveth by counsel from another, is drier and purer than that which cometh from his own understanding and judgment, which is ever infused and drenched in his affections and customs. So, as there is as much difference between the counsel that a friend giveth, and that a man giveth himself, as there is between the counsel of a friend and of a flatterer; for there is no such flatterer as is a man's self, and there is no such remedy against flattery of a man's self, as the liberty of a friend. Counsel is of two sorts,—the one concerning manners, the other concerning business; for the first, the best preservative to keep the mind in health, is the faithful admonition of a friend. The calling of a

<hr>

[16] Tapestry. Speaking hypercritically, Lord Bacon commits an anachronism here, as Arras did not manufacture tapestry till the middle ages.

[17] Plut. Vit. Themist. 28.

[18] Ap. Stob. Serm. v. 129.

man's self to a strict account is a medicine sometimes too piercing and corrosive; reading good books of morality is a little flat and dead; observing our faults in others is sometimes improper for our case; but the best receipt (best, I say, to work, and best to take), is the admonition of a friend. It is a strange thing to behold what gross errors and extreme absurdities many (especially of the greater sort) do commit for want of a friend to tell them of them, to the great damage both of their fame and fortune; for, as St. James saith, they are as men "that look sometimes into a glass, and presently forget their own shape and favor." [19] As for business, a man may think, if he will, that two eyes see no more than one; or, that a game-ster seeth always more than a looker-on; or, that a man in anger is as wise as he that has said over the four and twenty letters,[20] or, that a musket may be shot off as well upon the arm as upon a rest;[21] and such other fond and high imaginations, to think him-self all in all; but when all is done, the help of good counsel is that which setteth business straight. And if any man think that he will take counsel, but it shall be by pieces, asking counsel in one business of one man, and in another business of another man; it is well (that is to say, better, perhaps, than if he asked none at all); but he runneth two dangers,—one, that he shall not be faithfully counselled; for it is a rare thing, except it be from a perfect and entire friend, to have counsel given, but such as shall be bowed and

[19] James i. 23.

[20] He alludes to the recommendation which moralists have often given, that a person in anger should go through the alphabet to himself, before he allows himself to speak.

[21] In his day, the musket was fixed upon a stand, called the "rest," much as the gingals or matchlocks are used in the East at the present day.

crooked to some ends which he hath that giveth it; the other, that he shall have counsel given, hurtful and unsafe (though with good meaning), and mixed partly of mischief, and partly of remedy; even as if you would call a physician, that is thought good for the cure of the disease you complain of, but is unacquainted with your body; and, therefore, may put you in a way for a present cure, but overthroweth your health in some other kind, and so cure the disease and kill the patient. But a friend, wholly acquainted with a man's estate, will beware, by furthering present business, how he dasheth upon other inconvenience; and, therefore, rest not upon scattered counsels; they will rather distract and mislead, than settle and direct.

After these two noble fruits of friendship (peace in the affections, and support of the judgment), followeth the last fruit, which is like the pomegranate, full of many kernels; I mean aid, and bearing a part in all actions and occasions. Here the best way to represent to life and manifold use of friendship, is to cast and see how many things there are which a man cannot do himself; and then it will appear that it was a sparing speech of the ancients to say, "that a friend is another himself," for that a friend is far more than himself. Men have their time, and die many times in desire of some things which they principally take to heart; the bestowing of a child, the finishing of a work, or the like. If a man have a true friend, he may rest almost secure that the care of those things will continue after him; so that a man hath, as it were, two lives in his desires. A man hath a body, and that body is confined to a place; but where friendship is, all offices of life are, as it were, granted to him and his deputy, for he may exercise them by his friend.

How many things are there, which a man cannot, with any face or comeliness, say or do himself? A man can scarce allege his own merits with modesty, much less extol them; a man cannot sometimes brook to supplicate, or beg, and a number of the like; but all these things are graceful in a friend's mouth, which are blushing in a man's own. So, again, a man's person hath many proper relations which he cannot put off. A man cannot speak to his son but as a father; to his wife but as a husband; to his enemy but upon terms; whereas, a friend may speak as the case requires, and not as it sorteth with the person. But to enumerate these things were endless; I have given the rule, where a man cannot fitly play his own part. If he have not a friend, he may quit the stage.

XXVIII.—OF EXPENSE.

RICHES are for spending, and spending for honor and good actions; therefore, extraordinary expense must be limited by the worth of the occasion; for voluntary undoing may be as well for a man's country as for the kingdom of heaven; but ordinary expense ought to be limited by a man's estate, and governed with such regard, as it be within his compass, and not subject to deceit and abuse of servants, and ordered to the best show, that the bills may be less than the estimation abroad. Certainly, if a man will keep but of even hand, his ordinary expenses ought to be but to the half of his receipts; and, if he think to wax rich, but to the third part. It is no baseness for the greatest to descend and look into their own estate. Some forbear it, not upon negligence alone, but doubting to bring themselves into melancholy, in respect they shall find it broken; but wounds cannot be cured without searching. He that cannot look into his own estate at all, had need both choose well those whom he employeth, and change them often; for new are more timorous, and less subtle. He that can look into his estate but seldom, it behooveth him to turn all to certainties. A man had need, if he be plentiful in some kind of expense, to be as saving again in some other: as, if he be plentiful in diet, to be saving in apparel; if he be plentiful in the hall, to be saving in the stable; and the like. For he that is plentiful in expenses of all kinds, will hardly be preserved from decay. In clearing[1] of a man's estate, he may as well hurt himself in being too sudden, as in letting it run on too long; for hasty selling is commonly as disadvantageable as interest. Besides, he that clears at once will relapse; for, finding himself out of straits, he will revert to his customs; but he that cleareth by degrees induceth a habit of frugality, and gaineth as well upon his mind as upon his estate. Certainly, who hath a state to repair, may not despise small things; and, commonly, it is less dishonorable to abridge petty charges, than to stoop to petty gettings. A man ought warily to begin charges, which once begun will continue; but in matters that return not, he may be more magnificent.

XXIX.—OF THE TRUE GREATNESS OF KINGDOMS AND ESTATES.

THE speech of Themistocles, the Athenian, which was haughty and arrogant, in taking so much to himself, had been a grave and wise observation and censure, applied at large to others. Desired at a feast to

[1] From debts and incumbrances.

touch a lute, he said, "He could not fiddle, but yet he could make a small town a great city." [1] These words (holpen a little with a metaphor) may express two different abilities in those that deal in business of estate; for if a true survey be taken of counsellors and statesmen, there may be found (though rarely) those which can make a small state great, and yet cannot fiddle: as, on the other side there will be found a great many that can fiddle very cunningly, but yet are so far from being able to make a small state great, as their gift lieth the other way,—to bring a great and flourishing estate to ruin and decay. And certainly, those degenerate arts and shifts, whereby many counsellors and governors gain both favor with their masters and estimation with the vulgar, deserve no better name than fiddling; being things rather pleasing for the time, and graceful to themselves only, than tending to the weal and advancement of the state which they serve. There are also (no doubt) counsellors and governors which may be held sufficient, "negotiis pares," [2] able to manage affairs, and to keep them from precipices and manifest inconveniences; which, nevertheless, are far from the ability to raise and amplify an estate in power, means, and fortune. But be the workmen what they may be, let us speak of the work; that is, the true greatness of kingdoms and estates, and the means thereof. An argument fit for great and mighty princes to have in their hand; to the end, that neither by overmeasuring their forces, they lose themselves in vain enterprises: nor, on the other side, by undervaluing them, they descend to fearful and pusillanimous counsels.

The greatness of an estate, in bulk and territory,

[1] Plut. Vit. Themist. ad init.   [2] "Equal to business."

doth fall under measure; and the greatness of finances and revenue doth fall under computation. The population may appear by musters, and the number and greatness of cities and towns by cards and maps; but yet there is not anything amongst civil affairs more subject to error than the right valuation and true judgment concerning the power and forces of an estate. The kingdom of heaven is compared, not to any great kernel, or nut, but to a grain of mustard-seed;[3] which is one of the least grains, but hath in it a property and spirit hastily to get up and spread. So are there states great in territory, and yet not apt to enlarge or command; and some that have but a small dimension of stem, and yet apt to be the foundations of great monarchies.

Walled towns, stored arsenals and armories, goodly races of horse, chariots of war, elephants, ordnance, artillery, and the like; all this is but a sheep in a lion's skin, except the breed and disposition of the people be stout and warlike. Nay, number itself in armies importeth not much, where the people is of weak courage; for, as Virgil saith, "It never troubles a wolf how many the sheep be."[4] The army of the Persians in the plains of Arbela was such a vast sea of people, as it did somewhat astonish the commanders in Alexander's army, who came to him, therefore, and wished him to set upon them by night; but he answered, "He would not pilfer the victory;" and the defeat was

[3] He alludes to the following passage, St. Matthew xiii. 31: "Another parable put he forth unto them, saying, The kingdom of heaven is like to a grain of mustard-seed, which a man took and sowed in his field; which indeed is the least of all seeds; but when it is grown, it is the greatest among herbs, and becometh a tree, so that the birds of the air come and lodge in the branches thereof."

[4] Virg. Ecl. vii. 51.

easy.[5]—When Tigranes,[6] the Armenian, being en-camped upon a hill with four hundred thousand men, discovered the army of the Romans, being not above fourteen thousand, marching towards him, he made himself merry with it, and said, "Yonder men are too many for an ambassage, and too few for a fight;" but before the sun set, he found them enow to give him the chase with infinite slaughter. Many are the ex-amples of the great odds between number and cour-age; so that a man may truly make a judgment, that the principal point of greatness in any state is to have a race of military men. Neither is money the sinews of war (as it is trivially said), where the sinews of men's arms, in base and effeminate people, are failing: for Solon said well to Crœsus (when in ostentation he showed him his gold), "Sir, if any other come that hath better iron than you, he will be master of all this gold." Therefore, let any prince or state think soberly of his forces, except his militia of natives be of good and valiant soldiers; and let princes, on the other side, that have subjects of martial disposition, know their own strength unless they be otherwise wanting unto them-selves. As for mercenary forces (which is the help in this case) all examples show that, whatsoever estate or prince doth rest upon them, he may spread his feathers for a time, but he will mew them soon after.

The blessing of Judah and Issachar[7] will never

[5] Vide. *A. L.* i. vii. 11.

[6] He was vanquished by Lucullus, and finally submitted to Pompey.—*Plut. Vit. Lucull.* 27.

[7] He alludes to the prophetic words of Jacob on his death-bed, Gen. xlix, 9, 14, 15: "Judah is a lion's whelp; . . . he stooped down, he couched as a lion, and as an old lion. . . . Issachar is a strong ass couching down between two burdens: And he saw that rest was good, and the land that it was pleasant; and bowed his shoulder to bear, and became a servant unto tribute."

meet; that the same people, or nation, should be both the lion's whelp and the ass between burdens; neither will it be, that a people overlaid with taxes should ever become valiant and martial. It is true that taxes, levied by consent of the estate, do abate men's courage less; as it hath been seen notably in the excises of the Low Countries, and, in some degree, in the subsidies[8] of England; for, you must note, that we speak now of the heart, and not of the purse; so that, although the same tribute and tax, laid by consent or by imposing, be all one to the purse, yet it works diversely upon courage. So that you may conclude, that no people overcharged with tribute is fit for empire.

Let states that aim at greatness take heed how their nobility and gentlemen do multiply too fast; for that maketh the common subject grow to be a peasant and base swain, driven out of heart, and, in effect, but the gentleman's laborer. Even as you may see in coppice woods; if you leave your staddles[9] too thick, you shall never have clean underwood, but shrubs and bushes. So in countries, if the gentlemen be too many, the commons will be base; and you will bring it to that, that not the hundred poll will be fit for a helmet, especially as to the infantry, which is the nerve of an army; and so there will be great population and little strength. This which I speak of, hath been nowhere better seen than by comparing of England and France; whereof England, though far less in territory and population, hath been, nevertheless, an overmatch; in regard, the middle people of England make good soldiers, which the peasants of France do

[8] Sums of money voluntarily contributed by the people for the use of the sovereign.

[9] Young trees.

not. And herein the device of King Henry the Seventh (whereof I have spoken largely in the history of his life) was profound and admirable; in making farms and houses of husbandry of a standard, that is, maintained with such a proportion of land unto them as may breed a subject to live in convenient plenty, and no servile condition, and to keep the plough in the hands of the owners, and not mere hirelings; and thus, indeed, you shall attain to Virgil's character, which he gives to ancient Italy:—

> "Terra potens armis atque ubere glebæ." [10]

Neither is that state (which, for anything I know, is almost peculiar to England, and hardly to be found anywhere else, except it be, perhaps, in Poland), to be passed over; I mean the state of free servants and attendants upon noblemen and gentlemen, which are noways inferior unto the yeomanry for arms; and, therefore, out of all question, the splendor and magnificence, and great retinues, and hospitality of noblemen and gentlemen received into custom, do much conduce unto martial greatness; whereas, contrariwise, the close and reserved living of noblemen and gentlemen causeth a penury of military forces.

By all means, it is to be procured that the trunk of Nebuchadnezzar's tree of monarchy[11] be great

[10] "A land strong in arms and in the richness of the soil."—*Virg. Æn.* i. 535.

[11] He alludes to the dream of Nebuchadnezzar, which is mentioned Daniel iv. 10; "I saw, and behold a tree in the midst of the earth, and the height thereof was great. The tree grew, and was strong, and the height thereof reached unto heaven, and the sight thereof to the end of all the earth: the leaves thereof were fair, and the fruit thereof much, and in it was meat for all; the beasts of the field had shadow under it, and the fowls of the heaven dwelt in the boughs thereof. and all flesh was fed of it."

enough to bear the branches and the boughs; that is, that the natural subjects of the crown, or state, bear a sufficient proportion to the stranger subjects that they govern. Therefore, all states that are liberal of naturalization towards strangers are fit for empire; for to think that a handful of people can, with the greatest courage and policy in the world, embrace too large extent of dominion, it may hold for a time, but it will fail suddenly. The Spartans were a nice people in point of naturalization; whereby, while they kept their compass, they stood firm; but when they did spread, and their boughs were becoming too great for their stem, they became a windfall upon the sudden. Never any state was, in this point, so open to receive strangers into their body as were the Romans; therefore, it sorted with them accordingly, for they grew to the greatest monarchy. Their manner was to grant naturalization (which they called "jus civitatis"),[12] and to grant it in the highest degree, that is, not only "jus commercii,"[13] "jus connubii,"[14] "jus hæreditatis;"[15] but, also, "jus suffragii,"[16] and "jus honorum;"[17] and this not to singular persons alone, but likewise to whole families; yea, to cities and sometimes to nations. Add to this their custom of plantation of colonies, whereby the Roman plant was removed into the soil of other nations, and, putting both constitutions together, you will say, that it was not the Romans that spread upon the world, but it was the world that spread upon the Romans; and that was

[12] "Right of citizenship."
[13] "Right of trading."
[14] "Right of intermarriage."
[15] "Right of inheritance."
[16] "Right of suffrage."
[17] "Right of honors."

the sure way of greatness. I have marvelled sometimes at Spain, how they clasp and contain so large
dominions with so few natural Spaniards;[18] but sure
the whole compass of Spain is a very great body of a
tree, far above Rome and Sparta at the first; and,
besides, though they have not had that usage to natur-
alize liberally, yet they have that which is next to it;
that is, to employ, almost indifferently, all nations in
their militia of ordinary soldiers; yea, and sometimes
in their highest commands; nay, it seemeth at this
instant they are sensible of this want of natives, as
by the pragmatical sanction,[19] now published, appeareth.

It is certain that sedentary and within-door arts,
and delicate manufactures (that require rather the
finger than the arm), have in their nature a con-
trariety to a military disposition; and, generally, all
warlike people are a little idle, and love danger better
than travail; neither must they be too much broken
of it, if they shall be preserved in vigor. Therefore,
it was great advantage in the ancient states of Sparta,
Athens, Rome, and others, that they had the use of
slaves, which commonly did rid those manufactures;
but that is abolished, in greatest part, by the Christian law. That which cometh nearest to it is, to
leave those arts chiefly to strangers (which, for that
purpose, are the more easily to be received), and to
contain the principal bulk of the vulgar natives within those three kinds, tillers of the ground, free ser-

[18] Long since the time of Lord Bacon, as soon as these colonies
had arrived at a certain state of maturity, they at different
periods revolted from the mother country.

[19] The laws and ordinances promulgated by the sovereigns of
Spain were so called. The term was derived from the Byzantine
empire.

vants, and handicraftsmen of strong and manly arts;
as smiths, masons, carpenters, &c., not reckoning professed soldiers.

But, above all, for empire and greatness, it importeth most, that a nation do profess arms as their
principal honor, study, and occupation; for the things
which we formerly have spoken of are but habilita-
tions[20] towards arms; and what is habilitation without intention and act? Romulus, after his death (as
they report or feign), sent a present to the Romans,
that, above all, they should intend[21] arms, and then
they should prove the greatest empire of the world.
The fabric of the state of Sparta was wholly (though
not wisely) framed and composed to that scope and
end; the Persians and Macedonians had it for a
flash;[22] the Gauls, Germans, Goths, Saxons, Normans,
and others, had it for a time; the Turks have it at this
day, though in great declination. Of Christian Europe, they that have it are in effect only the Spaniards; but it is so plain, that every man profiteth in
that he most intendeth, that it needeth not to be stood
upon. It is enough to point at it, that no nation which
doth not directly profess arms, may look to have greatness fall into their mouths; and, on the other side,
it is a most certain oracle of time, that those states
that continue long in that profession (as the Romans
and Turks principally have done), do wonders; and
those that have professed arms but for an age have,
notwithstanding, commonly attained that greatness in
that age which maintained them long after, when their
profession and exercise of arms had grown to decay.

Incident to this point is, for a state to have those

[20] Qualifications.   [21] Attend to.
[22] For a short or transitory period.

laws or customs which may reach forth unto them just occasions (as may be pretended) of war; for there is that justice imprinted in the nature of men, that they enter not upon wars (whereof so many calamities do ensue), but upon some, at the least specious grounds and quarrels. The Turk hath at hand, for cause of war, the propagation of his law or sect, a quarrel that he may always command. The Romans, though they esteemed the extending the limits of their empire to be great honor to their generals when it was done, yet they never rested upon that alone to begin a war. First, therefore, let nations that pretend to greatness have this, that they be sensible of wrongs, either upon borderers, merchants, or politic ministers; and that they sit not too long upon a provocation: secondly, let them be pressed,[23] and ready to give aids and succors to their confederates, as it ever was with the Romans; insomuch, as if the confederate had leagues defensive with divers other states, and, upon invasion offered, did implore their aids severally, yet the Romans would ever be the foremost, and leave it to none other to have the honor. As for the wars, which were anciently made on the behalf of a kind of party, or tacit conformity of estate, I do not see how they may be well justified: as when the Romans made a war for the liberty of Græcia; or, when the Lacedæmonians and Athenians made wars to set up or pull down democracies and oligarchies; or when wars were made by foreigners, under the pretence of justice or protection, to deliver the subjects of others from tyranny and oppression, and the like. Let it suffice, that no estate expect to

[23] Be in a hurry.

be great, that is not awake upon any just occasion of arming.

Nobody can be healthful without exercise, neither natural body nor politic; and, certainly, to a kingdom, or estate, a just and honorable war is the true exercise. A civil war, indeed, is like the heat of a fever; but a foreign war is like the heat of exercise, and serveth to keep the body in health; for, in a slothful peace, both courages will effeminate and manners corrupt. But, howsoever it be for happiness, without all question for greatness, it maketh to be still, for the most part, in arms; and the strength of a veteran army (though it be a chargeable business) always on foot, is that which commonly giveth the law, or, at least, the reputation amongst all neighbor states, as may well be seen in Spain,[24] which hath had, in one part or other, a veteran army, almost continually, now by the space of sixscore years.

To be master of the sea is an abridgment of a monarchy. Cicero, writing to Atticus, of Pompey's preparation against Cæsar, saith, "Consilium Pompeii plane Themistocleum est; putat enim, qui mari potitur, eum rerum potiri;[25] and, without doubt Pompey had tired out Cæsar, if upon vain confidence he had not left that way. We see the great effects of battles by sea. The battle of Actium decided the empire of the world: the battle of Lepanto arrested the greatness of the Turk. There be many examples where sea-fights have been final to the war; but this is when princes, or states, have set up their rest upon

[24] It was its immense armaments that in a great measure consumed the vitals of Spain.

[25] "Pompey's plan is clearly that of Themistocles; for he believes that whoever is master of the sea will obtain the supreme power."—*Ad Att.* x. 8.

the battles. But thus much is certain, that he that commands the sea is at great liberty, and may take as much and as little of the war as he will; whereas, those that be strongest by land are many times, nevertheless, in great straits. Surely, at this day, with us of Europe, the vantage of strength at sea (which is one of the principal dowries of this kingdom of Great Britain) is great; both because most of the kingdoms of Europe are not merely inland, but girt with the sea most part of their compass; and because the wealth of both Indies seems, in great part, but an accessary to the command of the seas.

The wars of latter ages seem to be made in the dark, in respect of the glory and honor which reflected upon men from the wars in ancient time. There be now, for marital encouragement, some degrees and orders of chivalry, which, nevertheless, are conferred promiscuously upon soldiers and no soldiers; and some remembrance, perhaps, upon the escutcheon, and some hospitals for maimed soldiers, and such like things; but in ancient times, the trophies erected upon the place of the victory; the funeral laudatives,[26] and monuments for those that died in the wars; the crowns and garlands personal; the style of emperor which the great kings of the world after borrowed; the triumphs of the generals upon their return; the great donatives and largesses upon the disbanding of the armies; were things able to inflame all men's courages. But, above all, that of the triumph amongst the Romans was not pageants or gaudery, but one of the wisest and noblest institutions that ever was; for it contained three things: honor to the general, riches to the treasury out of the spoils, and donatives to the army. But

[26] Encomiums.

that honor, perhaps, were not fit for monarchies, except it be in the person of the monarch himself, or his sons; as it came to pass in times of Roman emperors who did impropriate the triumphs to themselves and their sons, for such wars as they did achieve in person, and left only for wars achieved by subjects, some triumphal garments and ensigns to the general.

To conclude. No man can by care-taking (as the Scripture saith) "add a cubit to his stature," [27] in this little model of a man's body; but in the great frame of kingdoms and commonwealths, it is in the power of princes, or estates, to add amplitude and greatness to their kingdom; for, by introducing such ordinances, constitutions, and customs, as we have now touched, they may sow greatness to their posterity and succession: but these things are commonly not observed, but left to take their chance.

XXX.—OF REGIMEN OF HEALTH.

THERE is a wisdom in this beyond the rules of physic. A man's own observation, what he finds good of, and what he finds hurt of, is the best physic to preserve health; but it is a safer conclusion to say, "This agreeth not well with me, therefore I will not continue it;" than this, "I find no offence of this, therefore I may use it:" for strength of nature in youth passeth over many excesses which are owing[1] a man till his age. Discern of the coming on of years, and think not to do the same things still; for age will not be defied. Beware of sudden change in any great

[27] St. Matthew vi. 27; St. Luke xii. 25.
[1] The effects of which must be felt in old age.

point of diet, and, if necessity enforce it, fit the rest
to it; for it is a secret both in nature and state, that
it is safer to change many things than one. Examine
thy customs of diet, sleep, exercise, apparel, and the
like; and try, in any thing thou shalt judge hurtful,
to discontinue it by little and little; but so, as if thou
dost find any inconvenience by the change, thou come
back to it again; for it is hard to distinguish that
which is generally held good and wholesome, from
that which is good particularly,[2] and fit for thine own
body. To be free-minded and cheerfully disposed at
hours of meat, and of sleep, and of exercise, is one of
the best precepts of long lasting. As for the passions
and studies of the mind, avoid envy, anxious fears,
anger fretting inwards, subtle and knotty inquisitions,
joys, and exhilarations in excess, sadness not communicated. Entertain hopes, mirth rather than joy,
variety of delights, rather than surfeit of them; wonder and admiration, and therefore novelties; studies
that fill the mind with splendid and illustrious objects, as histories, fables, and contemplations of nature. If you fly physic in health altogether, it will
be too strange for your body when you shall need it;
if you make it too familiar, it will work no extraordinary effect when sickness cometh. I commend
rather some diet, for certain seasons, than frequent
use of physic, except it be grown into a custom; for
those diets alter the body more, and trouble it less.
Despise no new accident[3] in your body, but ask
opinion[4] of it. In sickness, respect health principally;
and in health, action; for those that put their bodies

[2] Of benefit in your individual case.
[3] Any striking change in the constitution.
[4] Take medical advice.

to endure in health, may, in most sicknesses which are not very sharp, be cured only with diet and tendering. Celsus could never have spoken it as a physician, had he not been a wise man withal, when he giveth it for one of the great precepts of health and lasting, that a man do vary and interchange contraries, but with an inclination to the more benign extreme. Use fasting and full eating, but rather full eating;[5] watching and sleep, but rather sleep; sitting and exercise, but rather exercise, and the like; so shall nature be cherished, and yet taught masteries.[6] Physicians are some of them so pleasing and conformable to the humor of the patient, as they press not the true cure of the disease; and some other are so regular in proceeding according to art for the disease, as they respect not sufficiently the condition of the patient. Take one of a middle temper; or, if it may not be found in one man, combine two of either sort; and forget not to call as well the best acquainted with your body, as the best reputed of for his faculty.

XXXI.—OF SUSPICION.

SUSPICIONS amongst thoughts are like bats amongst birds, they ever fly by twilight. Certainly they are to be repressed, or at the least well guarded; for they cloud the mind, they lose friends, and they check with business, whereby business cannot go on currently and constantly. They dispose kings to tyranny, husbands to jealousy, wise men to irresolution and melancholy. They are defects, not in the heart but in the brain; for they take place in the stoutest na-

[5] Incline rather to fully satisfying your hunger.
[6] Celsus *de Med.* i. 1.

tures, as in the example of Henry the Seventh of
England. There was not a more suspicious man, nor
a more stout, and in such a composition they do small
hurt; for commonly they are not admitted, but with
examination, whether they be likely or no; but in fearful natures they gain ground too fast. There is nothing makes a man suspect much, more than to know
little; and, therefore, men should remedy suspicion
by procuring to know more, and not to keep their suspicions in smother. What would men have? Do they
think those they employ and deal with are saints?
Do they not think they will have their own ends, and
be truer to themselves than to them? Therefore, there
is no better way to moderate suspicions, than to account upon such suspicions as true, and yet to bridle
them as false: [1] for so far a man ought to make use
of suspicions as to provide, as if that should be true
that he suspects, yet it may do him no hurt. Suspicions that the mind of itself gathers are but buzzes;
but suspicions that are artificially nourished, and put
into men's heads by the tales and whisperings of
others, have stings. Certainly, the best mean, to clear
the way in this same wood of suspicions, is frankly to
communicate them with the party that he suspects:
for thereby he shall be sure to know more of the truth
of them than he did before; and withal, shall make that
party more circumspect, not to give further cause of
suspicion. But this would not be done to men of base
natures; for they, if they find themselves once suspected, will never be true. The Italian says, "Sospetto
licentia fede;" [2] as if suspicion did give a passport to
faith; but it ought rather to kindle it to discharge itself.

[1] To hope the best, but be fully prepared for the worst.
[2] "Suspicion is the passport to faith."

XXXII.—OF DISCOURSE

Some in their discourse desire rather commendation of wit, in being able to hold all arguments,[1] than
of judgment, in discerning what is true; as if it were
a praise to know what might be said and not what
should be thought. Some have certain common-
places and themes, wherein they are good, and want
variety; which kind of poverty is for the most part tedious, and, when it is once perceived, ridiculous. The
honorablest part of talk is to give the occasion,[2] and
again to moderate and pass to somewhat else; for then
a man leads the dance. It is good in discourse, and
speech of conversation, to vary and intermingle speech
of the present occasion with arguments, tales with
reasons, asking of questions with telling of opinions,
and jest with earnest; for it is a dull thing to tire, and,
as we say now, to jade any thing too far. As for jest,
there be certain things which ought to be privileged
from it; namely, religion, matters of state, great persons, any man's present business of importance, and
any case that deserveth pity; yet there be some that
think their wits have been asleep, except they dart
out somewhat that is piquant, and to the quick; that
is a vein which would be bridled:[3]—

"Parce, puer, stimulis, et fortius utere loris."[4]

And, generally, men ought to find the difference between saltness and bitterness. Certainly, he that hath

[1] A censure of this nature has been applied by some to Dr.
Johnson, and possibly with some reason.

[2] To start the subject.

[3] Requires to be bridled.

[4] He quotes here from Ovid: "Boy, spare the whip, and tightly
grasp the reins."—*Met.* ii. 127.

a satirical vein, as he maketh others afraid of his wit, so he had need be afraid of others' memory. He that questioneth much, shall learn much, and content much, but especially if he apply his questions to the skill of the persons whom he asketh: for he shall give them occasion to please themselves in speaking, and himself shall continually gather knowledge; but let his questions not be troublesome, for that is fit for a poser.[5] And let him be sure to leave other men their turns to speak; nay, if there be any that would reign and take up all the time, let him find means to take them off, and to bring others on, as musicians used to do with those that dance too long galliards.[6] If you dissemble sometimes your knowledge of that you are thought to know, you shall be thought, another time, to know that you know not. Speech of a man's self ought to be seldom, and well chosen. I knew one was wont to say in scorn, "He must needs be a wise man, he speaks so much of himself;" and there is but one case wherein a man may commend himself with good grace, and that is in commending virtue in another, especially if it be such a virtue whereunto himself pretendeth. Speech of touch[7] towards others should be sparingly used; for discourse ought to be as a field, without coming home to any man. I knew two noblemen, of the west part of England, whereof the one was given to scoff, but kept ever royal cheer in his house; the other would ask of those that had been at the other's table, "Tell, truly, was there never a flout[8] or

---

[5] One who tests or examines.

[6] The galliard was a light active dance, much in fashion in the time of Queen Elizabeth.

[7] Hits at, or remarks intended to be applied to, particular individuals.

[8] A slight or insult.

dry blow[9] given?" To which the guest would answer,
"Such and such a thing passed." The lord would say,
"I thought he would mar a good dinner." Discretion
of speech is more than eloquence; and to speak agreeably to him with whom we deal, is more than to speak
in good words, or in good order. A good continued
speech, without a good speech of interlocution, shows
slowness; and a good reply, or second speech, without a good settled speech, showeth shallowness and
weakness. As we see in beasts, that those that are
weakest in the course, are yet nimblest in the turn;
as it is betwixt the greyhound and the hare. To use
too many circumstances, ere one come to the matter,
is wearisome; to use none at all, is blunt.

XXXIII.—OF PLANTATIONS.[1]

PLANTATIONS are amongst ancient, primitive, and
heroical works. When the world was young, it begat
more children; but now it is old, it begets fewer; for
I may justly account new plantations to be the children of former kingdoms. I like a plantation in a
pure soil; that is, where people are not displanted,[2] to
the end to plant in others; for else it is rather an extirpation than a plantation. Planting of countries is
like planting of woods; for you must make account
to lose almost twenty years' profit, and expect your
recompense in the end; for the principal thing that

[9] A sarcastic remark.
[1] The old term for colonies.
[2] He perhaps alludes covertly to the conduct of the Spaniards
in extirpating the aboriginal inhabitants of the West India
Islands, against which the venerable Las Casas so eloquently but
vainly protested.

hath been the destruction of most plantations, hath been the base and hasty drawing of profit in the first years. It is true, speedy profit is not to be neglected, as far as may stand with the good of the plantation, but no further. It is a shameful and unblessed thing[s] to take the scum of people and wicked condemned men, to be the people with whom you plant; and not only so, but it spoileth the plantation; for they will ever live like rogues, and not fall to work; but be lazy, and do mischief, and spend victuals, and be quickly weary, and then certify over to their country to the discredit of the plantation. The people wherewith you plant ought to be gardeners, ploughmen, laborers, smiths, carpenters, joiners, fishermen, fowlers, with some few apothecaries, surgeons, cooks, and bakers. In a country of plantations, first look about what kind of victual the country yields of itself to hand; as chestnuts, walnuts, pine-apples, olives, dates, plums, cherries, wild honey, and the like, and make use of them. Then consider what victual, or esculent things there are, which grow speedily, and within the year; as parsnips, carrots, turnips, onions, radish, artichokes of Jerusalem, maize, and the like. For wheat, barley, and oats, they ask too much labor; but with pease and beans you may begin, both because they ask less labor, and because they serve for meat as well as for bread; and of rice, likewise, cometh a great increase, and it is a kind of meat. Above all, there ought to be brought store of biscuit, oatmeal, flour, meal, and the like, in the beginning, till bread may be had. For beasts, or birds, take chiefly such as are

[s] Of course, this censure would not apply to what is primarily and essentially a convict colony; the object of which is to drain the mother country of its impure superfluities

least subject to diseases, and multiply fastest; as swine, goats, cocks, hens, turkeys, geese, house-doves, and the like. The victual in plantations ought to be expended almost as in a besieged town, that is, with certain allowance; and let the main part of the ground employed to gardens or corn, be to a common stock; and to be laid in, and stored up, and then delivered out in proportion; besides some spots of ground that any particular person will manure for his own private use. Consider, likewise, what commodities the soil where the plantation is doth naturally yield, that they may some way help to defray the charge of the plantation; so it be not, as was said, to the untimely prejudice of the main business, as it hath fared with tobacco in Virginia.[4] Wood commonly aboundeth but too much; and therefore timber is fit to be one. If there be iron ore, and streams whereupon to set the mills, iron is a brave commodity where wood aboundeth. Making of bay-salt, if the climate be proper for it, would be put in experience; growing silk, likewise, if any be, is a likely commodity; pitch and tar, where store of firs and pines are, will not fail; so drugs and sweet woods, where they are, cannot but yield great profit; soap-ashes, likewise, and other things that may be thought of; but moil[5] not too much under ground, for the hope of mines is very uncertain, and useth to make the planters lazy in other things. For government, let it be in the hands of one, assisted with some counsel, and let them have commission to exercise martial laws, with some limitation; and, above all,

[4] Times have much changed since this was penned, tobacco is now the staple commodity, and the source of "the main business" of Virginia.

[5] To labor hard.

let men make that profit of being in the wilderness,
as they have God always, and his service, before their
eyes. Let not the government of the plantation depend upon too many counsellors and undertakers in
the country that planteth, but upon a temperate number; and let those be rather noblemen and gentlemen, than merchants, for they look ever to the present
gain. Let there be freedoms from custom, till the
plantation be of strength; and not only freedom from
custom, but freedom to carry their commodities where
they may make their best of them, except there be
some special cause of caution. Cram not in people,
by sending too fast company after company; but
rather hearken how they waste, and send supplies pro-
portionably; but so as the number may live well in
the plantation, and not by surcharge be in penury.
It hath been a great endangering to the health of
some plantations, that they have built along the sea
and rivers, in marish[6] and unwholesome grounds;
therefore, though you begin there, to avoid carriage
and other like discommodities, yet build still rather
upwards from the streams than along. It concerneth,
likewise, the health of the plantation, that they have
good store of salt with them, that they may use it in
their victuals when it shall be necessary. If you
plant where savages are, do not only entertain them
with trifles and gingles,[7] but use them justly and gra-
ciously, with sufficient guard, nevertheless; and do not
win their favor by helping them to invade their enemies, but for their defence it is not amiss; and send
oft of them over to the country that plants, that they
may see a better condition than their own, and com-

[6] Marshy; from the French *marais*, a marsh.
[7] Gewgaws, or spangles.

mend it when they return. When the plantation
grows to strength, then it is time to plant with women
as well as with men; that the plantation may spread
into generations, and not be ever pieced from without. It is the sinfullest thing in the world, to forsake or destitute a plantation once in forwardness;
for, besides the dishonor, it is the guiltiness of blood
of many commiserable persons.

XXXIV.—OF RICHES.

I CANNOT call riches better than the baggage of
virtue; the Roman word is better, "impedimenta;"
for as the baggage is to an army, so is riches to virtue;
it cannot be spared nor left behind, but it hindereth
the march; yea, and the care of it sometimes loseth
or disturbeth the victory. Of great riches there is no
real use, except it be in the distribution; the rest is
but conceit. So saith Solomon: "Where much is, there
are many to consume it; and what hath the owner,
but the sight of it with his eyes?" [1] The personal
fruition in any man cannot reach to feel great riches:
there is a custody of them, or a power of dole and
donative of them, or a fame of them, but no solid use
to the owner. Do you not see what feigned prices are
set upon little stones and rarities? and what works of
ostentation are undertaken, because there might seem
to be some use of great riches? But then you will
say, they may be of use to buy men out of dangers or

---

[1] He alludes to Ecclesiastes v. 11, the words of which are somewhat varied in our version: "When goods increase, they are
increased that eat them; and what good is there to the owners
thereof, saving the beholding of them with their eyes?"

troubles; as Solomon saith: "Riches are as a stronghold in the imagination of the rich man;"[2] but this is excellently expressed, that it is in imagination, and not always in fact; for, certainly, great riches have sold more men than they have bought out. Seek not proud riches, but such as thou mayest get justly, use soberly, distribute cheerfully, and leave contentedly; yet have no abstract nor friarly contempt of them, but distinguish, as Cicero saith well of Rabirius Posthumus: "In studio rei amplificandæ apparebat, non avaritiæ prædam, sed instrumentum bonitati quæri."[3] Hearken also to Solomon, and beware of hasty gathering of riches: "Qui festinat ad divitias, non erit insons."[4] The poets feign, that when Plutus (which is riches) is sent from Jupiter, he limps, and goes slowly; but when he is sent from Pluto, he runs, and is swift of foot; meaning, that riches gotten by good means and just labor pace slowly; but when they come by the death of others[5] (as by the course of inheritance, testaments, and the like), they come tumbling upon a man. But it might be applied likewise to Pluto, taking him for the devil; for when riches come from the devil (as by fraud and oppression, and unjust means), they come upon speed. The ways to enrich are many, and most of them foul: parsimony is one of the best, and yet is not innocent; for it withholdeth

[2] "The rich man's wealth is his strong city."—*Proverbs* x. 15; xviii. 11.

[3] "In his anxiety to increase his fortune, it was evident that not the gratification of avarice was sought, but the means of doing good."

[4] "He who hastens to riches will not be without guilt." In our version the words are: "He that maketh haste to be rich shall not be innocent."—*Proverbs* xxviii. 22.

[5] Pluto being the king of the infernal regions, or place of departed spirits.

men from works of liberality and charity. The improvement of the ground is the most natural obtaining of riches; for it is our great mother's blessing, the earth's, but it is slow; and yet, where men of great wealth do stoop to husbandry, it multiplieth riches exceedingly. I knew a nobleman, in England, that had the greatest audits[6] of any man in my time, a great grazier, a great sheep-master, a great timber-man, a great collier, a great corn-master, a great leadman, and so of iron, and a number of the like points of husbandry; so as the earth seemed a sea to him in respect of the perpetual importation. It was truly observed by one, "That himself came very hardly to a little riches, and very easily to great riches;" for when a man's stock is come to that, that he can expect the prime of markets,[7] and overcome those bargains, which for their greatness are few men's money, and be partner in the industries of younger men, he cannot but increase mainly. The gains of ordinary trades and vocations are honest, and furthered by two things, chiefly: by diligence, and by a good name for good and fair dealing; but the gains of bargains are of a more doubtful nature, when men shall wait upon others' necessity: broke by servants and instruments to draw them on; put off others cunningly that would be better chapmen; and the like practices, which are crafty and naught. As for the chopping of bargains, when a man buys not to hold, but to sell over again, that commonly grindeth double, both upon the seller and upon the buyer. Sharings do greatly enrich, if the hands be well chosen that are trusted. Usury is the certainest means of gain, though one of the worst;

[6] Rent-roll, or account taken of income.
[7] Wait till prices have risen.

as that whereby a man doth eat his bread, "in sudore
vultûs alieni;"[8] and, besides, doth plough upon Sun-
days; but yet certain though it be, it hath flaws, for
that the scriveners and brokers do value unsound men
to serve their own turn. The fortune, in being the
first in an invention, or in a privilege, doth cause
sometimes a wonderful overgrowth in riches, as it was
with the first sugar-man[9] in the Canaries; therefore,
if a man can play the true logician, to have as well
judgment as invention, he may do great matters, especially if the times be fit. He that resteth upon gains
certain, shall hardly grow to great riches; and he that
puts all upon adventures, doth oftentimes break and
come to poverty; it is good, therefore, to guard adventures with certainties that may uphold losses.
Monopolies, and coemption of wares for resale, where
they are not restrained, are great means to enrich; especially if the party have intelligence what things are
like to come into request, and so store himself before-
hand. Riches gotten by service, though it be of the
best rise, yet when they are gotten by flattery, feeding
humors, and other servile conditions, they may be
placed amongst the worst. As for fishing for testaments and executorships (as Tacitus saith of Seneca,
"Testamenta et orbos tanquam indagine capi"),[10] it
is yet worse, by how much men submit themselves to
meaner persons than in service. Believe not much
them that seem to despise riches, for they despise them
that despair of them; and none worse when they come

[8] "In the sweat of another's brow." He alludes to the words
of Genesis iii. 19: "In the sweat of thy face shalt thou eat
bread."

[9] Planter of sugar-canes.

[10] "Wills and childless persons were caught *by him,* as though
with a hunting-nest."—*Tacit. Ann.* xiii. 42.

to them. Be not penny-wise; riches have wings, and sometimes they fly away of themselves, sometimes they must be set flying to bring in more. Men leave their riches either to their kindred, or to the public; and moderate portions prosper best in both. A great state left to an heir, is as a lure to all the birds of prey round about to seize on him, if he be not the better stablished in years and judgment; likewise, glorious gifts and foundations are like sacrifices without salt, and but the painted sepulchres of alms, which soon will putrefy and corrupt inwardly. Therefore, measure not thine advancements by quantity, but frame them by measure, and defer not charities till death; for, certainly, if a man weigh it rightly, he that doth so is rather liberal of another man's than of his own.

XXXV.—OF PROPHECIES.

I MEAN not to speak of divine prophecies, nor of heathen oracles, nor of natural predictions; but only of prophecies that have been of certain memory, and from hidden causes. Saith the Pythonissa[1] to Saul, "To-morrow thou and thy sons shall be with me." Virgil hath these verses from Homer:—

> "Hic domus Æneæ cunctis dominabitur oris,
> Et nati natorum, et qui nascentur ab illis."[2]

[1] "Pythoness," used in the sense of witch. He alludes to the witch of Endor, and the words in Samuel xxviii. 19. He is, however, mistaken in attributing these words to the witch: it was the spirit of Samuel that said, "To-morrow shalt thou and thy sons be with me."

[2] "But the house of Æneas shall reign over every shore, both his children's children, and those who shall spring from them."—Æn. iii. 97.

A prophecy, as it seems, of the Roman empire
Seneca the tragedian hath these verses:—

> "Venient annis
> Sæcula seris, quibus Oceanus
> Vincula rerum laxet, et ingens
> Pateat Tellus, Tiphysque novos
> Detegat orbes; nec sit terris
> Ultima Thule."

A prophecy of the discovery of America. The daughter of Polycrates[4] dreamed that Jupiter bathed her
father, and Apollo anointed him; and it came to pass
that he was crucified in an open place, where the sun
made his body run with sweat, and the rain washed
it. Philip of Macedon dreamed he sealed up his
wife's belly, whereby he did expound it, that his wife
should be barren; but Aristander the soothsayer told
him his wife was with child, because men do not use
to seal vessels that are empty.[5] A phantasm that
appeared to M. Brutus in his tent, said to him, "Phil-
ippis iterum me videbis."[6] Tiberius said to Galba,
degustabis imperium."[7] In Vespasian's time, there
went a prophecy in the East, that those that should
come forth of Judea, should reign over the world;
which, though it may be was meant of our Saviour,

[3] "After the lapse of years, ages will come in which Ocean
shall relax his chains around the world, and a vast continent
shall appear, and Tiphys shall explore new regions, and Thule
shall be no longer the utmost verge of earth."—*Sen. Med.* ii. 375.

[4] He was the king of Samos, and was treacherously put to
death by Orœtes, the governor of Magnesia, in Asia Minor. His
daughter, in consequence of her dream, attempted to dissuade
him from visiting Orœtes, but in vain.—*Herod.* iii. 124.

[5] Plut. Vit. Alex. 2.

[6] "Thou shalt see me again at Philippi."—*Appian Bell. Civ.*
iv. 134.

[7] "Thou, also, Galba, shalt taste of empire."—*Suet. Vit.
Gall.* 4.

yet Tacitus expounds it of Vespasian.[8] Domitian
dreamed, the night before he was slain, that a golden
head was growing out of the nape of his neck;[9] and,
indeed, the succession that followed him, for many
years, made golden times. Henry the Sixth of England said of Henry the Seventh, when he was a lad,
and gave him water, "This is the lad that shall enjoy
the crown for which we strive." When I was in
France, I heard from one Dr. Pena, that the queen
mother,[10] who was given to curious arts, caused the
king her husband's nativity to be calculated under a
false name; and the astrologer gave a judgment, that
he should be killed in a duel; at which the queen
laughed, thinking her husband to be above challenges
and duels; but he was slain upon a course at tilt, the
splinters of the staff of Montgomery going in at his
beaver. The trivial prophecy which I heard when I
was a child, and Queen Elizabeth was in the flower
of her years, was,

> "When hempe is spunne,
> England's done;"

whereby it was generally conceived, that after the
princes had reigned which had the principal letters
of that word hempe (which were Henry, Edward,
Mary, Philip, and Elizabeth), England should come
to utter confusion; which, thanks be to God, is verified only in the change of the name; for that the king's
style is now no more of England, but of Britain.[11]

[8] Hist. v. 13.
[9] Suet. vit. Domit. 23.
[10] Catherine de Medicis, the wife of Henry II. of France, who
died from a wound accidentally received in a tournament.
[11] James I. being the first monarch of Great Britain.

There was also another prophecy before the year of
eighty-eight, which I do not well understand.

> "There shall be seen upon a day,
> Between the Baugh and the May,
> The black fleet of Norway.
> When that that is come and gone,
> England build houses of lime and stone,
> For after wars you shall have none."

It was generally conceived to be meant of the Spanish fleet that came in eighty-eight; for that the king
of Spain's surname, as they say, is Norway.   The
prediction of Regiomontanus,

> "Octogesimus octavus mirabilis annus," [12]

was thought likewise accomplished in the sending of
that great fleet, being the greatest in strength, though
not in number, of all that ever swam upon the sea.
As for Cleon's dream, [13] I think it was a jest; it was,
that he was devoured of a long dragon; and it was
expounded of a maker of sausages, that troubled him
exceedingly.   There are numbers of the like kind, especially if you include dreams, and predictions of astrology; but I have set down these few only of certain
credit, for example.   My judgment is, that they ought

---

[12] "The eighty-eighth will be a wondrous year."

[13] "Aristophanes, in his Comedy of the Knights, satirizes Cleon,
the Athenian demagogue.   He introduces a declaration of the
oracle, that the Eagle of hides (by whom Cleon was meant, his
father having been a tanner), should be conquered by a serpent,
which Demosthenes, one of the characters in the play, expounds
as meaning a maker of sausages.   How Lord Bacon could for a
moment doubt that this was a mere jest, it is difficult to conjec-
ture.   The following is a literal translation of a portion of the
passage from The Knights (l. 197): "But when a leather eagle
with crooked talons shall have seized with its jaws a serpent, a
stupid creature, a drinker of blood, then the tan-pickle of the
Paphlagonians is destroyed; but upon the sellers of sausages
the deity bestows great glory, unless they choose rather to sell
sausages."

all to be despised, and ought to serve but for winter talk by the fireside; though, when I say despised, I mean it as for belief; for otherwise, the spreading or publishing of them is in no sort to be despised, for they have done much mischief; and I see many severe laws made to suppress them. That that hath given them grace, and some credit, consisteth in three things. First, that men mark when they hit, and never mark when they miss;[14] as they do, generally, also of dreams. The second is, that probable conjectures, or obscure traditions, many times turn themselves into prophecies; while the nature of man, which coveteth divination, thinks it no peril to foretell that which indeed they do but collect, as that of Seneca's verse; for so much was then subject to demonstration, that the globe of the earth had great parts beyond the Atlantic, which might be probably conceived not to be all sea; and adding thereto the tradition in Plato's Timæus, and his Atlanticus,[15] it might encourage one to turn it to a prediction. The third and last (which is the great one), is, that almost all of them, being infinite in number, have been impostures, and, by idle and crafty brains, merely contrived and feigned, after the event past.

[14] This is a very just remark. So-called strange coincidences, and wonderful dreams that are verified, when the point is considered, are really not at all marvellous. We never hear of the 999 dreams that are not verified, but the thousandth that happens to precede its fulfilment is blazoned by unthinking people as a marvel. It would be a much more wonderful thing if dreams were not occasionally verified.

[15] Under this name he alludes to the Critias of Plato, in which an imaginary "terra incognita" is discoursed of under the name of the "New Atlantis." It has been conjectured from this by some, that Plato really did believe in the existence of a continent on the other side of the globe

XXXVI.—OF AMBITION.

AMBITION is like choler, which is a humor that maketh men active, earnest, full of alacrity, and stirring,
if it be not stopped; but if it be stopped, and cannot
have its way, it becometh adust,[1] and thereby malign
and venomous. So ambitious men, if they find the
way open for their rising, and still get forward, they
are rather busy than dangerous; but if they be checked
in their desires, they become secretly discontent, and
look upon men and matters with an evil eye, and are
best pleased when things go backward; which is the
worst property in a servant of a prince or state.
Therefore, it is good for princes, if they use ambitious
men, to handle it so, as they be still progressive, and
not retrograde; which, because it cannot be without
inconvenience, it is good not to use such natures at
all; for if they rise not with their service, they will
take order to make their service fall with them. But
since we have said, it were good not to use men of
ambitious natures, except it be upon necessity, it is
fit we speak in what cases they are o' necessity. Good
commanders in the wars must be taken, be they never
so ambitious; for the use of their service dispenseth
with the rest; and to take a soldier without ambition,
is to pull off his spurs. There is also great use of ambitious men in being screens to princes in matters of
danger and envy; for no man will take that part, except he be like a seeled[2] dove, that mounts and mounts,
because he cannot see about him. There is use, also,
of ambitious men, in pulling down the greatness of any

[1] Hot and fiery.
[2] With the eyes closed or blindfolded.

subject that overtops; as Tiberius used Macro[3] in the pulling down of Sejanus. Since, therefore, they must be used in such cases, there resteth to speak how they are to be bridled, that they may be less dangerous. There is less danger of them if they be of mean birth, than if they be noble; and if they be rather harsh of nature, than gracious and popular; and if they be rather new raised, than grown cunning and fortified in their greatness. It is counted by some a weakness in princes to have favorites; but it is, of all others, the best remedy against ambitious great ones; for when the way of pleasuring and displeasuring lieth by the favorite, it is impossible any other should be overgreat. Another means to curb them, is, to balance them by others as proud as they; but then there must be some middle counsellors, to keep things steady, for without that ballast, the ship will roll too much. At the least, a prince may animate and inure some meaner persons to be, as it were, scourges to ambitious men. As for the having of them obnoxious to[4] ruin, if they be of fearful natures, it may do well; but if they be stout and daring, it may precipitate their designs, and prove dangerous. As for the pulling of them down, if the affairs require it, and that it may not be done with safety suddenly, the only way is, the interchange continually of favors and disgraces, whereby they may not know what to expect, and be, as it were, in a wood. Of ambitions, it is less harmful the ambition to prevail in great things, than that other to appear in every thing; for that breeds confusion,

[3] He was a favorite of Tiberius, to whose murder by Nero he was said to have been an accessary. He afterwards prostituted his own wife to Caligula, by whom he was eventually put to death.
[4] Liable to.

and mars business; but yet, it is less danger to have
an ambitious man stirring in business, than great in
dependencies. He that seeketh to be eminent amongst
able men, hath a great task, but that is ever good for
the public; but he that plots to be the only figure
amongst ciphers, is the decay of a whole age. Honor
hath three things in it: the vantage-ground to do
good; the approach to kings and principal persons;
and the raising of a man's own fortunes. He that hath
the best of these intentions, when he aspireth, is an
honest man; and that prince that can discern of these
intentions in another that aspireth, is a wise prince.
Generally, let princes and states choose such ministers
as are more sensible of duty than of rising, and such
as love business rather upon conscience than upon
bravery; and let them discern a busy nature from a
willing mind.

XXXVII.—OF MASQUES AND TRIUMPHS.

THESE things are but toys to come amongst such
serious observations; but yet, since princes will have
such things, it is better they should be graced with
elegancy, than daubed with cost. Dancing to song is
a thing of great state and pleasure. I understand it
that the song be in choir, placed aloft, and accom-
panied with some broken music, and the ditty fitted
to the device. Acting in song, especially in dialogues,
hath an extreme good grace; I say acting, not dancing (for that is a mean and vulgar thing); and the
voices of the dialogue would be strong and manly (a
base and a tenor, no treble), and the ditty high and
tragical, not nice or dainty. Several choirs, placed
one over against another, and taking the voices by

catches anthem-wise, give great pleasure. Turning dances into figure is a childish curiosity; and, generally, let it be noted, that those things which I here set down are such as to naturally take the sense, and not respect petty wonderments. It is true, the alterations of scenes, so it be quietly and without noise, are things of great beauty and pleasure for they feed and relieve the eye before it be full of the same object. Let the scenes abound with light, specially colored and varied; and let the masquers, or any other that are to come down from the scene, have some motions upon the scene itself before their coming down; for it draws the eye strangely, and makes it with great pleasure to desire to see that it cannot perfectly discern. Let the songs be loud and cheerful, and not chirpings or pulings;[1] let the music, likewise, be sharp and loud, and well placed. The colors that show best by candlelight, are white, carnation, and a kind of sea-water green; and ouches,[2] or spangs,[3] as they are of no great cost, so they are of most glory. As for rich embroidery, it is lost and not discerned. Let the suits of the masquers be graceful, and such as become the person when the vizors are off; not after examples of known attires, Turks, soldiers, mariners, and the like. Let anti-masques[4] not be long; they have been commonly of fools, satyrs, baboons, wild men, antics,

---

[1] Chirpings like the noise of young birds.

[2] Jewels or necklaces.

[3] Spangles, or O's of gold or silver. Beckmann says that these were invented in the beginning of the seventeenth century. See Beckmann's Hist. of Inventions (Bohn's Stand. Lib.), vol. i. p. 424.

[4] Or antic-masques. These were ridiculous interludes dividing the acts of the more serious masque. These were performed by hired actors, while the masque was played by ladies and gentlemen. The rule was, the characters were to be neither serious nor hideous. The "Comus" of Milton is an admirable specimen of a masque.

beasts, sprites, witches, Ethiopes, pigmies, turquets,[5] nymphs, rustics, Cupids, statues moving, and the like. As for angels, it is not comical enough to put them in anti-masques; and any thing that is hideous, as devils, giants, is, on the other side, as unfit; but, chiefly, let the music of them be recreative, and with some strange changes. Some sweet odors suddenly coming forth, without any drops falling, are, in such a company as there is steam and heat, things of great pleasure and refreshment. Double masques, one of men, another of ladies, addeth state and variety; but all is nothing, except the room be kept clear and neat.

For justs, and tourneys, and barriers, the glories of them are chiefly in the chariots, wherein the challengers make their entry; especially if they be drawn with strange beasts, as lions, bears, camels, and the like; or in the devices of their entrance, or in the bravery of their liveries, or in the goodly furniture of their horses and armor. But enough of these toys.

XXXVIII.—OF NATURE IN MEN.

Nature is often hidden, sometimes overcome, seldom extinguished. Force maketh nature more violent in the return; doctrine and discourse maketh nature less importune, but custom only doth alter and subdue nature. He that seeketh victory over his nature, let him not set himself too great nor too small tasks; for the first will make him dejected by often failings, and the second will make him a small proceeder, though by often prevailings. And at the first, let him practice with helps, as swimmers do with blad-

[5] Turks.

ders, or rushes; but, after a time, let him practise with disadvantages, as dancers do with thick shoes; for it breeds great perfection, if the practice be harder than the use. Where nature is mighty, and therefore the victory hard, the degrees had need be, first, to stay and arrest nature in time; like to him that would say over the four and twenty letters when he was angry; then to go less in quantity: as if one should, in forbearing wine, come from drinking healths to a draught at a meal; and, lastly, to discontinue altogether; but if a man have the fortitude and resolution to enfranchise himself at once, that is the best:—

> "Optimus ille animi vindex lædentia pectus
> Vincula qui rupit, dedoluitque semel." [1]

Neither is the ancient rule amiss, to bend nature as a wand to a contrary extreme, whereby to set it right; understanding it where the contrary extreme is no vice. Let not a man force a habit upon himself with a perpetual continuance, but with some intermission, for both the pause reinforceth the new onset; and if a man that is not perfect be ever in practice, he shall as well practise his errors as his abilities, and induce one habit of both; and there is no means to help this but by seasonable intermissions. But let not a man trust his victory over his nature too far; for nature will lie buried a great time, and yet revive upon the occasion or temptation; like as it was with Æsop's damsel, turned from a cat to a woman, who sat very demurely at the board's end till a mouse ran before her. Therefore, let a man either

---

[1] "He is the best asserter *of the liberty* of his mind, who bursts the chains that gall his breast, and at the same moment ceases to grieve."—This quotation is from *Ovid's Remedy of Love*, 293.

avoid the occasion altogether, or put himself often to it, that he may be little moved with it. A man's nature is best perceived in privateness, for there is no affectation; in passion, for that putteth a man out of his precepts; and in a new case or experiment, for there custom leaveth him. They are happy men whose natures sort with their vocations; otherwise they may say, "Multum incola fuit anima mea," [2] when they converse in those things they do not affect. In studies, whatsoever a man commandeth upon himself, let him set hours for it: but whatsoever is agreeable to his nature, let him take no care for any set times; for his thoughts will fly to it of themselves, so as the spaces of other business or studies will suffice. A man's nature runs either to herbs or weeds; therefore, let him seasonably water the one, and destroy the other.

XXXIX.—OF CUSTOM AND EDUCATION.

MEN's thoughts are much according to their inclination;[1] their discourse and speeches according to their learning and infused opinions; but their deeds are, after, as they have been accustomed; and, therefore, as Machiavel well noteth (though in an evil-favored instance), there is no trusting to the force of nature, nor to the bravery of words, except it be corroborate by custom.[2] His instance is, that, for the achieving of a desperate conspiracy, a man should not rest upon the fierceness of any man's nature, or his resolute undertakings, but take such a one as hath

[2] "My soul has long been a sojourner."
[1] "The wish is father to the thought," is a proverbial saying of similar meaning.
[2] *Vide* Disc. Sop. Liv. iii. 6.

had his hands formerly in blood; but Machiavel knew not of a Friar Clement,[3] nor a Ravaillac,[4] nor a Jaureguy,[5] nor a Baltazar Gerard;[6] yet his rule holdeth still, that nature, nor the engagement of words, are not so forcible as custom. Only superstition is now so well advanced, that men of the first blood are as firm as butchers by occupation; and votary[7] resolution is made equipollent to custom, even in matter of blood. In other things, the predominancy of custom is everywhere visible, insomuch as a man would wonder to hear men profess, protest, engage, give great words, and then do just as they have done before, as if they were dead images and engines, moved only by the wheels of custom. We see, also, the reign or tyranny of custom, what it is.

The Indians[8] (I mean the sect of their wise men) lay themselves quietly upon a stack of wood, and so sacrifice themselves by fire; nay, the wives strive to be burned with the corpses of their husbands. The lads of Sparta, of ancient time, were wont to be scourged upon the altar of Diana, without so much

[3] Jacques Clement, a Dominican friar, who assassinated Henry III. of France, in 1589. The sombre fanatic was but twenty-five years of age; and he had announced the intention of killing with his own hands the great enemy of his faith. He was instigated by the Leaguers, and particularly by the Duchess of Montpensier, the sister of the Duke of Guise.

[4] He murdered Henry IV. of France, in 1610.

[5] Philip II. of Spain having, in 1582, set a price upon the head of William of Nassau, Prince of Orange, the leader of the Protestants, Jaureguy attempted to assassinate him, and severely wounded him.

[6] He assassinated William of Nassau, in 1584. It is supposed that this fanatic meditated the crime for six years.

[7] A resolution prompted by a vow of devotion to a particular principle or creed.

[8] He alludes to the Hindoos, and the ceremony of Suttee, encouraged by the Brahmins.

as quecking.[9] I remember, in the beginning of Queen Elizabeth's time of England, an Irish rebel condemned, put up a petition to the deputy that he might be hanged in a withe, and not in a halter, because it had been so used with former rebels. There be monks in Russia for penance, that will sit a whole night in a vessel of water, till they be engaged with hard ice. Many examples may be put of the force of custom, both upon mind and body; therefore, since custom is the principal magistrate of man's life, let men, by all means, endeavor to obtain good customs. Certainly, custom is most perfect when it beginneth in young years: this we call education, which is, in effect, but an early custom. So we see, in languages, the tongue is more pliant to all expressions and sounds, the joints are more supple to all feats of activity and motions in youth, than afterwards; for it is true, that late learners cannot so well take the ply, except it be in some minds that have not suffered themselves to fix, but have kept themselves open and prepared to receive continual amendment, which is exceeding rare. But if the force of custom, simple and separate, be great, the force of custom, copulate and conjoined and collegiate, is far greater; for there example teacheth, company comforteth, emulation quickeneth, glory raiseth; so as in such places the force of custom is in his exaltation. Certainly, the great multiplication of virtues upon human nature resteth upon societies well ordained and disciplined; for commonwealths and good governments do nourish virtue grown, but do not much mend the seeds; but the misery is, that the most effectual means are now applied to the ends least to be desired.

[9] Flinching.—*Vide* Cic. Tuscul. Disp. ii. 14.

XL.—OF FORTUNE.

It cannot be denied, but outward accidents conduce much to fortune; favor, opportunity, death of others, occasion fitting virtue; but, chiefly, the mould of a man's fortune is in his own hands: "Faber quisque fortunæ suæ,"[1] saith the poet; and the most frequent of external causes, is that the folly of one man is the fortune of another; for no man prospers so suddenly as by others' errors. "Serpens nisi serpentem comederit non fit draco."[2] Overt and apparent virtues bring forth praise: but there be secret and hidden virtues that bring forth fortune; certain deliveries of a man's self, which have no name. The Spanish name, "disemboltura,"[3] partly expresseth them, when there be not stonds[4] nor restiveness in a man's nature, but that the wheels of his mind keep way with the wheels of his fortune; for so Livy (after he had described Cato Major in these words, "In illo viro, tantum robur corporis et animi fuit, ut quocunque loco natus esset, fortunam sibi facturus videretur,")[5] falleth upon that,

[1] "Every man is the architect of his own fortune." Sallust, in his letters "De Republicâ Ordinandâ," attributes these words to Appius Claudius Cæcus, a Roman poet whose works are now lost. Lord Bacon, in the Latin translation of his Essays, which was made under his supervision, rendered the word "poet" "comicus;" by whom he probably meant Plautus, who has this line in his "Trinummus" (Act ii, sc. 2): "Nam sapiens quidem pol ipsus fingit fortunam sibi," which has the same meaning, though in somewhat different terms.

[2] "A serpent, unless it has devoured a serpent, does not become a dragon."

[3] Or "desenvoltura," implying readiness to adapt one's self to circumstances.

[4] Impediments, causes for hesitation.

[5] "In that man there was such great strength of body and mind, that, in whatever station he had been born, he seemed as though he should make his fortune."

that he had "versatile ingenium:" [6] therefore, if a man look sharply and attentively, he shall see Fortune; for though she be blind, yet she is not invisible. The way of Fortune, is like the milky way in the sky; which is a meeting, or knot, of a number of small stars, not seen asunder, but giving light together; so are there a number of little and scarce discerned virtues, or rather faculties and customs, that make men fortunate. The Italians note some of them, such as a man would little think. When they speak of one that cannot do amiss, they will throw in into his other conditions, that he hath "Poco di matto;" [7] and, certainly, there be not two more fortunate properties, than to have a little of the fool, and not too much of the honest; therefore, extreme lovers of their country, or masters, were never fortunate; neither can they be, for when a man placeth his thoughts without himself, he goeth not his own way. A hasty fortune maketh an enterpriser and remover (the French hath it better, "entreprenant," or "remuant"); but the exercised fortune maketh the able man. Fortune is to be honored and respected, and it be but for her daughters, Confidence and Reputation; for those two Felicity breedeth; the first within a man's self, the latter in others towards him. All wise men, to decline the envy of their own virtues, use to ascribe them to Providence and Fortune; for so they may the better assume them; and, besides, it is greatness in a man to be the care of the higher powers. So Cæsar said to the pilot in the tempest, "Cæsarem portas, et fortunam ejus." [8] So

[6] "A versatile genius."
[7] "A little of the fool."
[8] "Thou carriest Cæsar and his fortunes."—*Plut. Vit. Cæls.* 38.

Sylla chose the name of "Felix," [9] and not of "Magnus;" [10] and it hath been noted, that those who ascribe openly too much to their own wisdom and policy, end unfortunate.   It is written, that Timotheus[11] the Athenian, after he had, in the account he gave to the state of his government, often interlaced his speech, "and in this Fortune had no part," never prospered in any thing he undertook afterwards.   Certainly there be, whose fortunes are like Homer's verses, that have a slide[12] and easiness more than the verses of other poets; as Plutarch saith of Timoleon's fortune in respect of that of Agesilaus or Epaminondas; and that this should be, no doubt it is much in a man's self.

XLI.—OF USURY.[1]

MANY have made witty invectives against usury. They say it is pity the devil should have God's part, which is the tithe; that the usurer is the greatest Sabbath-breaker, because his plough goeth every Sunday; that the usurer is the drone that Virgil speaketh of—

"Ignavum fucos pecus a præsepibus arcent;" [2]

that the usurer breaketh the first law that was made for mankind after the fall, which was, "in sudore vultûs tui comedes panem tuum;" [3] not, "in sudore vul-

[9] "The Fortunate." He attributed his success to the intervention of Hercules, to whom he paid especial veneration.

[10] "The Great."—*Plut. Syll.* 34.

[11] A successful Athenian general, the son of Conon, and the friend of Plato.

[12] Fluency, or smoothness.

[1] Lord Bacon seems to use the word in the general sense of "lending money upon interest."

[2] "Drive from their hives the drones, a lazy race."—*Georgics,* b. iv. 168.

[3] "In the sweat of thy face shalt thou eat thy bread."—*Gen.* iii. 19.

tûs alieni;"[4] that usurers should have orangetawny[5] bonnets, because they do Judaize; that it is against nature for money to beget money, and the like. I say this only, that usury is a "concessum propter duritiem cordis;"[6] for, since there must be borrowing and lending, and men are so hard of heart as they will not lend freely, usury must be permitted. Some others have made suspicious and cunning propositions of banks, discovery of men's estates, and other inventions; but few have spoken of usury usefully. It is good to set before us the incommodities and commodities of usury, that the good may be either weighed out, or culled out; and warily to provide, that, while we make forth to that which is better, we meet not with that which is worse.

The discommodities of usury are, first, that it makes fewer merchants; for were it not for this lazy trade of usury, money would not lie still, but would, in great part, be employed upon merchandising, which is the "vena porta"[7] of wealth in a state. The second, that it makes poor merchants; for as a farmer cannot husband his ground so well if he sit at a great rent, so the merchant cannot drive his trade so well if he sit[8] at great usury. The third is incident to the other two; and that is, the decay of customs of kings, or states, which ebb or flow with merchandising. The fourth, that it bringeth the treasure of a realm or state into a few hands; for the usurer being at cer-

[4] "In the sweat of the face of another."

[5] In the middle ages the Jews were compelled, by legal enactment, to wear peculiar dresses and colors; one of these was orange.

[6] "A concession by reason of hardness of heart." He alludes to the words in St. Matthew xix. 8.

[7] See note to Essay xix.

[8] Hold.

tainties, and others at uncertainties, at the end of the game most of the money will be in the box; and ever a state flourisheth when wealth is more equally spread. The fifth, that it beats down the price of land; for the employment of money is chiefly either merchandising or purchasing, and usury waylays both. The sixth, that it doth dull and damp all industries, improvements, and new inventions, wherein money would be stirring, if it were not for this slug. The last, that it is the canker and ruin of many men's estates, which, in process of time, breeds a public poverty.

On the other side, the commodities of usury are, first, that, howsoever usury in some respect hindereth merchandising, yet in some other it advanceth it; for it is certain that the greatest part of trade is driven by young merchants upon borrowing at interest; so as if the usurer either call in, or keep back his money, there will ensue presently a great stand of trade. The second is, that, were it not for this easy borrowing upon interest, men's necessities would draw upon them a most sudden undoing, in that they would be forced to sell their means (be it lands or goods), far under foot; and so, whereas usury doth but gnaw upon them, bad markets would swallow them quite up. As for mortgaging or pawning, it will little mend the matter; for either men will not take pawns without use, or, if they do, they will look precisely for the forfeiture. I remember a cruel moneyed man in the country, that would say, "The devil take this usury, it keeps us from forfeitures of mortgages and bonds." The third and last is, that it is a vanity to conceive that there would be ordinary borrowing without profit; and it is impossible to conceive the number of inconveniences that will ensue, if borrowing be cramped.

Therefore, to speak of the abolishing of usury is idle; all states have ever had it in one kind or rate, or other; so as that opinion must be sent to Utopia.[9]

To speak now of the reformation and reglement[10] of usury, how the discommodities of it may be best avoided, and the commodities retained. It appears, by the balance of commodities and discommodities of usury, two things are to be reconciled; the one, that the tooth of usury be grinded, that it bite not too much; the other, that there be left open a means to invite moneyed men to lend to the merchants, for the continuing and quickening of trade. This cannot be done, except you introduce two several sorts of usury, a less and a greater; for if you reduce usury to one low rate, it will ease the common borrower, but the merchant will be to seek for money; and it is to be noted that the trade of merchandise being the most lucrative, may bear usury at a good rate; other contracts not so.

To serve both intentions, the way would be briefly thus: that there be two rates of usury; the one free and general for all; the other under license only to certain persons, and in certain places of merchandising. First, therefore, let usury in general be reduced to five in the hundred, and let that rate be proclaimed to be free and current; and let the state shut itself out to take any penalty for the same. This will preserve borrowing from any general stop or dryness; this will ease infinite borrowers in the country; this will, in good part, raise the price of land, because land purchased at sixteen years' purchase will yield six in

[9] The imaginary country described in Sir Thomas More's political romance of that name.
[10] Regulation.

the hundred, and somewhat more, whereas this rate
of interest yields but five. This, by like reason, will
encourage and edge industrious and profitable improvements, because many will rather venture in that
kind, than take five in the hundred, especially having
been used to greater profit. Secondly, let there be
certain persons licensed to lend to known merchants
upon usury, at a higher rate, and let it be with the
cautions following: Let the rate be, even with the
merchant himself, somewhat more easy than that he
used formerly to pay; for, by that means, all borrowers shall have some ease by this reformation, be
he merchant, or whosoever; let it be no bank or common stock, but every man be master of his own
money; not that I altogether mislike banks, but they
will hardly be brooked, in regard of certain suspicions.
Let the state be answered[11] some small matter for the
license, and the rest left to the lender; for if the abatement be but small, it will no whit discourage the lender;
for he, for example, that took before ten or nine
in the hundred, will sooner descend to eight in the
hundred, than give over his trade of usury, and go
from certain gains to gains of hazard. Let these licensed lenders be in number indefinite, but restrained
to certain principal cities and towns of merchandising; for then they will be hardly able to color other
men's moneys in the country, so as the license of
nine will not suck away the current rate of five; for
no man will send his moneys far off, nor put them
into unknown hands.

If it be objected, that this doth in a sort authorize
usury, which before was in some places but permis=

[11] Be paid

sive; the answer is, that it is better to mitigate usury by declaration, than to suffer it to rage by connivance.[12]

XLII.—OF YOUTH AND AGE.

A MAN that is young in years may be old in hours, if he have lost no time; but that happeneth rarely. Generally, youth is like the first cogitations, not so wise as the second; for there is a youth in thoughts as well as in ages; and yet the invention of young men is more lively than that of old, and imaginations stream into their minds better, and, as it were, more divinely. Natures that have much heat, and great and violent desires and perturbations, are not ripe for

[12] Our author was one of the earliest writers who treated the question of the interest of money with the enlightened views of a statesman and an economist. The taking of interest was considered, in his time, immoral.

Laws on this matter are extremely ancient. Moses forbids the Jews to require interest of each other. "Thou shalt not lend upon usury to thy brother; usury of money, usury of victuals, usury of any thing that is lent upon usury:

"Unto a stranger thou mayest lend upon usury; but unto thy brother thou shalt not lend upon usury."—*Deut.* xxiii. 19, 20.

Among the Greeks, the rate of interest was settled by agreement between the borrower and the lender, without any interference of the law. The customary rate varied from ten to thirty-three and one third per cent.

The Romans enacted laws against usurious interest; but their legal interest, admitted by the law of the Twelve Tables, was, according to some, twelve per cent., or, to others, one twelfth of the capital, i. e. eight and one third per cent. Justinian reduced it to six per cent.

In England, the legal rate of interest was, in Henry the Eighth's reign, ten per cent. It was reduced, in 1624, to eight per cent. It was further diminished, in 1672, to six per cent. And definitively, in 1713, fixed at five per cent., the ordinary rate of interest throughout Europe. In France, the rates of interest have been nearly similar at the same periods.

action till they have passed the meridian of their years: as it was with Julius Cæsar and Septimius Severus; of the latter of whom it is said, "Juventutem egit erroribus, imo furoribus plenam;"[1] and yet he was the ablest emperor, almost, of all the list; but reposed natures may do well in youth, as it is seen in Augustus Cæsar, Cosmus Duke of Florence, Gaston de Foix,[2] and others. On the other side, heat and vivacity in age is an excellent composition for business. Young men are fitter to invent than to judge, fitter for execution than for counsel, and fitter for new projects than for settled business; for the experience of age, in things that fall within the compass of it, directeth them; but in new things abuseth them. The errors of young men are the ruin of business; but the errors of aged men amount but to this, that more might have been done, or sooner.

Young men, in the conduct and manage of actions, embrace more than they can hold, stir more than they can quiet; fly to the end, without consideration of the means and degrees; pursue some few principles which they have chanced upon absurdly; care not to innovate, which draws unknown inconveniences; use extreme remedies at first; and that, which doubleth all errors, will not acknowledge or retract them, like an unready horse, that will neither stop nor turn. Men of age object too much, consult too long, adventure too little, repent too soon, and seldom drive business home to the full period, but content themselves

---

[1] "He passed his youth full of errors, of madness even."— *Spartian. Vit. Sev.*

[2] He was nephew of Louis the Twelfth of France, and commanded the French armies in Italy against the Spaniards. After a brilliant career, he was killed at the battle of Ravenna, in 1512.

with a mediocrity of success. Certainly, it is good
to compound employments of both; for that will be
good for the present, because the virtues of either age
may correct the defects of both; and good for succession, that young men may be learners, while men in
age are actors; and, lastly, good for externe accidents,
because authority followeth old men, and favor and
popularity youth; but, for the moral part, perhaps,
youth will have the preëminence, as age hath for the
politic. A certain rabbin, upon the text, "Your young
men shall see visions, and your old men shall dream
dreams," [3] inferreth that young men are admitted
nearer to God than old, because vision is a clearer
revelation than a dream; and, certainly, the more a
man drinketh of the world, the more it intoxicateth;
and age doth profit rather in the powers of understanding, than in the virtues of the will and affections. There be some have an over-early ripeness in
their years, which fadeth betimes; these are, first,
such as have brittle wits, the edge whereof is soon
turned; such as was Hermogenes[4] the rhetorician,
whose books are exceedingly subtle; who afterwards
waxed stupid. A second sort is of those that have
some natural dispositions, which have better grace in
youth than in age; such as is a fluent and luxuriant
speech, which becomes youth well, but not age; so
Tully saith of Hortensius: "Idem manebat, neque
idem decebat." [5] The third is of such as take too high
a strain at the first, and are magnanimous more than

---

[3] Joel ii. 28, quoted Acts ii. 17.

[4] He lived in the second century after Christ, and is said to
have lost his memory at the age of twenty-five.

[5] "He remained the same, but *with the advance of years* was
not so becoming."—*Cic. Brut.* 95.

tract of years can uphold; as was Scipio Africanus,
of whom Livy saith, in effect, "Ultima primis cede-
bant." [6]

XLIII.—OF BEAUTY.

VIRTUE is like a rich stone, best plain set; and surely
virtue is best in a body that is comely, though not of
delicate features, and that hath rather dignity of
presence than beauty of aspect; neither is it always
most seen, that very beautiful persons are otherwise
of great virtue; as if nature were rather busy not to
err, than in labor to produce excellency; and therefore they prove accomplished, but not of great spirit,
and study rather behavior than virtue.   But this
holds not always; for Augustus Cæsar, Titus Vespasianus, Philip le Bel of France, Edward the Fourth
of England,[1] Alcibiades of Athens, Ismael the Sophy
of Persia, were all high and great spirits, and yet the
most beautiful men of their times.   In beauty, that of
favor is more than that of color; and that of decent
and gracious motion, more than that of favor.[2]   That
is the best part of beauty, which a picture cannot
express; no, nor the first sight of the life.   There is
no excellent beauty that hath not some strangeness
in the proportion.   A man cannot tell whether Apelles,

---

[6] "The close was unequal to the beginning." This quotation
is not correct; the words are: "Memorabilior prima pars vita
quam postrema fuit,"—"The first part of his life was more distinguished than the latter."—*Livy* xxxviii. ch. 53.

[1] By the context, he would seem to consider "great spirit"
and "virtue" as convertible terms.   Edward IV., however, has
no claim to be considered as a virtuous or magnanimous man,
though he possessed great physical courage.

[2] Features.

or Albert Durer, were the more trifler; whereof the one would make a personage by geometrical proportions; the other, by taking the best parts out of divers faces to make one excellent. Such personages, I think, would please nobody but the painter that made them: not but I think a painter may make a better face than ever was; but he must do it by a kind of felicity (as a musician that maketh an excellent air in music), and not by rule. A man shall see faces, that, if you examine them part by part, you shall find never a good, and yet altogether do well. If it be true that the principal part of beauty is in decent motion, certainly it is no marvel, though persons in years seem many times more amiable; "Pulchrorum autumnus pulcher;"[3] for no youth can be comely but by pardon,[4] and considering the youth as to make up the comeliness. Beauty is as summer fruits, which are easy to corrupt, and cannot last; and, for the most part, it makes a dissolute youth, and an age a little out of countenance; but yet certainly again, if it light well, it maketh virtues shine, and vices blush.

XLIV.—OF DEFORMITY.

DEFORMED persons are commonly even with nature; for, as nature hath done ill by them, so do they by nature, being for the most part (as the Scripture saith) "void of natural affection;"[1] and so they have their revenge of nature. Certainly, there is a consent between the body and the mind, and where na-

---

[3] "The autumn of the beautiful is beautiful"
[4] By making allowances.
[1] Rom. i. 31; 2 Tim. iii. 3.

ture erreth in the one, she ventureth in the other:
"Ubi peccat in uno, periclitatur in altero." [2] But because there is in man an election, touching the frame
of his mind, and a necessity in the frame of his body,
the stars of natural inclination are sometimes ob-
scured by the sun of discipline and virtue; therefore,
it is good to consider of deformity, not as a sign
which is more deceivable, but as a cause which seldom faileth of the effect. Whosoever hath any thing
fixed in his person that doth induce contempt, hath
also a perpetual spur in himself to rescue and deliver
himself from scorn; therefore, all deformed persons
are extreme bold; first, as in their own defence, as
being exposed to scorn, but, in process of time, by a
general habit. Also, it stirreth in them industry, and
especially of this kind, to watch and observe the
weakness of others, that they may have somewhat to
repay. Again, in their superiors, it quencheth jealousy
towards them, as persons that they think they may at
pleasure despise; and it layeth their competitors and
emulators asleep, as never believing they should be
in possibility of advancement till they see them in
possession; so that upon the matter, in a great wit,
deformity is an advantage to rising. Kings in ancient
times (and at this present in some countries) were
wont to put great trust in eunuchs, because they that
are envious towards all are more obnoxious and officious towards one; but yet their trust towards them
hath rather been as to good spials,[3] and good whis-
perers, than good magistrates and officers; and much
like is the reason of deformed persons. Still the
ground is, they will, if they be of spirit, seek to free

[2] "Where she errs in the one, she ventures in the other."
[3] Spies.

themselves from scorn, which must be either by virtue
or malice; and, therefore, let it not be marvelled, if
sometimes they prove excellent persons; as was Agesi-
laüs, Zanger, the son of Solyman,[4] Æsop, Gasca president of Peru; and Socrates may go likewise amongst
them, with others.

XLV.—OF BUILDING.

Houses are built to live in, and not to look on,
therefore, let use be preferred before uniformity, except where both may be had. Leave the goodly fabrics of houses, for beauty only, to the enchanted palaces of the poets, who build them with small cost.
He that builds a fair house upon an ill seat[1] com-
mitteth himself to prison; neither do I reckon it an
ill seat only where the air is unwholesome, but likewise where the air is unequal. As you shall see many
fine seats set upon a knap[2] of ground environed with
higher hills round about it, whereby the heat of the
sun is pent in, and the wind gathereth as in troughs;
so as you shall have, and that suddenly, as great diversity of heat and cold as if you dwelt in several
places. Neither is it ill air only that maketh an ill
seat; but ill ways, ill markets, and, if you will consult with Momus,[3] ill neighbors. I speak not of many
more: want of water, want of wood, shade, and shelter, want of fruitfulness, and mixture of grounds of
several natures; want of prospect, want of level

[4] Solyman the Magnificent, Sultan of the Turks.
[1] Site.
[2] Knoll.
[3] Have a liking for cheerful society. Momus being the god of
mirth.

grounds, want of places at some near distance for sports of hunting, hawking, and races; too near the sea, too remote; having the commodity of navigable rivers, or the discommodity of their overflowing; too far off from great cities, which may hinder business; or too near them, which lurcheth[4] all provisions, and maketh every thing dear; where a man hath a great living laid together, and where he is scanted; all which, as it is impossible perhaps to find together, so it is good to know them, and think of them, that a man may take as many as he can; and if he have several dwellings, that he sort them so, that what he wanteth in the one he may find in the other. Lucullus answered Pompey well, who, when he saw his stately galleries and rooms so large and lightsome, in one of his houses, said, "Surely, an excellent place for summer, but how do you do in winter?" Lucullus answered, "Why, do you not think me as wise as some fowls are, that ever change their abode towards the winter?" [5]

To pass from the seat to the house itself, we will do as Cicero doth in the orator's art, who writes books De Oratore, and a book he entitles Orator; whereof the former delivers the precepts of the art, and the latter the perfection. We will therefore describe a princely palace, making a brief model thereof; for it is strange to see, now in Europe, such huge buildings as the Vatican and Escurial,[6] and some others be, and yet scarce a very fair room in them.

First, therefore, I say, you cannot have a perfect

[4] Eats up.
[5] Plut. Vit. Lucull. 39.
[6] A vast edifice, about twenty miles from Madrid, founded by Philip II.

palace, except you have two several sides; a side for the banquet, as is spoken of in the book of Esther,[7] and a side for the household; the one for feasts and triumphs, and the other for dwelling. I understand both these sides to be not only returns, but parts of the front, and to be uniform without, though severally partitioned within; and to be on both sides of a great and stately tower in the midst of the front, that, as it were, joineth them together on either hand. I would have, on the side of the banquet in front, one only goodly room above stairs, of some forty foot high; and under it a room for a dressing or preparing place, at times of triumphs. On the other side, which is the household side, I wish it divided at the first into a hall and a chapel, (with a partition between), both of good state and bigness; and those not to go all the length, but to have at the further end a winter and a summer parlor, both fair; and under these rooms a fair and large cellar sunk under ground; and likewise some privy kitchens, with butteries, and pantries, and the like. As for the tower, I would have it two stories, of eighteen foot high apiece above the two wings; and a goodly leads upon the top, railed, with statues interposed; and the same tower to be divided into rooms, as shall be thought fit. The stairs likewise to the upper rooms, let them be upon a fair open newel,[8] and finely railed in with images of wood cast into a brass color, and a very fair landing-place at the top. But this to be, if you do not point any of the lower rooms for a dining-place of servants; for, other-

[7] Esth. i. 5; "The King made a feast unto all the people that were present in Shushan the palace, both unto great and small, seven days, in the court of the garden of the king's palace."

[8] The cylinder formed by the small end of the steps of winding stairs.

wise, you shall have the servants' dinner after your
own; for the steam of it will come up as in a tunnel.[9]
And so much for the front; only I understand the
height of the first stairs to be sixteen foot, which is
the height of the lower room.

Beyond this front is there to be a fair court, but
three sides of it of a far lower building than the front;
and in all the four corners of that court fair stair-
cases, cast into turrets on the outside, and not within
the row of buildings themselves; but those towers
are not to be of the height of the front, but rather
proportionable to the lower building. Let the court
not be paved, for that striketh up a great heat in
summer, and much cold in winter; but only some side
alleys with a cross, and the quarters to graze, being
kept shorn, but not too near shorn. The row of return on the banquet side, let it be all stately galleries;
in which galleries let there be three or five fine cupo-
las in the length of it, placed at equal distance, and
fine colored windows of several works; on the household side, chambers of presence and ordinary enter-
tainments, with some bedchambers; and let all three
sides be a double house, without thorough lights on
the sides, that you may have rooms from the sun,
both for forenoon and afternoon. Cast it, also, that
you may have rooms both for summer and winter;
shady for summer, and warm for winter. You shall
have sometimes fair houses so full of glass, that one
cannot tell where to become[10] to be out of the sun or
cold. For imbowed[11] windows, I hold them of good
use; (in cities, indeed, upright[12] do better, in respect

[9] The funnel of a chimney.
[10] Where to go.
[11] Bow, or bay, windows.
[12] Flush with the wall.

of the uniformity towards the street;) for they be
pretty retiring places for conference; and, besides,
they keep both the wind and sun off; for that which
would strike almost through the room doth scarce
pass the window: but let them be but few, four in
the court, on the sides only.

Beyond this court, let there be an inward court,
of the same square and height, which is to be environed with the garden on all sides; and in the inside,
cloistered on all sides upon decent and beautiful
arches, as high as the first story; on the under story
towards the garden, let it be turned to grotto, or place
of shade, or estivation; and only have opening and
windows towards the garden, and be level upon the
floor, no whit sunk under ground to avoid all damp-
ishness; and let there be a fountain, or some fair work
of statues in the midst of this court, and to be paved
as the other court was. These buildings to be for
privy lodgings on both sides, and the end for privy
galleries; whereof you must foresee that one of them
be for an infirmary, if the prince or any special person should be sick, with chambers, bedchamber, "an-
ticamera," [13] and "recamera," [14] joining to it; this
upon the second story. Upon the ground story, a
fair gallery, open, upon pillars; and upon the third
story, likewise, an open gallery upon pillars, to take
the prospect and freshness of the garden. At both
corners of the further side, by way of return, let there
be two delicate or rich cabinets, daintily paved, richly
hanged, glazed with crystalline glass, and a rich
cupola in the midst, and all other elegancy that can
be thought upon. In the upper gallery, too, I wish

[13] Antechamber.
[14] Withdrawing-room.

that there may be, if the place will yield it, some
fountains running in divers places from the wall, with
some fine avoidances.[15] And thus much for the model
of the palace, save that you must have, before you
come to the front, three courts: a green court plain,
with a wall about it; a second court of the same, but
more garnished with little turrets, or rather embellish-
ments, upon the wall; and a third court, to make a
square with the front, but not to be built, nor yet inclosed with a naked wall, but inclosed with terraces
leaded aloft, and fairly garnished on the three sides,
and cloistered on the inside with pillars, and not with
arches below. As for offices, let them stand at distance, with some low galleries to pass from them to
the palace itself.

XLVI.—OF GARDENS.

God Almighty first planted a garden; and, indeed,
it is the purest of human pleasures; it is the greatest
refreshment to the spirits of man; without which
buildings and palaces are but gross handyworks; and
a man shall ever see, that, when ages grow to civility
and elegancy, men come to build stately, sooner than
to garden finely; as if gardening were the greater
perfection. I do hold it, in the royal ordering of gardens, there ought to be gardens for all the months in
the year, in which, severally, things of beauty may be
then in season. For December, and January, and the
latter part of November, you must take such things
as are green all winter: holly, ivy, bays, juniper, cy-
press-trees, yew, pineapple-trees;[1] fir-trees, rosemary,

[15] Watercourses.
[1] Pine trees.

lavender; periwinkle, the white, the purple, and the blue; germander, flags, orange-trees, lemon-trees, and myrtles, if they be stoved;[2] and sweet marjoram, warm set. There followeth, for the latter part of January and February, the mezereon-tree, which then blossoms; crocus vernus, both the yellow and the gray; primroses, anemones, the early tulip, the hyacinthus orientalis, chamaïris fritellaria. For March, there come violets, especially the single blue, which are the earliest; the yellow daffodil, the daisy, the almond-tree in blossom, the peach-tree in blossom, the cornelian-tree in blossom, sweet-brier. In April, follow the double white violet, the wall-flower, the stock-gillyflower, the cowslip, flower-de-luces, and lilies of all natures; rosemary flowers, the tulip, the double peony, the pale daffodil, the French honeysuckle, the cherry-tree in blossom, the damascene[3] and plum-trees in blossom, the white thorn in leaf, the lilac-tree. In May and June come pinks of all sorts, especially the blush-pink; roses of all kinds, except the musk, which comes later; honeysuckles, strawberries, bugloss, columbine, the French marigold, flos Africanus, cherry-tree in fruit, ribes,[4] figs in fruit, rasps, vine-flowers, lavender in flowers, the sweet satyrian, with the white flower; herba muscaria, lilum convallium, the apple-tree in blossom. In July come gilly-flowers of all varieties, musk-roses, the lime-tree in blossom, early pears, and plums in fruit, genitings,[5] codlins. In August come plums of all sorts in fruit, pears, apricots, barberries, filberts, musk-melons,

[2] Kept warm in a greenhouse.
[3] The damson, or plum of Damascus.
[4] Currants.
[5] An apple that is gathered very early.

monk-hoods, of all colors. In September come grapes,
apples, poppies of all colors, peaches, melocotones[6]
nectarines, cornelians,[7] wardens,[8] quinces. In Octo-
ber, and the beginning of November, come services,
medlars, bullaces, roses cut or removed to come late,
hollyoaks, and such like. These particulars are for
the climate of London; but my meaning is perceived,
that you may have "ver perpetuum," [9] as the place
affords.

And because the breath of flowers is far sweeter
in the air (where it comes and goes, like the warbling
of music), than in the hand, therefore nothing is more
fit for that delight, than to know what be the flowers
and plants that do best perfume the air. Roses,
damask and red, are fast flowers[10] of their smell, so
that you may walk by a whole row of them, and find
nothing of their sweetness; yea, though it be in a
morning's dew. Bays, likewise, yield no smell as they
grow, rosemary little, nor sweet marjoram; that which,
above all others, yields the sweetest smell in the air,
is the violet, especially the white double violet, which
comes twice a year, about the middle of April, and
about Bartholomewtide. Next to that is the musk-
rose; then the strawberry leaves dying, with a most
excellent cordial smell; then the flower of the vines,
it is a little dust like the dust of a bent,[11] which grows
upon the cluster in the first coming forth; then sweet-

[6] A kind of quince, so called from "cotoneum," or "cydonium,"
the Latin name of the quince.
[7] The fruit of the cornel-tree.
[8] The warden was a large pear, so called from its keeping well.
Warden-pie was formerly much esteemed in this country.
[9] Perpetual spring.
[10] Flowers that do not send forth their smell at any distance.
[11] A species of grass of the genus argostis.

brier, then wall-flowers, which are very delightful to be set under a parlor or lower chamber window; then pinks and gillyflowers, specially the matted pink and clove gillyflower; then the flowers of the lime-tree; then the honeysuckles, so they be somewhat afar off. Of bean-flowers[12] I speak not, because they are field-flowers; but those which perfume the air most delightfully, not passed by as the rest, but being trodden upon and crushed, are three; that is, burnet, wild thyme, and water-mints; therefore you are to set whole alleys of them, to have the pleasure when you walk or tread.

For gardens (speaking of those which are indeed prince-like, as we have done of buildings), the contents ought not well to be under thirty acres of ground, and to be divided into three parts; a green in the entrance, a heath, or desert, in the going forth, and the main garden in the midst, besides alleys on both sides; and I like well that four acres of ground be assigned to the green, six to the heath, four and four to either side, and twelve to the main garden. The green hath two pleasures: the one, because nothing is more pleasant to the eye than green grass kept finely shorn; the other, because it will give you a fair alley in the midst, by which you may go in front upon a stately hedge, which is to inclose the garden. But because the alley will be long, and in great heat of the year, or day, you ought not to buy the shade in the garden by going in the sun through the green; therefore you are, of either side the green, to plant a covert alley, upon carpenter's work, about twelve foot in height, by which you may go in shade into the

[12] The blossoms of the bean.

garden. As for the making of knots or figures, with divers colored earths, that they may lie under the windows of the house on that side which the garden stands, they be but toys; you may see as good sights many times in tarts. The garden is best to be square, encompassed on all the four sides with a stately arched hedge: the arches to be upon pillars of carpenter's work, of some ten foot high, and six foot broad, and the spaces between of the same dimension with the breadth of the arch. Over the arches let there be an entire hedge of some four foot high, framed also upon carpenter's work; and upon the upper hedge, over every arch a little turret, with a belly enough to receive a cage of birds; and over every space between the arches some other little figure, with broad plates of round colored glass gilt, for the sun to play upon; but this hedge I intend to be raised upon a bank, not steep, but gently slope, of some six foot, set all with flowers. Also, I understand that this square of the garden should not be the whole breadth of the ground, but to leave on either side ground enough for diversity of side alleys, unto which the two covert alleys of the green may deliver you;[13] but there must be no alleys with hedges at either end of this great inclosure; not at the hither end, for letting[14] your prospect upon this fair hedge from the green; nor at the further end for letting your prospect from the hedge through the arches upon the heath.

For the ordering of the ground within the great hedge, I leave it to variety of device; advising, nevertheless, that whatsoever form you cast it into first, it be not too bushy, or full of work; wherein I, for my

[13] Bring or lead you.
[14] Impeding.

part, do not like images cut out in juniper or other garden stuff; they be for children. Little low hedges, round like welts, with some pretty pyramids, I like well; and in some places fair columns, upon frames of carpenter's work. I would also have the alleys spacious and fair. You may have closer alleys upon the side grounds, but none in the main garden. I wish, also, in the very middle, a fair mount, with three ascents and alleys, enough for four to walk abreast; which I would have to be perfect circles, without any bulwarks or embossments; and the whole mount to be thirty foot high, and some fine banqueting-house, with some chimneys neatly cast, and without too much glass.

For fountains, they are a great beauty and refreshment; but pools mar all, and make the garden unwholesome, and full of flies and frogs. Fountains I intend to be of two natures; the one that sprinkleth or spouteth water; the other, a fair receipt of water, of some thirty or forty foot square, but without fish, or slime, or mud. For the first, the ornaments of images, gilt or of marble, which are in use, do well; but the main matter is so to convey the water, as it never stay, either in the bowls or in the cistern; that the water be never by rest discolored, green, or red, or the like, or gather any mossiness or putrefaction; besides that, it is to be cleansed every day by the hand; also, some steps up to it, and some fine pavement about it, doth well. As for the other kind of fountain, which we may call a bathing-pool, it may admit much curiosity and beauty, wherewith we will not trouble ourselves: as, that the bottom be finely paved, and with images; the sides likewise; and withal, embellished with colored glass, and such things of lustre; encompassed, also, with fine rails of low statues. But the main point is the same that we mentioned in the former kind of fountain; which is, that the water be in perpetual motion, fed by a water higher than the pool, and delivered into it by fair spouts, and then discharged away under ground, by some equality of bores, that it stay little; and for fine devices, of arching water[15] without spilling, and making it rise in several forms (of feathers, drinking-glasses, canopies, and the like), they be pretty things to look on, but nothing to health and sweetness.

For the heath, which was the third part of our plot, I wish it to be framed as much as may be to a natural wildness. Trees I would have none in it, but some thickets made only of sweet-brier and honeysuckle, and some wild vine amongst; and the ground set with violets, strawberries, and primroses; for these are sweet, and prosper in the shade, and these to be in the heath here and there, not in any order. I like also little heaps, in the nature of molehills (such as are in wild heaths), to be set, some with wild thyme, some with pinks, some with germander, that gives a good flower to the eye; some with periwinkle, some with violets, some with strawberries, some with cowslips, some with daisies, some with red roses, some with lilum convallium,[16] some with sweet-williams red, some with bear's-foot, and the like low flowers, being withal sweet and sightly; part of which heaps to be with standards of little bushes pricked upon their top, and part without; the standards to be roses, juniper, holly, barberries (but here and there, because of the

[15] Causing the water to fall in a perfect arch, without any spray escaping from the jet.
[16] Lilies of the valley.

smell of their blossom), red currants, gooseberries,
rosemary, bays, sweetbrier, and such like; but these
standards to be kept with cutting, that they grow not
out of course.

For the side grounds, you are to fill them with
variety of alleys, private, to give a full shade; some
of them wheresoever the sun be. You are to frame
some of them likewise for shelter, that when the wind
blows sharp, you may walk as in a gallery: and those
alleys must be likewise hedged at both ends, to keep
out the wind; and these closer alleys must be ever
finely gravelled, and no grass, because of going wet.
In many of these alleys, likewise, you are to set fruit-
trees of all sorts, as well upon the walls as in ranges;[17]
and this should be generally observed, that the borders
wherein you plant your fruit-trees be fair, and large,
and low, and not steep; and set with fine flowers, but
thin and sparingly, lest they deceive[18] the trees. At
the end of both the side grounds I would have a mount
of some pretty height, leaving the wall of the inclosure breast high, to look abroad into the fields.

For the main garden, I do not deny but there
should be some fair alleys ranged on both sides with
fruit-trees, and some pretty tufts of fruit-trees and
arbors with seats, set in some decent order; but these
to be by no means set too thick, but to leave the main
garden so as it be not close, but the air open and free.
For as for shade, I would have you rest upon the alleys
of the side grounds, there to walk, if you be disposed,
in the heat of the year or day; but to make account[19]
that the main garden is for the more temperate parts

[17] In rows.
[18] Insidiously subtract nourishment from.
[19] To consider or expect.

of the year, and in the heat of summer for the morning and the evening or overcast days.

For aviaries, I like them not, except they be of that largeness as they may be turfed, and have living plants and bushes set in them; that the birds may have more scope and natural nestling, and that no foulness appear in the floor of the aviary. So I have made a platform of a princely garden, partly by precept, partly by drawing; not a model, but some general lines of it; and in this I have spared for no cost. But it is nothing for great princes, that, for the most part, taking advice with workmen, with no less cost set their things together, and sometimes add statues and such things for state and magnificence, but nothing to the true pleasure of a garden.

XLVII.—OF NEGOTIATING.

IT is generally better to deal by speech than by letter; and by the mediation of a third, than by a man's self. Letters are good, when a man would draw an answer by letter back again; or when it may serve for a man's justification afterwards to produce his own letter, or where it may be danger to be interrupted or heard by pieces. To deal in person is good, when a man's face breedeth regard, as commonly with inferiors; or in tender cases, where a man's eye upon the countenance of him with whom he speaketh, may give him a direction how far to go; and, generally, where a man will reserve to himself liberty, either to disavow or to expound. In choice of instruments, it is better to choose men of a plainer sort, that are like to do that that is committed to them, and to report

back again faithfully the success, than tnose that are
cunning to contrive out of other men's business somewhat to grace themselves, and will help the matter in
report, for satisfaction sake.   Use also such persons
as affect[1] the business wherein they are employed,
for that quickeneth much; and such as are fit for the
matter, as bold men for expostulation, fairspoken men
for persuasion, crafty men for inquiry and observation, froward and absurd men for business that doth
not well bear out itself. Use also such as have been
lucky and prevailed before in things wherein you
have employed them; for that breeds confidence, and
they will strive to maintain their prescription. It is
better to sound a person with whom one deals afar
off, than to fall upon the point at first, except you
mean to surprise him by some short question. It is
better dealing with men in appetite,[2] than with those
that are where they would be. If a man deal with
another upon conditions, the start of first performance is all; which a man cannot reasonably demand,
except either the nature of the thing be such, which
must go before; or else a man can persuade the other
party, that he shall still need him in some other thing;
or else that he be counted the honester man. All practice is to discover, or to work. Men discover themselves in trust, in passion, at unawares; and, of necessity, when they would have somewhat done, and cannot find an apt pretext. If you would work any
man, you must either know his nature and fashions,
and so lead him; or his ends, and so persuade him; or

[1] Love, are pleased with.
[2] It is more advantageous to deal with men whose desires are
not yet satisfied, than with those who have gained all they have
wished for, and are likely to be proof against inducements.

his weakness and disadvantages, and so awe him; or those that have interest in him, and so govern him. In dealing with cunning persons, we must ever consider their ends, to interpret their speeches; and it is good to say little to them, and that which they least look for. In all negotiations of difficulty, a man may not look to sow and reap at once; but must prepare business, and so ripen it by degrees.

XLVIII.—OF FOLLOWERS AND FRIENDS.

COSTLY followers are not to be liked, lest, while a man maketh his train longer, he make his wings shorter. I reckon to be costly, not them alone which charge the purse, but which are wearisome and importune in suits. Ordinary followers ought to challenge no higher conditions than countenance, recommendation, and protection from wrongs. Factious followers are worse to be liked, which follow not upon affection to him with whom they range themselves, but upon discontentment conceived against some other; whereupon commonly ensueth that ill intelligence, that we many times see between great personages. Likewise glorious[1] followers, who make themselves as trumpets of the commendations of those they follow, are full of inconvenience, for they taint business through want of secrecy; and they export honor from a man, and make him a return in envy. There is a kind of followers, likewise, which are dangerous, being indeed espials; which inquire the secrets of the house, and bear tales of them to others; yet such men, many times, are in great favor, for they are officious, and commonly exchange tales. The following, by cer-

[1] In the sense of the Latin "gloriosus," "boastful," "bragging."

tain estates[2] of men, answerable to that which a great
person himself professeth (as of soldiers to him that
hath been employed in the wars, and the like), hath
ever been a thing civil and well taken even in monarchies, so it be without too much pomp or popularity.
But the most honorable kind of following, is to be
followed as one that apprehendeth to advance virtue
and desert in all sorts of persons; and yet, where
there is no eminent odds in sufficiency, it is better to
take with the more passable, than with the more able;
and, besides, to speak truth in base times, active men
are of more use than virtuous. It is true, that, in government, it is good to use men of one rank equally;
for to countenance some extraordinarily, is to make
them insolent, and the rest discontent, because they
may claim a due: but, contrariwise, in favor, to use
men with much difference and election is good: for
it maketh the persons preferred more thankful, and
the rest more officious, because all is of favor. It is
good discretion not to make too much of any man at
the first, because one cannot hold out that proportion.
To be governed, as we call it, by one, is not safe, for
it shows softness,[3] and gives a freedom to scandal and
disreputation; for those that would not censure, or
speak ill of a man immediately, will talk more boldly
of those that are so great with them, and thereby
wound their honor; yet to be distracted with many is
worse, for it makes men to be of the last impression,
and full of change. To take advice of some few
friends is ever honorable; for lookers-on many times
see more than gamesters, and the vale best discov-
ereth the hill. There is little friendship in the world,

[2] Professions or classes.
[3] Weakness, or indecision of character

and least of all between equals, which was wont[4] to be magnified. That that is, is between superior and inferior,[5] whose fortunes may comprehend the one the other.

XLIX.—OF SUITORS.

Many ill matters and projects are undertaken; and private suits to putrefy the public good. Many good matters are undertaken with bad minds; I mean not only corrupt minds, but crafty minds, that intend not performance. Some embrace suits, which never mean to deal effectually in them; but if they see there may be life in the matter, by some other mean they will be content to win a thank, or take a second reward, or, at least, to make use, in the mean time, of the suitor's hopes. Some take hold of suits only for an occasion to cross some other, or to make an information, whereof they could not otherwise have apt

[4] He probably alludes to the ancient stories of the friendship of Orestes and Pylades, Theseus and Pirithoüs, Damon and Pythias, and others, and the maxims of the ancient philosophers. Aristotle considers that equality in circumstances and station is one requisite of friendship. Seneca and Quintus Curtius express the same opinion. It seems hardly probable that Lord Bacon reflected deeply when he penned this passage, for between equals, jealousy, the most insidious of all the enemies of friendship, has the least chance of originating. Dr. Johnson says: "Friendship is seldom lasting but between equals, or where the superiority on one side is reduced by some equivalent advantage on the other. Benefits which cannot be repaid, and obligations which cannot be discharged, are not commonly found to increase affection; they excite gratitude indeed, and heighten veneration, but commonly take away that easy freedom and familiarity of intercourse, without which, though there may be fidelity, and zeal, and admiration, there cannot be friendship."— *The Rambler*, No. 64.

[5] In such a case, gratitude and admiration exist on the one hand, esteem and confidence on the other.

pretext, without care what become of the suit when
that turn is served; or, generally, to make other men's
business a kind of entertainment to bring in their own:
nay, some undertake suits with a full purpose to let
them fall, to the end to gratify the adverse party, or
competitor. Surely, there is in some sort a right in
every suit; either a right of equity, if it be a suit
of controversy, or a right of desert, if it be a suit of
petition. If affection lead a man to favor the wrong
side in justice, let him rather use his countenance to
compound the matter than to carry it. If affection
lead a man to favor the less worthy in desert, let him
do it without depraving[1] or disabling the better de-
server. In suits which a man doth not well understand, it is good to refer them to some friend of trust
and judgment, that may report whether he may deal
in them with honor; but let him choose well his refer-
endaries,[2] for else he may be led by the nose. Suitors
are so distasted[3] with delays and abuses, that plain
dealing in denying to deal in suits at first, and report-
ing the success barely,[4] and in challenging no more
thanks than one hath deserved, is grown not only
honorable, but also gracious. In suits of favor, the
first coming ought to take little place;[5] so far forth[6]
consideration may be had of his trust, that if intelligence of the matter could not otherwise have been
had but by him, advantage be not taken of the note,[7]
but the party left to his other means, and in some sort
recompensed for his discovery. To be ignorant of the

---

[1] Lowering, or humiliating.   [2] Referees.   [3] Disgusted.

[4] Giving no false color to the degree of success which has at
tended the prosecution of the suit.

[5] To have little effect.

[6] To this extent.

[7] Of the information

value of a suit is simplicity; as well as to be ignorant
of the right thereof, is want of conscience. Secrecy
in suits is a great mean of obtaining; for voicing them
to be in forwardness may discourage some kind of
suitors, but doth quicken and awake others. But
timing of the suit is the principal; timing, I say, not
only in respect of the person that should grant it, but
in respect of those which are like to cross it. Let a
man, in the choice of his mean, rather choose the fittest mean, than the greatest mean; and rather them
that deal in certain things, than those that are general. The reparation of a denial is sometimes equal
to the first grant, if a man show himself neither dejected nor discontented. "Iniquum petas, ut æquum
feras," [8] is a good rule, where a man hath strength of
favor; but otherwise a man were better rise in his suit;
for he that would have ventured at first to have lost
the suitor, will not, in the conclusion, lose both the
suitor and his own former favor. Nothing is thought
so easy a request to a great person as his letter: and
yet if it be not in a good cause, it is so much out of his
reputation. There are no worse instruments than
these general contrivers of suits; for they are but a
kind of poison and infection to public proceedings.

L.—OF STUDIES.[1]

STUDIES serve for delight, for ornament, and for
ability. Their chief use for delight, is in privateness
and retiring; for ornament, is in discourse; and for

[8] "Ask what is exorbitant, that you may obtain what is moderate."

[1] This formed the first essay in the earliest edition of the
work.

ability, is in the judgment and disposition of business; for expert men can execute, and perhaps judge of particulars one by one; but the general counsels, and the plots and marshalling of affairs, come best from those that are learned. To spend too much time in studies, is sloth; to use them too much for ornament, is affectation: to make judgment wholly by their rules, is the humor of a scholar. They perfect nature, and are perfected by experience; for natural abilities are like natural plants, that need pruning by study; and studies themselves do give forth directions too much at large, except they be bounded in by experience. Crafty men contemn studies, simple men admire them, and wise men use them; for they teach not their own use; but that is a wisdom without them and above them, won by observation. Read not to contradict and confute, nor to believe and take for granted, nor to find talk and discourse, but to weigh and consider. Some books are to be tasted, others to be swallowed, and some few to be chewed and digested; that is, some books are to be read only in parts; others to be read, but not curiously;[2] and some few to be read wholly, and with diligence and attention. Some books also may be read by deputy, and extracts made of them by others; but that would be only in the less important arguments and the meaner sort of books; else distilled books are, like common distilled waters, flashy[3] things. Reading maketh a full man; conference a ready man; and writing an exact man; and, therefore, if a man write little, he had need have a great memory; if he confer little, he had need have a present wit; and if he read little, he had

[2] Attentively.
[3] Vapid: without taste or spirit.

need have much cunning, to seem to know that he doth
not. Histories make men wise; poets, witty; the
mathematics, subtile; natural philosophy, deep; moral,
grave; logic and rhetoric, able to contend: "Abeunt
studia in mores;" [4] nay, there is no stand or impediment in the wit, but may be wrought out by fit studies.
Like as diseases of the body may have appropriate
exercises, bowling is good for the stone and reins,
shooting for the lungs and breast, gentle walking for
the stomach, riding for the head and the like; so, if a
man's wit be wandering, let him study the mathematics; for in demonstrations, if his wit be called
away never so little, he must begin again; if his wit
be not apt to distinguish or find difference, let him
study the schoolmen, for they are "Cymini sectores." [5]
If he be not apt to beat over matters, and to call up
one thing to prove and illustrate another, let him study
the lawyers' cases; so every defect of the mind may
have a special receipt.

LI.—OF FACTION.

MANY have an opinion not wise, that for a prince
to govern his estate, or for a great person to govern
his proceedings, according to the respect of factions,
is a principal part of policy; whereas, contrariwise,
the chiefest wisdom is, either in ordering those things
which are general, and wherein men of several fac-

[4] "Studies become habits."
[5] "Splitters of cummin-seeds;" or, as we now say, "splitters
of straws," or "hairs." Butler says of Hudibras:—

"He could distinguish and divide
A hair 'twixt south and southwest side."

tions do nevertheless agree, or in dealing with correspondence to particular persons, one by one; but I say not, that the consideration of factions is to be neglected. Mean men in their rising must adhere; but great men, that have strength in themselves, were better to maintain themselves indifferent and neutral; yet, even in beginners, to adhere so moderately, as he be a man of the one faction, which is most passable with the other, commonly giveth best way. The lower and weaker faction is the firmer in conjunction; and it is often seen, that a few that are stiff, do tire out a great number that are more moderate. When one of the factions is extinguished, the remaining subdivideth; as the faction between Lucullus and the rest of the nobles of the senate (which they called "optimates"), held out a while against the faction of Pompey and Cæsar; but when the senate's authority was pulled down, Cæsar and Pompey soon after brake. The faction or party of Antonius and Octavianus Cæsar, against Brutus and Cassius, held out likewise for a time; but when Brutus and Cassius were overthrown, then soon after Antonius and Octavianus brake and subdivided. These examples are of wars, but the same holdeth in private factions; and, therefore, those that are seconds in factions do many times, when the faction subdivideth, prove principals; but many times also they prove ciphers, and cashiered, for many a man's strength is in opposition; and when that faileth, he groweth out of use. It is commonly seen, that men once placed, take in with the contrary faction to that by which they enter; thinking, belike, that they have the first sure, and now are ready for a new purchase. The traitor in faction lightly goeth away with it; for when matters have stuck long in balancing, the winning of some one man casteth them,[1] and he getteth all the thanks. The even carriage between two factions proceedeth not always of moderation, but of a trueness to a man's self, with end to make use of both. Certainly, in Italy, they hold it a little suspect in popes, when they have often in their mouth, "Padre commune;" [2] and take it to be a sign of one that meaneth to refer all to the greatness of his own house. Kings had need beware how they side themselves, and make themselves as of a faction or party; for leagues within the state are ever pernicious to monarchies; for they raise an obligation paramount to obligation of sovereignty, and make the king "tanquam unus ex nobis," [3] as was to be seen in the League of France. When factions are carried too high and too violently, it is a sign of weakness in princes, and much to the prejudice both of their authority and business. The motions of factions under kings, ought to be like the motions (as the astronomers speak) of the inferior orbs, which may have their proper motions, but yet still are quietly carried by the higher motion of "primum mobile." [4]

LII.—OF CEREMONIES AND RESPECTS.

He that is only real, had need have exceeding great parts of virtue; as the stone had need to be rich that is set without foil; but if a man mark it well, it is in

[1] Causes one side to preponderate.
[2] "The common father."
[3] "As one of us." Henry the Third of France, favoring the league formed by the Duke of Guise and Cardinal De Lorraine against the Protestants, soon found that, through the adoption of that policy, he had forfeited the respect of his subjects.
[4] See a note to Essay 15.

praise and commendation of men, as it is in gettings
and gains; for the proverb is true, that "Light gains
make heavy purses;" for light gains come thick,
whereas great come but now and then. So it is true,
that small matters win great commendation, because
they are continually in use and in note; whereas the
occasion of any great virtue cometh but on festivals;
therefore it doth much add to a man's reputation,
and is (as Queen Isabella[1] said) like perpetual letters commendatory, to have good forms. To attain
them, it almost sufficeth not to despise them; for so
shall a man observe them in others; and let him trust
himself with the rest; for if he labor too much to express them, he shall lose their grace, which is to be
natural and unaffected. Some men's behavior is like
a verse, wherein every syllable is measured; how can
a man comprehend great matters, that breaketh his
mind too much to small observations? Not to use
ceremonies at all, is to teach others not to use them
again, and so diminisheth respect to himself; especially they be not to be omitted to strangers and for-
mal natures; but the dwelling upon them, and exalt-
ing them above the moon, is not only tedious, but doth
diminish the faith and credit of him that speaks; and,
certainly, there is a kind of conveying of effectual and
imprinting passages amongst compliments, which is
of singular use, if a man can hit upon it. Amongst a
man's peers, a man shall be sure of familiarity, and,
therefore, it is good a little to keep state; amongst a
man's inferiors, one shall be sure of reverence, and
therefore it is good a little to be familiar. He that is
too much in any thing, so that he giveth another oc-

[1] Of Castile. She was the wife of Ferdinand of Arragon, and
was the patroness of Columbus.

casion of satiety, maketh himself cheap. To apply one's self to others, is good, so it be with demonstration that a man doth it upon regard, and not upon facility. It is a good precept, generally in seconding another, yet to add somewhat of one's own; as, if you will grant his opinion, let it be with some distinction; if you will follow his motion, let it be with condition; if you allow his counsel, let it be with alleging further reason. Men had need beware how they be too perfect in compliments; for be they never so sufficient otherwise, their enviers will be sure to give them that attribute to the disadvantage of their greater virtues. It is loss, also, in business, to be too full of respects, or to be too curious in observing times and opportunities. Solomon saith, "He that considereth the wind shall not sow, and he that looketh to the clouds shall not reap." [2] A wise man will make more opportunities than he finds. Men's behavior should be like their apparel, not too strait or point device,[3] but free for exercise or motion.

LIII.—OF PRAISE.

PRAISE is the reflection of virtue; but it is glass, or body, which giveth the reflection. If it be from the common people, it is commonly false and naught, and rather followeth vain persons than virtuous; for the common people understand not many excellent virtues. The lowest virtues draw praise from them, the

[2] The words in our version are: "He that observeth the wind shall not sow, and he that regardeth the clouds shall not reap."— *Ecclesiastes* xi. 1.

[3] Exact in the extreme. Point-de-vice was originally the name of a kind of lace of very fine pattern.

middle virtues work in them astonishment or admiration, but of the highest virtues they have no sense
or perceiving at all; but shows and "species virtutibus
similes," [1] serve best with them. Certainly, fame is
like a river, that beareth up things light and swollen,
and drowns things weighty and solid; but if persons
of quality and judgment concur, then it is (as the
Scripture saith), "Nomen bonum instar unguenti
fragrantis:" [2] it filleth all round about, and will not
easily away; for the odors of ointments are more dur-
able than those of flowers. There be so many false
points of praise, that a man may justly hold it a suspect. Some praises proceed merely of flattery; and
if he be an ordinary flatterer, he will have certain common attributes, which may serve every man; if he be
a cunning flatterer, he will follow the arch-flatterer,
which is a man's self, and wherein a man thinketh
best of himself, therein the flatterer will uphold him
most. But if he be an impudent flatterer, look wherein a man is conscious to himself that he is most defective, and is most out of countenance in himself,
that will the flatterer entitle him to, perforce, "spretâ
conscientiâ." [3] Some praises come of good wishes and
respects, which is a form due in civility to kings and
great persons, "laudando præcipere;" [4] when, by telling men what they are, they represent to them what
they should be; some men are praised maliciously to
their hurt, thereby to stir envy and jealousy towards

---

[1] "Appearances resembling virtues."

[2] "A good name is like sweet-smelling ointment." The words
in our version are, "A good name is better than precious ointment."—*Ecclesiastes* vii. 1.

[3] "Disregarding *his own* conscience."

[4] "To instruct under the form of praise."

them: "Pessimum genus inimicorum laudantium;" [5] insomuch as it was a proverb amongst the Grecians, that "he that was praised to his hurt, should have a push[6] rise upon his nose;" as we say that a blister will rise upon one's tongue that tells a lie; certainly, moderate praise, used with opportunity, and not vulgar, is that which doth the good. Solomon saith: "He that praiseth his friend aloud, rising early, it shall be to him no better than a curse." [7] Too much magnifying of man or matter doth irritate contradiction, and procure envy and scorn. To praise a man's self cannot be decent, except it be in rare cases; but to praise a man's office[8] or profession, he may do it with good grace, and with a kind of magnanimity. The cardinals of Rome, which are theologues,[9] and friars, and schoolmen, have a phrase of notable contempt and scorn towards civil business; for they call all temporal business of wars, embassages, judicature, and other employments, sbirrerie, which is under-sheriffries, as if they were but matters for under-sheriffs and catchpoles; though many times those under-sheriffries do more good than their high speculations. St. Paul, when he boasts of himself, he doth oft interlace, "I speak like a fool:" [10] but speaking of his calling, he saith, "Magnificabo apostolatum meum." [11]

[5] "The worst kind of enemies are those who flatter."

[6] A pimple filled with "pus," or "purulent matter." The word is still used in the east of England.

[7] The words in our version are: "He that blesseth his friend with a loud voice, rising early in the morning, it shall be counted a curse to him."—*Proverbs* xxvii. 14.

[8] In other words, to show what we call an *esprit de corps.*

[9] Theologians.

[10] 2 Cor. xi. 23.

[11] "I will magnify my apostleship." He alludes to the words in Romans xi. 13: "Inasmuch as I am the apostle of the Gentiles, I magnify mine office."

LIV.—OF VAINGLORY.

It was prettily devised of Æsop, the fly sat upon
the axle-tree of the chariot-wheel, and said, "What
a dust do I raise!" So are there some vain persons,
that, whatsoever goeth alone, or moveth upon greater
means, if they have never so little hand in it, they
think it is they that carry it. They that are glorious,
must needs be factious; for all bravery[1] stands upon
comparisons. They must needs be violent, to make
good their own vaunts; neither can they be secret,
and therefore not effectual; but, according to the
French proverb, "Beaucoup de bruit, peu de fruit;"—
"much bruit,[2] little fruit." Yet, certainly, there is
use of this quality in civil affairs: where there is an
opinion[3] and fame to be created, either of virtue or
greatness, these men are good trumpeters. Again, as
Titus Livius noteth, in the case of Antiochus and the
Ætolians,[4] there are sometimes great effects of cross
lies; as if a man that negotiates between two princes,
to draw them to join in a war against the third, doth
extol the forces of either of them above measure, the
one to the other; and sometimes he that deals between
man and man, raiseth his own credit with both, by
pretending greater interest than he hath in either;
and in these, and the like kinds, it often falls out,
that somewhat is produced of nothing; for lies are
sufficient to breed opinion, and opinion brings on substance. In military commanders and soldiers, vain-

[1] Vaunting, or boasting.
[2] Noise. We have a corresponding proverb: "Great cry and
little wool."
[3] A high or good opinion.
[4] *Vide* Liv. xxxvii. 48.

glory is an essential point; for as iron sharpens iron, so by glory one courage sharpeneth another. In cases of great enterprise upon charge[5] and adventure, a composition of glorious natures doth put life into business; and those that are of solid and sober natures, have more of the ballast than of the sail. In fame of learning, the flight will be slow without some feathers of ostentation: "Qui de contemnendâ gloriâ libros scribunt, nomen suum inscribunt."[6] Socrates, Aristotle, Galen, were men full of ostentation: certainly, vainglory helpeth to perpetuate a man's memory; and virtue was never so beholden to human nature, as it received its due at the second hand. Neither had the fame of Cicero, Seneca, Plinius Secundus,[7] borne her age so well if it had not been joined with some vanity in themselves; like unto varnish, that makes ceilings not only shine, but last. But all this while, when I speak of vainglory, I mean not of that property that Tacitus doth attribute to Mucianus, "Omnium, quæ dixerat feceratque, arte quâdam ostentator;"[8] for that[9] proceeds not of vanity, but of natural magnanimity and discretion; and, in some persons, is not

[5] By express command.
[6] "Those who write books on despising glory, set their names in the title-page." He quotes from Cicero's "Tusculanæ Disputationes," b. i. c. 15, whose words are: "Quid nostri philosophi? Nonne in his libris ipsis, quos scribunt de contemnendâ gloriâ, sua nomina inscribunt."—"What do our philosophers do? Do they not, in those very books which they write on despising glory, set their names in the title-page?"
[7] Pliny the Younger, the nephew of the elder Pliny, the naturalist.
[8] "One who set off every thing he said and did with a certain skill." Mucianus was an intriguing general in the times of Otho and Vitellius.—*Hist.* xi. 80.
[9] Namely, the property of which he was speaking, and not that mentioned by Tacitus.

only comely, but gracious; for excusations,[10] cessions,[11] modesty itself, well governed, are but arts of ostentation; and amongst those arts there is none better than that which Plinius Secundus speaketh of, which is to be liberal of praise and commendation to others, in that wherein a man's self hath any perfection. For, saith Pliny, very wittily, "In commending another, you do yourself right;[12] for he that you commend is either superior to you in that you commend, or inferior: if he be inferior, if he be to be commended, you much more; if he be superior, if he be not to be commended, you much less." Glorious[13] men are the scorn of wise men, the admiration of fools, the idols of parasites, and the slaves of their own vaunts.

LV.—OF HONOR AND REPUTATION.

THE winning of honor is but the revealing of a man's virtue and worth without disadvantage; for some in their actions do woo and affect honor and reputation; which sort of men are commonly much talked of, but inwardly little admired; and some, contrariwise, darken their virtue in the show of it, so as they be undervalued in opinion. If a man perform that which hath not been attempted before, or attempted and given over, or hath been achieved, but not with so good circumstance, he shall purchase more honor than by affecting a matter of greater difficulty or virtue, wherein he is but a follower. If a

[10] Apologies.
[11] Concessions.
[12] Plin. Epist. vi. 17.
[13] Boastful.

man so temper his actions, as in some one of them he doth content every faction or combination of people, the music will be the fuller.   A man is an ill husband of his honor that entereth into any action, the failing wherein may disgrace him more than the carrying of it through can honor him.   Honor that is gained and broken upon another hath the quickest reflection, like diamonds cut with facets; and therefore let a man contend to excel any competitors of his in honor, in outshooting them, if he can, in their own bow.   Discreet followers and servants help much to reputation: "Omnis fama a domesticis emanat."[1]   Envy, which is the canker of honor, is best extinguished by declaring a man's self in his ends, rather to seek merit than fame; and by attributing a man's successes rather to Divine providence and felicity, than to his own virtue or policy.   The true marshalling of the degrees of sovereign honor are these.   In the first place are "conditores imperiorum,"[2] founders of states and commonwealths; such as were Romulus, Cyrus, Cæsar, Ottoman,[3] Ismael: in the second place are "legislatores," lawgivers, which are also called second founders, or "perpetui principes,"[4] because they govern by their ordinances after they are gone; such were Lycurgus, Solon, Justinian, Edgar,[5] Alphonsus of Castile, th

[1] "All fame emanates from servants."—*Q. Cic. de Petit. Consul,* v. 17.

[2] "Founders of empires."

[3] He alludes to Ottoman, or Othman I., the founder of the dynasty now reigning at Constantinople.   From him, the Turkish empire received the appellation of "Othoman," or "Ottoman" Porte.

[4] "Perpetual rulers."

[5] Surnamed the Peaceful, who ascended the throne of England A. D. 959.   He was eminent as a legislator, and a rigid assertor of justice.   Hume considers his reign "one of the most fortunate that we meet with in the ancient English history."

Wise, that made the "Siete Partidas:"[6] in the third
place are "liberatores," or "salvatores,"[7] such as compound the long miseries of civil wars, or deliver their
countries from servitude of strangers or tyrants, as
Augustus Cæsar, Vespasianus, Aurelianus, Theodor-
icus, King Henry the Seventh of England, King
Henry the Fourth of France: in the fourth place are
"propagatores," or "propugnatores imperii,"[8] such as
in honorable wars enlarge their territories, or make
noble defence against invaders: and, in the last place
are "patres patriæ,"[9] which reign justly, and make the
times good wherein they live; both which last kinds
need no examples, they are in such number. Degrees of honor in subjects are, first, "participes curarum,"[10] those upon whom princes do discharge the
greatest weight of their affairs, their right hands, as
we call them; the next are "duces belli,"[11] great leaders, such as are princes' lieutenants, and do them
notable services in the wars; the third are "gratiosi,"
favorites, such as exceed not this scantling,[12] to be
solace to the sovereign, and harmless to the people;
and the fourth "negotiis pares,"[13] such as have great
places under princes, and execute their places with

[6] These were a general collection of the Spanish laws, made
by Alphonso X. of Castile, arranged under their proper titles.
The work was commenced by Don Ferdinand his father, to put
an end to the contradictory decisions in the Castilian courts of
justice. It was divided into seven parts, whence its name "Siete
Partidas." It did not, however, become the law of Castile till
nearly eighty years after.

[7] "Deliverers," or "preservers."
[8] "Extenders," or "defenders of the empire."
[9] "Fathers of their country."
[10] "Participators in cares."
[11] "Leaders in war."
[12] Proportion, dimensions.
[13] "Equal to their duties."

sufficiency, There is an honor, likewise, which may
be ranked amongst the greatest, which happeneth
rarely; that is, of such as sacrifice themselves to death
or danger for the good of their country; as was M.
Regulus, and the two Decii.

LVI.—OF JUDICATURE.

Judges ought to remember that their office is "jus
dicere,"[1] and not "jus dare;"[2] to interpret law, and
not to make law, or give law; else will it be like the
authority claimed by the Church of Rome, which,
under pretext of exposition of Scripture, doth not
stick to add and alter, and to pronounce that which
they do not find, and, by show of antiquity, to introduce novelty. Judges ought to be more learned than
witty, more reverend than plausible, and more advised than confident. Above all things, integrity is
their portion and proper virtue. "Cursed (saith the
law)[3] is he that removeth the landmark." The mis-
layer of a mere stone is to blame; but it is the unjust
judge that is the capital remover of landmarks, when
he defineth amiss of lands and property. One foul
sentence doth more hurt than many foul examples;
for these do but corrupt the stream, the other corrupteth the fountain: so saith Solomon, "Fons turba-
tus et vena corrupta est justus cadens in causâ suâ
coram adversario."[4] The office of judges may have

[1] "To expound the law."
[2] "To make the law."
[3] The Mosaic law. He alludes to Deuteronomy xxvii. 17
"Cursed be he that removeth his neighbor's landmark."
[4] "A righteous man falling down before the wicked is as a
troubled fountain and a corrupt spring."—*Proverbs* xxv. 26.

reference unto the parties that sue, unto the advocates that plead, unto the clerks and ministers of justice underneath them, and to the sovereign or state above them.

First, for the causes or parties that sue. "There be (saith the Scripture) that turn judgment into wormwood;"[5] and surely there be, also, that turn it into vinegar; for injustice maketh it bitter, and delays make it sour. The principal duty of a judge is to suppress force and fraud; whereof force is the more pernicious when it is open, and fraud when it is close and disguised. Add thereto contentious suits, which ought to be spewed out, as the surfeit of courts. A judge ought to prepare his way to a just sentence, as God useth to prepare his way, by raising valleys and taking down hills; so when there appeareth on either side a high hand, violent prosecution, cunning advantages taken, combination, power, great counsel, then is the virtue of a judge seen to make inequality equal, that he may plant his judgment as upon an even ground. "Qui fortiter emungit, elicit sanguinem;"[6] and where the wine-press is hard wrought, it yields a harsh wine, that tastes of the grape-stone. Judges must beware of hard constructions and strained inferences; for there is no worse torture than the torture of laws. Especially in case of laws penal, they ought to have care that that which was meant for terror be not turned into rigor; and that they bring not upon the people that shower whereof the Scripture

[5] "Ye who turn judgment to wormwood, and leave off righteousness in the earth."—*Amos* v. 7.

[6] "He who wrings the nose strongly brings blood."—*Proverbs* xxx. 33: "Surely, the churning of milk bringeth forth butter, and the wringing of the nose bringeth forth blood; so the forcing of wrath bringeth forth strife."

speaketh, "Pluet super eos laqueos;" [7] for penal laws
pressed,[8] are a shower of snares upon the people.
Therefore let penal laws, if they have been sleepers of
long, or if they be grown unfit for the present time, be
by wise judges confined in the execution; "Judicis offi-
cium est, ut res, ita tempora rerum," &c.[9] In causes of
life and death, judges ought (as far as law permitteth)
in justice to remember mercy; to cast a severe eye
upon the example, but a merciful eye upon the person.

Secondly, for the advocates and counsel that plead.
Patience[10] and gravity of hearing is an essential part
of justice, and an overspeaking judge is no well-tuned
cymbal. It is no grace to a judge first to find that
which he might have heard in due time from the bar;
or to show quickness of conceit in cutting off evidence
or counsel too short, or to prevent information by
questions, though pertinent. The parts of a judge
in hearing are four: to direct the evidence; to moderate length, repetition, or impertinency of speech; to
recapitulate, select, and collate the material points of
that which hath been said; and to give the rule or
sentence. Whatsoever is above these is too much, and
proceedeth either of glory, and willingness to speak,
or of impatience to hear, or of shortness of memory,
or of want of a staid and equal attention. It is a
strange thing to see that the boldness of advocates
should prevail with judges; whereas, they should

[7] "He will rain snares upon them." Psalm xi. 6: "Upon the
wicked he shall rain snares, fire, and brimstone, and an horrible
tempest."

[8] Strained.

[9] "It is the duty of a judge to consider not only the facts, but
the circumstances of the case."—*Ovid. Trist.* I. i. 37.

[10] Pliny the Younger, Ep. B. 6, E. 2, has the observation:
"Patientiam . . . quæ pars magna justitiæ est;" "Patience
which is a great part of justice."

imitate God in whose seat they sit, who represseth the presumptuous, and giveth grace to the modest; but it is more strange, that judges should have noted favorites, which cannot but cause multiplication of fees, and suspicion of by-ways. There is due from the judge to the advocate some commendation and gracing, where causes are well handled and fair pleaded, especially towards the side which obtaineth not;[11] for that upholds in the client the reputation of his counsel, and beats down in him the conceit[12] of his cause. There is likewise due to the public a civil reprehension of advocates, where there appeareth cunning counsel, gross neglect, slight information, indiscreet pressing, or an over-bold defence; and let not the counsel at the bar chop[13] with the judge, nor wind himself into the handling of the cause anew after the judge hath declared his sentence; but, on the other side, let not the judge meet the cause half-way, nor give occasion to the party to say, his counsel or proofs were not heard.

Thirdly, for that that concerns clerks and ministers. The place of justice is a hallowed place; and, therefore, not only the bench, but the foot-pace and precincts, and purprise thereof, ought to be preserved without scandal and corruption; for, certainly, "Grapes (as the Scripture saith) will not be gathered of thorns or thistles;[14] neither can justice yield her fruit with sweetness amongst the briers and brambles of catching and polling[15] clerks and ministers. The

[11] Is not successful.
[12] Makes him to feel less confident of the goodness of his cause.
[13] Altercate, or bandy words with the judge.
[14] "Do men gather grapes of thorns, or figs of thistles?"—*St. Matthew* vii. 16.
[15] Plundering.

attendance of courts is subject to four bad instruments: first, certain persons that are sowers of suits,
which make the court swell, and the country pine:
the second sort is of those that engage courts in quarrels of jurisdiction, and are not truly "amici curiæ,"[16]
but "parasiti curiæ,"[17] in puffing a court up beyond
her bounds for their own scraps and advantage: the
third sort is of those that may be accounted the left
hands of courts; persons that are full of nimble and
sinister tricks and shifts, whereby they pervert the
plain and direct courses of courts, and bring justice
into oblique lines and labyrinths: and the fourth is
the poller and exacter of fees; which justifies the common resemblance of the courts of justice to the bush,
whereunto while the sheep flies for defence in weather,
he is sure to lose part of his fleece.   On the other side,
an ancient clerk, skilful in precedents, wary in proceeding, and understanding in the business of the
court, is an excellent finger of a court, and doth many
times point the way to the judge himself.

Fourthly, for that which may concern the sovereign and estate.   Judges ought, above all, to remember the conclusion of the Roman Twelve Tables,[18]
"Salus populi suprema lex;"[19] and to know that laws,
except they be in order to that end, are but things
captious, and oracles not well inspired; therefore it
is a happy thing in a state, when kings and states do
often consult with judges; and again, when judges do
often consult with the king and state: the one, when
there is matter of law intervenient in business of
state; the other, when there is some consideration of

[16] "Friends of the court."
[17] "Parasites," or "flatterers of the court."
[18] Which were compiled by the decemvirs.
[19] "The safety of the people is the supreme law."

state intervenient in matter of law; for many times the things deduced to judgment may be "meum"[20] and "tuum,"[21] when the reason and consequence thereof may trench to point of estate. I call matter of estate, not only the parts of sovereignty, but whatsoever introduceth any great alteration, or dangerous precedent, or concerneth manifestly any great portion of people; and let no man weakly conceive, that just laws and true policy have any antipathy for they are like the spirits and sinews, that one moves with the other. Let judges also remember, that Solomon's throne was supported by lions[22] on both sides; let them be lions, but yet lions under the throne, being circumspect that they do not check or oppose any points of sovereignty. Let not judges also be so ignorant of their own right, as to think there is not left to them, as a principal part of their office, a wise use and application of laws; for they may remember what the apostle saith of a greater law than theirs: "Nos scimus quia lex bona est, modo quis eâ utatur legitime."[23]

LVII.—OF ANGER.

To seek to extinguish anger utterly is but a bravery[1] of the Stoics. We have better oracles: "Be angry,

[20] "Mine."   [21] "Yours."

[22] He alludes to 1 Kings x. 19, 30: "The throne had six steps, and the top of the throne was round behind; and there were stays on either side on the place of the seat, and two lions stood beside the stays. And twelve lions stood there on the one side and on the other upon the six steps." The same verses are repeated in 1 Chronicles ix. 18, 19.

[23] "We know that the law is good, if a man use it lawfully."— 1 *Timothy* i. 8.

[1] A boast.

but sin not; let not the sun go down upon your anger."[2] Anger must be limited and confined, both in race and in time. We will first speak how the natural inclination and habit, "to be angry," may be attempered and calmed; secondly, how the particular motions of anger may be repressed, or, at least, refrained from doing mischief; thirdly, how to raise anger, or appease anger in another.

For the first, there is no other way but to meditate and ruminate well upon the effects of anger, how it troubles man's life; and the best time to do this is, to look back upon anger when the fit is thoroughly over. Seneca saith well, "that anger is like ruin, which breaks itself upon that it falls."[3] The Scripture exhorteth us "to possess our souls in patience;"[4] whosoever is out of patience, is out of possession of his soul. Men must not turn bees:—

"Animasque in vulnere ponunt." [5]

Anger is certainly a kind of baseness; as it appears well in the weakness of those subjects in whom it reigns, children, women, old folks, sick folks. Only men must beware that they carry their anger rather with scorn than with fear; so that they may seem rather to be above the injury than below it; which is a thing easily done, if a man will give law to himself in it.

For the second point, the causes and motives of anger are chiefly three. First, to be too sensible of

[2] In our version it is thus rendered: "Be ye angry, and sin not; let not the sun go down upon your wrath."—*Ephesians* iv. 26.
[3] Sen. De Ira i. 1.
[4] "In your patience possess ye your souls."—*Luke* xvi. 19.
[5] "And leave their lives in the wound." The quotation is from Virgil's Georgics, iv. 238.

hurt, for no man is angry that feels not himself nurt and therefore tender and delicate persons must need be oft angry, they have so many things to trouble them, which more robust natures have little sense of: the next is, the apprehension and construction of the injury offered, to be, in the circumstances thereof, full of contempt; for contempt is that which putteth an edge upon anger, as much, or more, than the hurt itself; and therefore, when men are ingenious in picking out circumstances of contempt, they do kindle their anger much: lastly, opinion of the touch[6] of a man's reputation doth multiply and sharpen anger; wherein the remedy is, that a man should have, as Gonsalvo was wont to say, "Telam honoris crassiorem."[7] But in all refrainings of anger, it is the best remedy to win time, and to make a man's self believe that the opportunity of his revenge is not yet come; but that he foresees a time for it, and so to still himself in the mean time, and reserve it.

To contain anger from mischief, though it take hold of a man, there be two things whereof you must have special caution: the one, of extreme bitterness of words, especially if they be aculeate and proper,[8] for "communia maledicta"[9] are nothing so much; and, again, that in anger a man reveal no secrets, for that makes him not fit for society: the other, that you do not peremptorily break off in any business in a fit of anger; but, howsoever you show bitterness, do not act any thing that is not revocable.

For raising and appeasing anger in another, it is done chiefly by choosing of times when men are

[6] Susceptibility upon.
[7] "A thicker covering for his honor."
[8] Pointed and peculiarly appropriate to the party attacked.
[9] "Ordinary abuse."

frowardest and worst disposed to incense them; again, by gathering (as was touched before) all that you can find out to aggravate the contempt: and the two remedies are by the contraries; the former to take good times, when first to relate to a man an angry business, for the first impression is much; and the other is, to sever, as much as may be, the construction of the injury from the point of contempt; imputing it to misunderstanding, fear, passion, or what you will.

LVIII.—OF VICISSITUDE OF THINGS

SOLOMON saith, "There is no new thing upon the earth;"[1] so that as Plato[2] had an imagination that all knowledge was but remembrance, so Solomon giveth his sentence, "That all novelty is but oblivion;"[3] whereby you may see, that the river of Lethe runneth as well above ground as below. There is an abstruse astrologer that saith, if it were not for two things that are constant (the one is, that the fixed stars ever stand at like distance one from another, and never come nearer together, nor go further asunder; the other, that the diurnal motion perpetually keepeth time), no individual would last one moment; certain it is, that the matter is in a perpetual flux, and never at a

[1] "The thing that hath been, it is that which shall be; and that which is done, is that which shall be done; and there is no new thing under the sun. Is there any thing whereof it may be said, See, this is new? It hath been already of old time, which was before us."—*Ecclesiastes* i. 9, 10.

[2] In his Phædo.

[3] "There is no remembrance of former things: neither shall there be any remembrance of things that are to come, with those that shall come hereafter."—*Ecclesiastes* i. 11.

stay. The great winding-sheets that bury all things in oblivion, are two,—deluges and earthquakes. As for conflagrations and great droughts, they do not merely dispeople, but destroy. Phaeton's car went but a day; and the three years' drought in the time of Elias,[4] was but particular,[5] and left people alive. As for the great burnings by lightnings, which are often in the West Indies,[6] they are but narrow;[7] but in the other two destructions, by deluge and earth-quake, it is further to be noted, that the remnant of people which happen to be reserved, are commonly ignorant and mountainous people, that can give no account of the time past; so that the oblivion is all one, as if none had been left. If you consider well of the people of the West Indies, it is very probable that they are a newer, or a younger people than the people of the old world; and it is much more likely that the destruction that hath heretofore been there, was not by earthquakes, (as the Egyptian priest told Solon, concerning the Island of Atlantis,[8] that it was swallowed by an earthquake), but rather that it was desolated by a particular deluge, for earthquakes are seldom in those parts; but, on the other side, they have such pouring rivers, as the rivers of Asia, and Africa, and Europe, are but brooks to them. Their

[4] "And Elijah the Tishbite, who was of the inhabitants of Gilead, said unto Ahab, As the Lord God of Israel liveth, be-fore whom I stand, there shall not be dew nor rain these years, but according to my word."—1 *Kings* xvii. 1. "And it came to pass after many days, that the word of the Lord came to Elijah in the third year, saying, Go, show thyself unto Ahab; and I will send rain upon the earth."—1 *Kings* xviii. 1.

[5] Confined to a limited space.

[6] The whole of the continent of America then discovered is included under this name.

[7] Limited.

[8] *Vide* Plat. Tim. iii. 24, seq.

Andes, likewise, or mountains, are far higher than those with us; whereby it seems, that the remnants of generations of men were in such a particular deluge saved. As for the observation that Machiavel hath, that the jealousy of sects doth much extinguish the memory of things,[9] traducing Gregory the Great, that he did what in him lay to extinguish all heathen antiquities, I do not find that those zeals do any great effects, nor last long; as it appeared in the succession of Sabinian,[10] who did revive the former antiquities.

The vicissitude, or mutations, in the superior globe, are no fit matter for this present argument. It may be, Plato's great year,[11] if the world should last so long, would have some effect, not in renewing the state of like individuals (for that is the fume[12] of those that conceive the celestial bodies have more accurate influences upon these things below, than indeed they have), but in gross. Comets, out of question, have likewise power and effect over the gross and mass of things; but they are rather gazed, and waited upon[13] in their journey, than wisely observed in their effects, especially in their respective effects; that is, what kind of comet for magnitude, color, version of the beams, placing in the region of heaven, or lasting, produceth what kind of effects.

[9] Mach. Disc. Sop. Liv. ii. 2.

[10] Sabinianus of Volaterra was elected Bishop of Rome on the death of Gregory the Great, A. D. 604. He was of an avaricious disposition, and thereby incurred the popular hatred. He died in eighteen months after his election.

[11] This Cicero speaks of as "the great year of the mathematicians." "On the Nature of the Gods," B. 4, ch. 20. By some it was supposed to occur after a period of 12,954 years, while, according to others, it was of 25,920 years' duration.—*Plat. Tim.* lii. 38, seq.

[12] Conceit.

[13] Observed.

There is a toy,[14] which I have heard, and I would not have it given over, but waited upon a little. They say it is observed in the Low Countries (I know not in what part), that every five and thirty years the same kind and suit of years and weather comes about again; as great frosts, great wet, great droughts, warm winters, summers with little heat, and the like; and they call it the prime. It is a thing I do the rather mention, because, computing backwards, I have found some concurrence.

But to leave these points of nature, and to come to men. The greatest vicissitude of things amongst men, is the vicissitude of sects and religions; for those orbs rule in men's minds most. The true religion is built upon the rock; the rest are tossed upon the waves of time. To speak, therefore, of the causes of new sects, and to give some counsel concerning them, as far as the weakness of human judgment can give stay to so great revolutions.

When the religion formerly received is rent by discords, and when the holiness of the professors of religion is decayed and full of scandal, and, withal, the times be stupid, ignorant, and barbarous, you may doubt the springing up of a new sect; if then, also, there should arise any extravagant and strange spirit to make himself author thereof; all which points held when Mahomet published his law. If a new sect have not two properties, fear it not, for it will not spread. The one is the supplanting or the opposing of authority established, for nothing is more popular than that; the other is, the giving license to pleasures and a voluptuous life; for as for speculative heresies (such as were in ancient times the

[14] A curious fancy or odd conceit.

Arians, and now the Arminians),[15] though they work mightily upon men's wits, yet they do not produce any great alterations in states, except it be by the help of civil occasions. There be three manner of plantations of new sects: by the power of signs and miracles; by the eloquence and wisdom of speech and persuasion; and by the sword. For martyrdoms, I reckon them amongst miracles, because they seem to exceed the strength of human nature; and I may do the like of superlative and admirable holiness of life. Surely, there is no better way to stop the rising of new sects and schisms, than to reform abuses; to compound the smaller differences; to proceed mildly, and not with sanguinary persecutions; and rather to take off the principal authors, by winning and advancing them, than to enrage them by violence and bitterness.

The changes and vicissitude in wars are many, but chiefly in three things: in the seats or stages of the war, in the weapons, and in the manner of the conduct. Wars, in ancient time, seemed more to move from east to west; for the Persians, Assyrians, Arabians, Tartars (which were the invaders), were all eastern people. It is true the Gauls were western; but we read but of two incursions of theirs, the one to Gallo-Græcia, the other to Rome: but east and west have no certain points of heaven; and no more have the wars, either from the east or west, any certainty of observation; but north and south are fixed; and it hath seldom or never been seen that the far southern

---

[15] The followers of Arminius, or James Harmensen, a celebrated divine of the 16th and 17th centuries. Though called a heresy by Bacon, his opinions have been for two centuries, and still are, held by a large portion of the Church of England.

people have invaded the northern, but contrariwise;
whereby it is manifest that the northern tract of the
world is in nature the more martial region, be it in
respect of the stars of that hemisphere,[16] or of the
great continents that are upon the north; whereas,
the south part, for aught that is known, is almost all
sea; or (which is most apparent) of the cold of the
northern parts, which is that which, without aid of
discipline, doth make the bodies hardest, and the
courage warmest.

Upon the breaking and shivering of a great state
and empire, you may be sure to have wars; for great
empires, while they stand, do enervate and destroy
the forces of the natives which they have subdued,
resting upon their own protecting forces; and then,
when they fail also, all goes to ruin, and they become
a prey. So was it in the decay of the Roman empire,
and likewise in the empire of Almaigne,[17] after
Charles the Great,[18] every bird taking a feather, and
were not unlike to befall to Spain, if it should break.
The great accessions and unions of kingdoms do likewise stir up wars; for when a state grows to an over-
power, it is like a great flood, that will be sure to
overflow, as it hath been seen in the states of Rome,
Turkey, Spain, and others. Look when the world
hath fewest barbarous people, but such as commonly
will not marry or generate, except they know means
to live (as it is almost everywhere at this day, except
Tartary), there is no danger of inundations of people; but when there be great shoals of people, which

[16] A belief in astrology, or at least the influence of the stars
was almost universal in the time of Bacon.
[17] Germany.
[18] Charlemagne.

go on to populate, without foreseeing means of life and sustenation, it is of necessity that once in an age or two they discharge a portion of their people upon other nations, which the ancient northern people were wont to do by lot; casting lots what part should stay at home, and what should seek their fortunes. When a warlike state grows soft and effeminate, they may be sure of a war, for commonly such states are grown rich in the time of their degenerating; and so the prey inviteth, and their decay in valor encourageth a war.

As for the weapons, it hardly falleth under rule and observation, yet we see even they have returns and vicissitudes; for certain it is that ordnance was known in the city of the Oxidraces, in India, and was that which the Macedonians[19] called thunder and lightning, and magic; and it is well known that the use of ordnance hath been in China above two thousand years. The conditions of weapons, and their improvements are, first, the fetching[20] afar off, for that outruns the danger, as it is seen in ordnance and muskets; secondly, the strength of the percussion, wherein, likewise, ordnance do exceed all arietations,[21] and ancient inventions; the third is, the commodious use of them, as that they may serve in all weathers, that the carriage may be light and manageable, and the like.

For the conduct of the war: at the first, men rested extremely upon number; they did put the wars likewise upon main force and valor, pointing days for pitched fields, and so trying it out upon an even

[19] When led thither by Alexander the Great.
[20] Striking.
[21] Application of the "aries," or battering-ram.

match; and they were more ignorant in ranging and arraying their battles. After they grew to rest upon number, rather competent than vast, they grew to advantages of place, cunning diversions, and the like, and they grew more skilful in the ordering of their battles.

In the youth of a state, arms do flourish; in the middle age of a state, learning; and then both of them together for a time; in the declining age of a state, mechanical arts and merchandise. Learning hath its infancy when it is but beginning, and almost childish; then its youth, when it is luxuriant and juvenile; then its strength of years, when it is solid and reduced; and, lastly, its old age, when it waxeth dry and exhaust. But it is not good to look too long upon these turning wheels of vicissitude, lest we become giddy; as for the philology of them, that is but a circle of tales, and therefore not fit for this writing

APPENDIX TO ESSAYS.

I.—A FRAGMENT OF AN ESSAY OF FAME.[1]

THE poets make fame a monster; they describe her in part finely and elegantly, and in part gravely and sententiously; they say, Look, how many feathers she hath, so many eyes she hath underneath, so many tongues, so many voices, she pricks up so many ears!

This is a flourish: there follow excellent parables; as that she gathereth strength in going; that she goeth upon the ground, and yet hideth her head in the clouds; that in the daytime she sitteth in a watch-tower, and flieth most by night; that she mingleth things done with things not done; and that she is a terror to great cities; but that which passeth all the rest is, they do recount that the Earth, mother of the giants that made war against Jupiter, and were by him destroyed, thereupon in anger brought forth Fame; for certain it is that rebels, figured by the giants, and seditious fames and libels, are but brothers and sisters, masculine and feminine. But now, if a man can tame this monster, and bring her to feed at the hand and govern her, and with her fly other ravening fowl, and kill them, it is somewhat worth; but we are infected with the style of the poets. To speak now in a sad and serious manner, there is not in all the politics a place less handled, and more worthy to

[1] This fragment was found among Lord Bacon's papers and published by Dr. Rawley in his Resuscitatio.

be handled, than this of fame. We will, therefore, speak of these points. What are false fames, and what are true fames, and how they may be best discerned; how fames may be sown and raised; how they may be spread and multiplied; and how they may be checked and lay dead; and other things concerning the nature of fame. Fame is of that force, as there is scarcely any great action wherein it hath not a great part, especially in the war. Mucianus undid Vitellius by a fame that he scattered, that Vitellius had in purpose to remove the legions of Syria into Germany, and the legions of Germany into Syria; whereupon the legions of Syria were infinitely inflamed.[2] Julius Cæsar took Pompey unprovided, and laid asleep his industry and preparations by a fame that he cunningly gave out, how Cæsar's own soldiers loved him not; and being wearied with the wars, and laden with the spoils of Gaul, would forsake him as soon as he came into Italy.[3] Livia settled all things for the succession of her son Tiberius, by continually giving out that her husband Augustus was upon recovery and amendment;[4] and it is a usual thing with the bashaws to conceal the death of the Grand Turk from the janizaries and men of war, to save the sacking of Constantinople, and other towns, as their manner is. Themistocles made Xerxes, king of Persia, post apace out of Græcia, by giving out that the Grecians had a purpose to break his bridge of ships which he had made athwart Hellespont.[5] There be a thousand such like examples, and the more they are, the less they

[2] Tac. Hist. ii. 80.
[3] Cæs. de Bell. Civ. i. 6.
[4] Tac. Ann. i. 5.
[5] *Vide* Herod. viii. 108, 109.

need to be repeated, because a man meeteth with them everywhere; therefore, let all wise governors have as great a watch and care over fames, as they have of the actions and designs themselves.

II.—OF A KING.

1. A KING is a mortal God on earth, unto whom the living God hath lent his own name as a great honor; but withal told him he should die like a man lest he should be proud and flatter himself, that God hath, with his name, imparted unto him his nature also.

2. Of all kind of men, God is the least beholden unto them; for he doth most for them, and they do, ordinarily, least for him.

3. A king that would not feel his crown too heavy for him, must wear it every day; but if he think it too light, he knoweth not of what metal it is made.

4. He must make religion the rule of government, and not to balance the scale; for he that casteth in religion only to make the scales even, his own weight is contained in those characters: "Mene, mene, tekel, upharsin: He is found too light, his kingdom shall be taken from him."

5. And that king that holds not religion the best reason of state, is void of all piety and justice, the supporters of a king.

6. He must be able to give counsel himself, but not rely thereupon; for though happy events justify their counsels, yet it is better that the evil event of good advice be rather imputed to a subject than a sovereign.

7. He is a fountain of honor, which should not run with a waste-pipe, lest the courtiers sell the water,

and then, as Papists say of their holy wells, it loses the virtue.

8. He is the life of the law, not only as he is *Lex loquens* himself, but because he animateth the dead letter, making it active towards all his subjects *præmio et pœna.*

9. A wise king must do less in altering his laws than he may; for new government is ever dangerous. It being true in the body politic, as in the corporal, that *omnis subita immutatio est periculosa;* and though it be for the better, yet it is not without a fearful apprehension; for he that changeth the fundamental laws of a kingdom, thinketh there is no good title to a crown, but by conquest.

10. A king that setteth to sale seats of justice, oppresseth the people; for he teacheth his judges to sell justice; and *pretio parata pretio venditur justitia.*

11. Bounty and magnificence are virtues very regal, but a prodigal king is nearer a tyrant than a parsimonious; for store at home draweth not his contemplations abroad, but want supplieth itself of what is next, and many times the next way. A king therein must be wise, and know what he may justly do.

12. That king which is not feared, is not loved; and he that is well seen in his craft, must as well study to be feared as loved; yet not loved for fear, but feared for love.

13. Therefore, as he must always resemble Him whose great name he beareth, and that as in manifesting the sweet influence of his mercy on the severe stroke of his justice sometimes, so in this not to suffer a man of death to live; for, besides that the land doth mourn, the restraint of justice towards sin doth more retard the affection of love, than the extent of mercy

doth inflame it; and sure, where love is [ill] bestowed, fear is quite lost.

14. His greatest enemies are his flatterers; for though they ever speak on his side, yet their words still make against him.

15. The love which a king oweth to a weal public should not be overstrained to any one particular; yet that his more especial favor do reflect upon some worthy ones, is somewhat necessary, because there are few of that capacity.

16. He must have a special care of five things, if he would not have his crown to be but to him *infelix felicitas.*

First, that *simulata sanctitas* be not in the church; for that is *duplex iniquitas.*

Secondly, that *inutilis æquitas* sit not in the chancery; for that is *inepta misericordia.*

Thirdly, that *utilis iniquitas* keep not the exchequer; for that is *crudele latrocinium.*

Fourthly, that *fidelis temeritas* be not his general; for that will bring but *seram pœnitentiam.*

Fifthly, that *infidelis prudentia* be not his secretary; for that is *anguis sub viridi herbâ.*

To conclude: as he is of the greatest power, so he is subject to the greatest cares, made the servant of his people, or else he were without a calling at all.

He, then, that honoreth him not is next an atheist, wanting the fear of God in his heart.

III.—ON DEATH.

1. I HAVE often thought upon death, and I find it the least of all evils. All that which is past is as a dream; and he that hopes or depends upon time

coming, dreams waking. So much of our life as we have discovered is already dead; and all those hours which we share, even from the breasts of our mothers, until we return to our grandmother the earth, are part of our dying days, whereof even this is one, and those that succeed are of the same nature, for we die daily; and, as others have given place to us, so we must, in the end, give way to others.

2. Physicians, in the name of death, include all sorrow, anguish, disease, calamity, or whatsoever can fall in the life of man, either grievous or unwelcome. But these things are familiar unto us, and we suffer them every hour; therefore we die daily, and I am older since I affirmed it.

3. I know many wise men that fear to die, for the change is bitter, and flesh would refuse to prove it; besides, the expectation brings terror, and that exceeds the evil. But I do not believe that any man fears to be dead, but only the stroke of death; and such are my hopes, that if Heaven be pleased, and nature renew but my lease for twenty-one years more without asking longer days, I shall be strong enough to acknowledge without mourning, that I was begotten mortal. Virtue walks not in the highway, though she go *per alta;* this is strength and the blood to virtue, to contemn things that be desired, and to neglect that which is feared.

4. Why should man be in love with his fetters, though of gold? Art thou drowned in security? Then I say thou art perfectly dead. For though thou movest, yet thy soul is buried within thee, and thy good angel either forsakes his guard, or sleeps. There is nothing under heaven, saving a true friend (who cannot be counted within the number of movables),

unto which my heart doth lean. And this dear freedom hath begotten me this peace, that I mourn not
for that end which must be, nor spend one wish to
have one minute added to the uncertain date of my
years. It was no mean apprehension of Lucian, who
says of Menippus, that in his travels through hell, he
knew not the kings of the earth from other men but
only by their louder cryings and tears, which were
fostered in them through the remorseful memory of
the good days they had seen, and the fruitful hav-
ings which they so unwillingly left behind them. He
that was well seated, looked back at his portion, and
was loath to forsake his farm; and others, either mind-
ing marriages, pleasures, profit, or preferment, desired to be excused from death's banquet. They had
made an appointment with earth, looking at the blessings, not the hand that enlarged them, forgetting how
unclothedly they came hither, or with what naked
ornaments they were arrayed.

5. But were we servants of the precept given, and
observers of the heathens' rule, *Memento mori*, and
not become benighted with this seeming felicity, we
should enjoy it as men prepared to lose, and not wind
up our thoughts upon so perishing a fortune. He that
is not slackly strong (as the servants of pleasure),
how can he be found unready to quit the vail and
false visage of his perfection? The soul having
shaken off her flesh, doth then set up for herself, and
contemning things that are under, shows what finger
hath enforced her; for the souls of idiots are of the
same piece with those of statesmen, but now and
then nature is at a fault, and this good guest of ours
takes soil in an imperfect body, and so is slackened
from showing her wonders, like an excellent musician,

which cannot utter himself upon a defective instrument.

6. But see how I am swerved, and lose my course, touching at the soul that doth least hold action with death, who hath the surest property in this frail act; his style is the end of all flesh, and the beginning of incorruption.

This ruler of monuments leads men, for the most part, out of this world with their heels forward, in token that he is contrary to life, which being obtained, sends men headlong into this wretched theatre, where, being arrived, their first language is that of mourning. Nor, in my own thoughts, can I compare men more fitly to any thing than to the Indian fig-tree, which, being ripened to his full height, is said to decline his branches down to the earth, whereof she conceives again, and they become roots in their own stock.

So man, having derived his being from the earth, first lives the life of a tree, drawing his nourishment as a plant, and made ripe for death, he tends downwards, and is sown again in his mother the earth, where he perisheth not, but expects a quickening.

7. So we see death exempts not a man from being, but only presents an alteration; yet there are some men (I think) that stand otherwise persuaded. Death finds not a worse friend than an alderman, to whose door I never knew him welcome; but he is an importunate guest, and will not be said nay.

And though they themselves shall affirm that they are not within, yet the answer will not be taken; and that which heightens their fear is, that they know they are in danger to forfeit their flesh, but are not wise of the payment-day, which sickly uncertainty is the occasion that (for the most part) they step out of this world unfurnished for their general account, and, being all unprovided, desire yet to hold their gravity, preparing their souls to answer in scarlet.

Thus I gather, that death is unagreeable to most citizens, because they commonly die intestate; this being a rule, that when their will is made, they think themselves nearer a grave than before. Now they, out of the wisdom of thousands, think to scare destiny, from which there is no appeal, by not making a will, or to live longer by protestation of their unwillingness to die. They are, for the most part, well made in this world (accounting their treasure by legions, as men do devils). Their fortune looks towards them, and they are willing to anchor at it, and desire (if it be possible) to put the evil day far off from them, and to adjourn their ungrateful and killing period.

No, these are not the men which have bespoken death, or whose looks are assured to entertain a thought of him.

8. Death arrives gracious only to such as sit in darkness, or lie heavy burdened with grief and irons; to the poor Christian, that sits bound in the galley; to despairful widows, pensive prisoners, and deposed kings; to them whose fortune runs back, and whose spirits mutiny: unto such, death is a redeemer, and the grave a place for retiredness and rest.

These wait upon the shore of death, and waft unto him to draw near, wishing above all others to see his star, that they might be led to his place; wooing the remorseless sisters to wind down the watch of their life, and to break them off before the hour.

9. But death is a doleful messenger to a usurer, and fate untimely cuts their thread; for it is never men-

tioned by him, but when rumors of war and civil tumults put him in mind thereof.

And when many hands are armed, and the peace of a city in disorder, and the foot of the common soldiers sounds an alarm on his stairs, then perhaps such a one (broken in thoughts of his moneys abroad, and cursing the monuments of coin which are in his house) can be content to think of death, and (being hasty of perdition) will perhaps hang himself, lest his throat should be cut; provided that he may do it in his study, surrounded with wealth, to which his eye sends a faint and languishing salute, even upon the turning off; remembering always, that he have time and liberty, by writing, to depute himself as his own heir.

For that is a great peace to his end, and reconciles him wonderfully upon the point.

10. Herein we all dally with ourselves, and are without proof of necessity. I am not of those, that dare promise to pine away myself in vainglory, and I hold such to be but feat boldness, and them that dare commit it, to be vain. Yet, for my part, I think nature should do me great wrong, if I should be so long in dying, as I was in being born.

To speak truth, no man knows the lists of his own patience, nor can divine how able he shall be in his sufferings, till the storm come (the perfectest virtue being tried in action); but I would (out of a care to do the best business well) ever keep a guard, and stand upon keeping faith and a good conscience.

11. And if wishes might find place, I would die together, and not my mind often, and my body once; that is, I would prepare for the messengers of death, sickness, and affliction, and not wait long, or be attempted by the violence of pain.

Herein I do not profess myself a Stoic, to hold grief no evil, but opinion, and a thing indifferent.

But I consent with Cæsar, that the suddenest passage is easiest, and there is nothing more awakens our resolve and readiness to die than the quieted conscience, strengthened with opinion that we shall be well spoken of upon earth by those that are just, and of the family of virtue; the opposite whereof is a fury to man, and makes even life unsweet.

Therefore, what is more heavy than evil fame deserved? Or, likewise, who can see worse days, than he that, yet living, doth follow at the funerals of his own reputation?

I have laid up many hopes, that I am privileged from that kind of mourning, and could wish the like peace to all those with whom I wage love.

12. I might say much of the commodities that death can sell a man; but, briefly, death is a friend of ours, and he that is not ready to entertain him, is not at home. Whilst I am, my ambition is not to foreflow the tide; I have but so to make my interest of it as I may account for it; I would wish nothing but what might better my days, nor desire any greater place than the front of good opinion. I make not love to the continuance of days, but to the goodness of them; nor wish to die, but refer myself to my hour, which the great Dispenser of all things hath appointed me; yet, as I am frail, and suffered for the first fault, were it given me to choose, I should not be earnest to see the evening of my age; that extremity, of itself, being a disease, and a mere return into infancy; so that, if perpetuity of life might be given me, I should think what the Greek poet said; "Such an age is a mortal evil." And since I must needs be dead, I require it

may not be done before mine enemies, that I be not stript before I be cold; but before my friends. The night is even now: but that name is lost; it is not now late, but early. Mine eyes begin to discharge their watch, and compound with this fleshly weakness for a time of perpetual rest; and I shall presently be as happy for a few hours, as I had died the first hour I was born.

The Wisdom of the Ancients

PREFACE.

THE earliest antiquity lies buried in silence and
oblivion, excepting the remains we have of it in sacred
writ. This silence was succeeded by poetical fables,
and these, at length, by the writings we now enjoy;
so that the concealed and secret learning of the ancients seems separated from the history and knowledge of the following ages by a veil, or partition-wall
of fables, interposing between the things that are lost
and those that remain.[1]

Many may imagine that I am here entering upon a
work of fancy, or amusement, and design to use a
poetical liberty, in explaining poetical fables. It is
true, fables, in general, are composed of ductile matter,
that may be drawn into great variety by a witty talent or an inventive genius, and be delivered of plausible meanings which they never contained. But this
procedure has already been carried to excess; and

[1] Varro distributes the ages of the world into three periods;
viz: the unknown, the fabulous, and the historical. Of the
former, we have no accounts but in Scripture; for the second,
we must consult the ancient poets, such as Hesiod, Homer, or
those who wrote still earlier, and then again come back to Ovid,
who, in his Metamorphoses, seems, in imitation perhaps of some
ancient Greek poet, to have intended a complete collection, or a
kind of continued and connected history of the fabulous age, especially with regard to changes, revolutions, or transformations.

great numbers, to procure the sanction of antiquity to their own notions and inventions, have miserably wrested and abused the fables of the ancients.

Nor is this only a late or unfrequent practice, but of ancient date and common even to this day. Thus Chrysippus, like an interpreter of dreams, attributed the opinions of the Stoics to the poets of old; and the chemists, at present, more childishly apply the poetical transformations to their experiments of the furnace. And though I have well weighed and considered all this, and thoroughly seen into the levity which the mind indulges for allegories and allusions, yet I cannot but retain a high value for the ancient mythology. And, certainly, it were very injudicious to suffer the fondness and licentiousness of a few to detract from the honor of allegory and parable in general. This would be rash, and almost profane; for, since religion delights in such shadows and disguises, to abolish them were, in a manner, to prohibit all intercourse betwixt things divine and human.

Upon deliberate consideration, my judgment is, that a concealed instruction and allegory was originally intended in many of the ancient fables. This opinion may, in some respect, be owing to the veneration I have for antiquity, but more to observing that some fables discover a great and evident similitude, relation, and connection with the thing they signify, as well in the structure of the fable as in the propriety of the names whereby the persons or actors are characterized; insomuch, that no one could positively deny a sense and meaning to be from the first intended, and purposely shadowed out in them. For who can hear that Fame, after the giants were destroyed, sprung up as their posthumous sister, and not

apply it to the clamor of parties and the seditious
rumors which commonly fly about for a time upon
the quelling of insurrections? Or who can read how
the giant Typhon cut out and carried away Jupiter's
sinews—which Mercury afterwards stole, and again
restored to Jupiter—and not presently observe that
this allegory denotes strong and powerful rebellions,
which cut away from kings their sinews, both of
money and authority; and that the way to have them
restored is by lenity, affability, and prudent edicts,
which soon reconcile, and, as it were, steal upon the
affections of the subject? Or who, upon hearing that
memorable expedition of the gods against the giants,
when the braying of Silenus's ass greatly contributed
in putting the giants to flight, does not clearly conceive that this directly points at the monstrous enterprises of rebellious subjects, which are frequently
frustrated and disappointed by vain fears and empty
rumors?

Again, the conformity and purport of the names is
frequently manifest and self-evident. Thus Metis,
the wife of Jupiter, plainly signifies counsel; Typhon,
swelling; Pan, universality; Nemesis, revenge, &c.
Nor is it a wonder, if sometimes a piece of history or
other things are introduced, by way of ornament; or,
if the times of the action are confounded; or, if part
of one fable be tacked to another; or, if the allegory
be new turned; for all this must necessarily happen,
as the fables were the inventions of men who lived in
different ages, and had different views; some of them
being ancient, others more modern; some having an
eye to natural philosophy, and others to morality or
civil policy.

It may pass for a further indication of a concealed

and secret meaning, that some of these fables are so absurd and idle in their narration, as to show and proclaim an allegory, even afar off. A fable that carries probability with it may be supposed invented for pleasure, or in imitation of history; but those that could never be conceived or related in this way must surely have a different use. For example, what a monstrous fiction is this, that Jupiter should take Metis to wife, and as soon as he found her pregnant eat her up, whereby he also conceived, and out of his head brought forth Pallas armed. Certainly no mortal could, but for the sake of the moral it couches, invent such an absurd dream as this, so much out of the road of thought!

But the argument of most weight with me is this, that many of these fables by no means appear to have been invented by the persons who relate and divulge them, whether Homer, Hesiod, or others; for if I were assured they first flowed from those later times and authors that transmit them to us, I should never expect any thing singularly great or noble from such an origin. But whoever attentively considers the thing, will find that these fables are delivered down and related by those writers, not as matters then first invented and proposed, but as things received and embraced in earlier ages. Besides, as they are differently related by writers nearly of the same ages, it is easily perceived that the relators drew from the common stock of ancient tradition, and varied but in point of embellishment, which is their own. And this principally raises my esteem of these fables, which I receive, not as the product of the age, or invention of the poets, but as sacred relics, gentle whispers, and the breath of better times, that from the traditions of

more ancient nations came, at length, into the flutes
and trumpets of the Greeks. But if any one shall,
notwithstanding this, contend that allegories are always adventitious, or imposed upon the ancient fables,
and no way native or genuinely contained in them, we
might here leave him undisturbed in that gravity of
judgment he affects (though we cannot help accounting it somewhat dull and phlegmatic), and, if it were
worth the trouble, proceed to another kind of argument.

Men have proposed to answer two different and
contrary ends by the use of parable; for parables
serve as well to instruct or illustrate as to wrap up
and envelop; so that though, for the present, we drop
the concealed use, and suppose the ancient fables to
be vague, undeterminate things, formed for amusement, still, the other use must remain, and can never
be given up. And every man, of any learning, must
readily allow that this method of instructing is grave,
sober, or exceedingly useful, and sometimes necessary
in the sciences, as it opens an easy and familiar passage to the human understanding, in all new discoveries that are abstruse and out of the road of vulgar
opinions. Hence, in the first ages, when such inventions and conclusions of the human reason as are
now trite and common were new and little known, all
things abounded with fables, parables, similes, comparisons, and allusions, which were not intended to
conceal, but to inform and teach, whilst the minds of
men continued rude and unpractised in matters of
subtilty and speculation, or even impatient, and in a
manner incapable of receiving such things as did not
fall directly under and strike the senses. For as hier-
oglyphics were in use before writing, so were parables

in use before arguments. And even to this day, if any man would let new light in upon the human understanding, and conquer prejudice, without raising contests, animosities, opposition, or disturbance, he must still go in the same path, and have recourse to the like method of allegory, metaphor, and allusion.

To conclude, the knowledge of the early ages was either great or happy; great, if they by design made this use of trope and figure; happy, if, whilst they had other views, they afforded matter and occasion to such noble contemplations. Let either be the case, our pains, perhaps, will not be misemployed, whether we illustrate antiquity or things themselves.

The like, indeed, has been attempted by others; but, to speak ingenuously, their great and voluminous labors have almost destroyed the energy, the efficacy, and grace of the thing; whilst, being unskilled in nature, and their learning no more than that of commonplace, they have applied the sense of the parables to certain general and vulgar matters, without reaching to their real purport, genuine interpretation, and full depth. For myself, therefore, I expect to appear new in these common things, because, leaving untouched such as are sufficiently plain and open, I shall drive only at those that are either deep or rich.

The Wisdom of the Ancients

A SERIES OF MYTHOLOGICAL FABLES.[1]

I.—CASSANDRA, OR DIVINATION.

EXPLAINED OF TOO FREE AND UNSEASONABLE ADVICE.

THE poets relate, that Apollo, falling in love with Cassandra, was still deluded and put off by her, yet fed with hopes, till she had got from him the gift of prophesy; and, having now obtained her end, she flatly rejected his suit. Apollo, unable to recall his rash gift, yet enraged to be outwitted by a girl, annexed this penalty to it, that though she should always prophesy true, she should never be believed; whence her divinations were always slighted, even when she again and again predicted the ruin of her country.

EXPLANATION.—This fable seems invented to express the insignificance of unseasonable advice. For they who are conceited, stubborn, or intractable, and listen not to the instructions of Apollo, the god of harmony, so as to learn and observe the modulations and measures of affairs, the sharps and flats of discourse, the difference between judicious and vulgar ears, and the proper times of speech and silence, let

[1] Most of these fables are contained in Ovid's Metamorphoses and Fasti, and are fully explained in Bohn's Classical Library translation.

them be ever so intelligent, and ever so frank of their
advice, or their counsels ever so good and just, yet
all their endeavors, either of persuasion or force, are
of little significance, and rather hasten the ruin of
those they advise. But, at last, when the calamitous
event has made the sufferers feel the effect of their
neglect, they too late reverence their advisers, as deep,
foreseeing, and faithful prophets.

Of this, we have a remarkable instance in Cato of
Utica, who discovered afar off, and long foretold, the
approaching ruin of his country, both in the first conspiracy, and as it was prosecuted in the civil war between Cæsar and Pompey, yet did no good the while,
but rather hurt the commonwealth, and hurried on its
destruction, which Cicero wisely observed in these
words: "Cato, indeed, judges excellently, but preju-
dices the state; for he speaks as in the commonwealth of Plato, and not as in the dregs of Romulus."

II.—TYPHON, OR A REBEL.

EXPLAINED OF REBELLION.

THE fable runs, that Juno, enraged at Jupiter's
bringing forth Pallas without her assistance, incessantly solicited all the gods and goddesses, that she
might produce without Jupiter; and having by violence and importunity obtained the grant, she struck
the earth, and thence immediately sprung up Typhon,
a huge and dreadful monster, whom she committed to
the nursing of a serpent. As soon as he was grown
up, this monster waged war on Jupiter, and taking
him prisoner, in the battle, carried him away on his
shoulders, into a remote and obscure quarter; and

there cutting out the sinews of his hands and feet,
he bore them off, leaving Jupiter behind miserably
maimed and mangled.

But Mercury afterwards stole these sinews from
Typhon, and restored them to Jupiter. Hence, recovering his strength, Jupiter again pursues the monster; first wounds him with a stroke of his thunder,
when serpents arose from the blood of the wound;
and now the monster being dismayed, and taking to
flight, Jupiter next darted Mount Ætna upon him,
and crushed him with the weight.

EXPLANATION.—This fable seems designed to express
the various fates of kings, and the turns that rebellions sometimes take, in kingdoms. For princes may
be justly esteemed married to their states, as Jupiter
to Juno; but it sometimes happens, that, being depraved by long wielding of the sceptre, and growing
tyrannical, they would engross all to themselves, and,
slighting the counsel of their senators and nobles, conceive by themselves; that is, govern according to their
own arbitrary will and pleasure. This inflames the
people, and makes them endeavor to create and set
up some head of their own. Such designs are generally set on foot by the secret motion and instigation
of the peers and nobles, under whose connivance the
common sort are prepared for rising; whence proceeds
a swell in the state, which is appositely denoted by
the nursing of Typhon. This growing posture of affairs is fed by the natural depravity and malignant
dispositions of the vulgar, which to kings is an en-
venomed serpent. And now the disaffected, uniting
their force, at length break out into open rebellion,
which, producing infinite mischiefs, both to prince

and people, is represented by the horrid and multiplied deformity of Typhon, with his hundred heads, denoting the divided powers; his flaming mouths, denoting fire and devastation; his girdles of snakes, denoting sieges and destruction; his iron hands, slaughter and cruelty; his eagle's talons, rapine and plunder; his plumed body, perpetual rumors, contradictory accounts, &c. And sometimes these rebellions grow so high, that kings are obliged, as if carried on the backs of the rebels, to quit the throne, and retire to some remote and obscure part of their dominions, with the loss of their sinews, both of money and majesty.

But if now they prudently bear this reverse of fortune, they may, in a short time, by the assistance of Mercury, recover their sinews again; that is, by becoming moderate and affable; reconciling the minds and affections of the people to them, by gracious speeches and prudent proclamations, which will win over the subject cheerfully to afford new aids and supplies, and add fresh vigor to authority. But prudent and wary princes here seldom incline to try fortune by a war, yet do their utmost, by some grand exploit, to crush the reputation of the rebels; and if the attempt succeeds, the rebels, conscious of the wound received, and distrustful of their cause, first betake themselves to broken and empty threats, like the hissings of serpents; and next, when matters are grown desperate, to flight. And now, when they thus begin to shrink, it is safe and seasonable for kings to pursue them with their forces, and the whole strength of the kingdom; thus effectually quashing and suppressing them, as it were by the weight of a mountain.

III.—THE CYCLOPS, OR THE MINISTERS OF TERROR.

EXPLAINED OF BASE COURT OFFICERS.

IT is related that the Cyclops, for their savageness and cruelty, were by Jupiter first thrown into Tartarus, and there condemned to perpetual imprisonment; but that afterwards Tellus persuaded Jupiter it would be for his service to release them, and employ them in forging thunderbolts. This he accordingly did; and they, with unwearied pains and diligence, hammered out his bolts, and other instruments of terror, with a frightful and continual din of the anvil.

It happened, long after, that Jupiter was displeased with Æsculapius, the son of Apollo, for having, by the art of medicine, restored a dead man to life; but concealing his indignation, because the action in itself was pious and illustrious, he secretly incensed the Cyclops against him, who, without remorse, presently slew him with their thunderbolts: in revenge whereof, Apollo, with Jupiter's connivance, shot them all dead with his arrows.

EXPLANATION.—This fable seems to point at the behavior of princes, who, having cruel, bloody, and oppressive ministers, first punish and displace them; but afterwards, by the advice of Tellus, that is, some earthly-minded and ignoble person, employ them again, to serve a turn, when there is occasion for cruelty in execution, or severity in exaction; but these ministers being base in their nature, whet by their former disgrace, and well aware of what is expected from them, use double diligence in their office; till, proceeding unwarily, and over-eager to gain favor, they sometimes, from the private nods, and ambiguous orders of their prince, perform some odious or execrable action: when princes, to decline the envy themselves, and knowing they shall never want such tools at their back, drop them, and give them up to the friends and followers of the injured person; thus exposing them, as sacrifices to revenge and popular odium: whence, with great applause, acclamations, and good wishes to the prince, these miscreants at last meet with their desert.

IV.—NARCISSUS, OR SELF-LOVE.

NARCISSUS is said to have been extremely beautiful and comely, but intolerably proud and disdainful; so that, pleased with himself, and scorning the world, he led a solitary life in the woods; hunting only with a few followers, who were his professed admirers, amongst whom the nymph Echo was his constant attendant. In this method of life, it was once his fate to approach a clear fountain, where he laid himself down to rest, in the noonday heat; when, beholding his image in the water, he fell into such a rapture and admiration of himself, that he could by no means be got away, but remained continually fixed and gazing, till at length he was turned into a flower, of his own name, which appears early in the spring, and is consecrated to the infernal deities, Pluto, Proserpine, and the Furies.

EXPLANATION.—This fable seems to paint the behavior and fortune of those, who, for their beauty, or other endowments, wherewith nature (without any industry of their own) has graced and adorned them, are extravagantly fond of themselves: for men of such a disposition generally affect retirement, and absence from public affairs; as a life of business must necessarily subject them to many neglects and contempts, which might disturb and ruffle their minds: whence such persons commonly lead a solitary, private, and shadowy life: see little company, and those only such as highly admire and reverence them; or, like an echo, assent to all they say.

And they who are depraved, and rendered still fonder of themselves by this custom, grow strangely indolent, inactive, and perfectly stupid. The Narcissus, a spring flower, is an elegant emblem of this temper, which at first flourishes, and is talked of, but, when ripe, frustrates the expectation conceived of it.

And that this flower should be sacred to the infernal powers, carries out the allusion still further; because men of this humor are perfectly useless in all respects: for whatever yields no fruit, but passes, and is no more, like the way of a ship in the sea, was by the ancients consecrated to the infernal shades and powers.

V.—THE RIVER STYX, OR LEAGUES.

EXPLAINED OF NECESSITY, IN THE OATHS OR SOLEMN LEAGUES OF PRINCES.

THE only solemn oath, by which the gods irrevocably obliged themselves, is a well known thing, and makes a part of many ancient fables. To this oath they did not invoke any celestial divinity, or divine attribute, but only called to witness the River Styx, which, with many meanders, surrounds the infernal court of Dis. For this form alone, and none but this, was held inviolable and obligatory; and the punishment of falsifying it, was that dreaded one of being excluded, for a certain number of years, from the table of the gods.

EXPLANATION.—This fable seems invented to show the nature of the compacts and confederacies of princes; which, though ever so solemnly and religiously sworn to, prove but little the more binding for it: so that oaths, in this case, seem used rather for decorum, reputation, and ceremony, than for fidelity, security, and effectuating. And though these oaths were strengthened with the bonds of affinity, which are the links and ties of nature, and again, by mutual services and good offices, yet we see all this will generally give way to ambition, convenience, and the thirst of power: the rather, because it is easy for princes, under various specious pretences, to defend, disguise, and conceal their ambitious desires and insincerity, having no judge to call them to account. There is, however, one true and proper confirmation of their faith, though no celestial divinity, but that great divinity of princes, Necessity; or, the danger of the state; and the securing of advantage.

This necessity is elegantly represented by Styx, the fatal river that can never be crossed back. And this deity it was, which Iphicrates the Athenian invoked in making a league; and because he roundly and openly avows what most others studiously conceal, it may be proper to give his own words. Observing that the Lacedæmonians were inventing and propos-

ing a variety of securities, sanctions, and bonds of
alliance, he interrupted them thus: "There may, indeed, my friends, be one bond and means of security
between us; and that is, for you to demonstrate you
have delivered into our hands, such things as that, if
you had the greatest desire to hurt us, you could not
be able." Therefore, if the power of offending be
taken away, or if, by a breach of compact, there be
danger of destruction or diminution to the state or
tribute, then it is that covenants will be ratified, and
confirmed, as it were by the Stygian oath, whilst there
remains an impending danger of being prohibited and
excluded from the banquet of the gods; by which expression the ancients denoted the rights and preroga-
tives, the affluence and the felicities, of empire and
dominion.

VI.—PAN, OR NATURE.[1]

EXPLAINED OF NATURAL PHILOSOPHY.

THE ancients have, with great exactness, delineated
universal nature under the person of Pan. They leave
his origin doubtful; some asserting him the son of
Mercury, and others the common offspring of all Penelope's suitors. The latter supposition doubtless occasioned some later rivals to entitle this ancient fable
Penelope; a thing frequently practised when the earlier relations are applied to more modern characters
and persons, though sometimes with great absurdity
and ignorance, as in the present case; for Pan was
one ncientest gods, and long before the time
besides, Penelope was venerated by an-

[1] H   te Pan.

tiquity for her matronal chastity. A third sort will have him the issue of Jupiter and Hybris, that is, Reproach. But whatever his origin was, the Destinies are allowed his sisters.

He is described by antiquity, with pyramidal horns reaching up to heaven, a rough and shaggy body, a very long beard, of a biform figure, human above, half brute below, ending in goat's feet. His arms, or ensigns of power, are, a pipe in his left hand, composed of seven reeds; in his right a crook; and he wore for his mantle a leopard's skin.

His attributes and titles were the god of hunters, shepherds, and all the rural inhabitants; president of the mountains; and, after Mercury, the next messenger of the gods. He was also held the leader and ruler of the Nymphs, who continually danced and frisked about him, attended with the Satyrs and their elders, the Sileni. He had also the power of striking terrors, especially such as were vain and superstitious; whence they came to be called panic terrors.[2]

Few actions are recorded of him; only a principal one is, that he challenged Cupid at wrestling, and was worsted. He also catched the giant Typhon in a net, and held him fast. They relate further of him, that when Ceres, growing disconsolate for the rape of Proserpine, hid herself, and all the gods took the utmost pains to find her, by going out different ways for that purpose, Pan only had the good fortune to meet her, as he was hunting, and discovered her to the rest. He likewise had the assurance to rival Apollo in music, and in the judgment of Midas was preferred; but the judge had, though with great .... and

[2] Cicero, Epistle to Atticus. 5.

secrecy, a pair of ass's ears fastened on him for his sentence.[3]

There is very little said of his amours; which may seem strange among such a multitude of gods, so profusely amorous. He is only reported to have been very fond of Echo, who was also esteemed his wife; and one nymph more, called Syrinx, with the love of whom Cupid inflamed him for his insolent challenge; so he is reported once to have solicited the moon to accompany him apart into the deep woods.

Lastly, Pan had no descendant, which also is a wonder, when the male gods were so extremely prolific; only he was the reputed father of a servant-girl called Iambe, who used to divert strangers with her ridiculous prattling stories.

This fable is perhaps the noblest of all antiquity, and pregnant with the mysteries and secrets of nature. Pan, as the name imports, represents the universe, about whose origin there are two opinions, viz: that it either sprung from Mercury, that is, the divine word, according to the Scriptures and philosophical divines, or from the confused seeds of things. For they who allow only one beginning of all things, either ascribe it to God, or, if they suppose a material beginning, acknowledge it to be various in its powers; so that the whole dispute comes to these points, viz: either that nature proceeds from Mercury, or from Penelope and all her suiters."[4]

[3] Ovid. Metamorphoses, b. ii.

[4] This refers to the confused mixture of things, as sung by Virgil:—

> "Namque canebat uti magnum per inane coacta
> Semina terrarumque animæque marisque fuissent;
> Et liquidi simul ignis; ut his exordia primis
> Omnia, et ipse tener mundi concreverit orbis."—
>
> *Ecl.* vi. C.

The third origin of Pan seems borrowed by the Greeks from the Hebrew mysteries, either by means of the Egyptians, or otherwise; for it relates to the state of the world, not in its first creation, but as made subject to death and corruption after the fall; and in this state it was and remains, the offspring of God and Sin, or Jupiter and Reproach. And therefore these three several accounts of Pan's birth may seem true, if duly distinguished in respect of things and times. For this Pan, or the universal nature of things, which we view and contemplate, had its origin from the divine word and confused matter, first created by God himself, with the subsequent introduction of sin, and, consequently, corruption.

The Destinies, or the natures and fates of things, are justly made Pan's sisters, as the chain of natural causes links together the rise, duration, and corruption; the exaltation, degeneration, and workings; the processes, the effects, and changes, of all that can any way happen to things.

Horns are given him, broad at the roots, but narrow and sharp at the top, because the nature of all things seems pyramidal; for individuals are infinite, but being collected into a variety of species, they rise up into kinds, and these again ascend, and are contracted into generals, till at length nature may seem collected to a point. And no wonder if Pan's horns reach to the heavens, since the sublimities of nature, or abstract ideas, reach in a manner to things divine; for there is a short and ready passage from metaphysics to natural theology.

Pan's body, or the body of nature, is, with great propriety and elegance, painted shaggy and hairy, as representing the rays of things; for rays are as the

hair or fleece of nature, and more or less worn by all
bodies. This evidently appears in vision, and in all
effects and operations at a distance; for whatever
operates thus, may be properly said to emit rays.[5]
But particularly the beard of Pan is exceeding long,
because the rays of the celestial bodies penetrate, and
act to a prodigious distance, and have descended into
the interior of the earth, so far as to change its surface; and the sun himself, when clouded on its upper
part, appears to the eye bearded.

Again, the body of nature is justly described biform,
because of the difference between its superior and inferior parts, as the former, for their beauty, regularity of motion, and influence over the earth, may be
properly represented by the human figure, and the
latter, because of their disorder, irregularity, and subjection to the celestial bodies, are by the brutal. This
biform figure also represents the participation of one
species with another; for there appear to be no simple
natures, but all participate or consist of two: thus,
man has somewhat of the brute, the brute somewhat
of the plant, the plant somewhat of the mineral; so
that all natural bodies have really two faces, or consist of a superior and an inferior species.

There lies a curious allegory in the making of Pan
goat-footed, on account of the motion of ascent which
the terrestrial bodies have towards the air and
heavens; for the goat is a clambering creature, that
delights in climbing up rocks and precipices; and in
the same manner the matters destined to this lower
globe strongly affect to rise upwards, as appears from
the clouds and meteors.

[5] This is always supposed to be the case in vision, the mathematical demonstrations in optics proceeding invariably upon
the assumption of this phenomenon.

Pan's arms, or the ensigns he bears in his hands, are of two kinds—the one an emblem of harmony, the other of empire. His pipe, composed of seven reeds, plainly denotes the consent and harmony, or the concords and discords of things, produced by the motion of the seven planets. His crook, also, contains a fine representation of the ways of nature, which are partly straight and partly crooked; thus the staff, having an extraordinary bend towards the top, denotes that the works of Divine Providence are generally brought about by remote means, or in a circuit, as if somewhat else were intended rather than the effect produced, as in the sending of Joseph into Egypt, &c. So likewise in human government, they who sit at the helm, manage and wind the people more successfully by pretext and oblique courses, than they could by such as are direct and straight; so that, in effect, all sceptres are crooked at the top.

Pan's mantle, or clothing, is with great ingenuity made of a leopard's skin, because of the spots; in like manner the heavens are sprinkled with stars, the sea with islands, the earth with flowers, and almost each particular thing is variegated, or wears a mottled coat.

The office of Pan could not be more livelily expressed than by making him the god of hunters; for every natural action, every motion and process, is no other than a chase. Thus arts and sciences hunt out their works, and human schemes and counsels their several ends; and all living creatures either hunt out their aliment, pursue their prey, or seek their pleasures, and this in a skilful and sagacious manner.[a] He is

[a] "Torva leæna lupum sequitur, lupus ipse capellam:
Florentem cytisum sequitur lasciva capella."
Virgil, Ecl. ii. 63.

also styled the god of the rural inhabitants, because
men in this situation live more according to nature
than they do in cities and courts, where nature is so
corrupted with effeminate arts, that the saying of the
poet may be verified:—

—pars minima est ipsa puella sui.[7]

He is likewise particularly styled President of the
Mountains, because in mountains and lofty places
the nature of things lies more open and exposed to the
eye and the understanding.

In his being called the messenger of the gods, next
after Mercury, lies a divine allegory, as next after the
Word of God, the image of the world is the herald of
the Divine power and wisdom, according to the expression of the Psalmist: "The heavens declare the
glory of God, and the firmament showeth his handi-
work."[8]

Pan is delighted with the company of the Nymphs,
that is, the souls of all living creatures are the delight
of the world; and he is properly called their governor,
because each of them follows its own nature, as a
leader, and all dance about their own respective rings,
with infinite variety and never-ceasing motion. And
with these continually join the Satyrs and Sileni, that
is, youth and age; for all things have a kind of young,
cheerful, and dancing time; and again their time of
slowness, tottering, and creeping. And whoever, in
a true light, considers the motions and endeavors of
both these ages, like another Democritus, will perhaps find them as odd and strange as the gesticula-
tions and antic motions of the Satyrs and Sileni.

[7] Ovid, Rem. Amoris, v. 343. Mart. Epist.
[8] Psalm xix. 1.

The power he had of striking terrors contains a very sensible doctrine; for nature has implanted fear in all living creatures, as well to keep them from risking their lives, as to guard against injuries and violence; and yet this nature or passion keeps not its bounds, but with just and profitable fears always mixes such as are vain and senseless; so that all things, if we could see their insides, would appear full of panic terrors. Thus mankind, particularly the vulgar, labor under a high degree of superstition, which is nothing more than a panic-dread, that principally reigns in unsettled and troublesome times.

The presumption of Pan in challenging Cupid to the conflict denotes that matter has an appetite and tendency to a dissolution of the world, and falling back to its first chaos again, unless this depravity and inclination were restrained and subdued by a more powerful concord and agreement of things, properly expressed by Love, or Cupid: it is therefore well for mankind, and the state of all things, that Pan was thrown and conquered in the struggle.

His catching and detaining Typhon in the net receives a similar explanation; for whatever vast and unusual swells, which the word typhon signifies, may sometimes be raised in nature, as in the sea, the clouds, the earth, or the like, yet nature catches, entangles, and holds all such outrages and insurrections in her inextricable net, wove, as it were, of adamant.

That part of the fable which attributes the discovery of lost Ceres to Pan whilst he was hunting—a happiness denied the other gods, though they diligently and expressly sought her—contains an exceeding just and prudent admonition; viz: that we are not to expect the discovery of things useful in common life, as

that of corn, denoted by Ceres, from abstract philosophies, as if these were the gods of the first order,—
no, not though we used our utmost endeavors this
way,—but only from Pan; that is, a sagacious experience and general knowledge of nature, which is often
found, even by accident, to stumble upon such discoveries whilst the pursuit was directed another way.

The event of his contending with Apollo in music
affords us a useful instruction, that may help to
humble the human reason and judgment, which is too
apt to boast and glory in itself. There seem to be
two kinds of harmony,—the one of Divine providence,
the other of human reason; but the government of
the world, the administration of its affairs, and the
more secret Divine judgments, sound harsh and dis-
sonant to human ears or human judgment; and though
this ignorance be justly rewarded with asses' ears,
yet they are put on and worn, not openly, but with
great secrecy; nor is the deformity of the thing seen
or observed by the vulgar.

We must not find it strange if no amours are related of Pan besides his marriage with Echo; for nature enjoys itself, and in itself all other things. He
that loves, desires enjoyment, but in profusion there
is no room for desire; and therefore Pan, remaining
content with himself, has no passion unless it be for
discourse, which is well shadowed out by Echo, or
talk, or, when it is more accurate, by Syrinx, or writing.[9] But Echo makes a most excellent wife for Pan,
as being no other than genuine philosophy, which
faithfully repeats his words, or only transcribes exactly as nature dictates; thus representing the true

[9] Syrinx, signifying a reed, or the ancient pen.

image and reflection of the world without adding a tittle.

It tends, also, to the support and perfection of Pan, or nature, to be without offspring; for the world generates in its parts, and not in the way of a whole, as wanting a body external to itself wherewith to generate.

Lastly, for the supposed or spurious prattling daughter of Pan, it is an excellent addition to the fable, and aptly represents the talkative philosophies that have at all times been stirring, and filled the world with idle tales; being ever barren, empty, and servile, though sometimes indeed diverting and entertaining, and sometimes again troublesome and importunate.

VII.—PERSEUS,[1] OR WAR.

EXPLAINED OF THE PREPARATION AND CONDUCT NECESSARY TO WAR.

"THE fable relates, that Perseus was dispatched from the east, by Pallas, to cut off Medusa's head, who had committed great ravage upon the people of the west; for this Medusa was so dire a monster, as to turn into stone all those who but looked upon her. She was a Gorgon, and the only mortal one of the three, the other two being invulnerable. Perseus, therefore, preparing himself for this grand enterprise, had presents made him from three of the gods: Mercury gave him wings for his heels; Pluto, a helmet; and Pallas, a shield and a mirror. But, though he was now so well equipped, he posted not directly to Medusa, but first turned aside to the Greæ, who were half-sisters to

[1] Ovid. Metam. b. iv.

the Gorgons. These Greæ were grayheaded, and like
old women, from their birth, having among them all
three but one eye, and one tooth, which, as they had
occasion to go out, they each wore by turns, and laid
them down again upon coming back. This eye and
this tooth they lent to Perseus, who now judging himself sufficiently furnished, he, without further stop,
flies swiftly away to Medusa, and finds her asleep.
But not venturing his eyes, for fear she should wake,
he turned his head aside, and viewed her in Pallas's
mirror, and thus directing his stroke, cut off her head;
when immediately, from the gushing blood, there
darted Pegasus winged. Perseus now inserted Medusa's head into Pallas's shield, which thence retained
the faculty of astonishing and benumbing all who
looked on it."

This fable seems invented to show the prudent
method of choosing, undertaking, and conducting a
war; and, accordingly, lays down three useful precepts about it, as if they were the precepts of Pallas.

The first is, that no prince should be over-solicitous
to subdue a neighboring nation; for the method of
enlarging an empire is very different from that of
increasing an estate. Regard is justly had to con-
tiguity, or adjacency, in private lands and possessions;
but in the extending of empire, the occasion, the facility, and advantage of a war, are to be regarded instead of vicinity. It is certain that the Romans, at
the time they stretched but little beyond Liguria to
the west, had by their arms subdued the provinces as
far as Mount Taurus to the east. And thus Perseus
readily undertook a very long expedition, even from
the east to the extremities of the west.

The second precept is, that the cause of the war be

just and honorable; for this adds alacrity both to the soldiers, and the people who find the supplies; procures aids, alliances, and numerous other conveniences. Now there is no cause of war more just and laudable than the suppressing of tyranny; by which a people are dispirited, benumbed, or left without life and vigor, as at the sight of Medusa.

Lastly, it is prudently added, that, as there were three of the Gorgons, who represent war, Perseus singled her out for this expedition that was mortal; which affords this precept, that such kind of wars should be chose as may be brought to a conclusion without pursuing vast and infinite hopes.

Again, Perseus's setting-out is extremely well adapted to his undertaking, and in a manner commands success; he received dispatch from Mercury, secrecy from Pluto, and foresight from Pallas. It also contains an excellent allegory, that the wings given him by Mercury were for his heels, not for his shoulders; because expedition is not so much required in the first preparations for war, as in the subsequent matters, that administer to the first; for there is no error more frequent in war, than, after brisk preparations, to halt for subsidiary forces and effective supplies.

The allegory of Pluto's helmet, rendering men invisible and secret, is sufficiently evident of itself; but the mystery of the shield and the mirror lies deeper; and denotes, that not only a prudent caution must be had to defend, like the shield, but also such an address and penetration as may discover the strength, the motions, the counsels, and designs of the enemy; like the mirror of Pallas.

But though Perseus may now seem extremely well

prepared, there still remains the most important thing of all; before he enters upon the war, he must of necessity consult the Greæ. These Greæ are treasons; half, but degenerate sisters of the Gorgons; who are representatives of wars; for wars are generous and noble; but treasons base and vile. The Greæ are elegantly described as hoary-headed, and like old women from their birth; on account of the perpetual cares, fears, and trepidations attending traitors. Their force, also, before it breaks out into open revolt, consists either in an eye or a tooth; for all faction, alienated from a state, is both watchful and biting; and this eye and tooth are, as it were, common to all the disaffected; because whatever they learn and know is transmitted from one to another, as by the hands of faction. And for the tooth, they all bite with the same: and clamor with one throat; so that each of them singly expresses the multitude.

These Greæ, therefore, must be prevailed upon by Perseus to lend him their eye and their tooth; the eye to give him indications, and make discoveries; the tooth for sowing rumors, raising envy, and stirring up the minds of the people. And when all these things are thus disposed and prepared, then follows the action of the war.

He finds Medusa asleep; for whoever undertakes a war with prudence, generally falls upon the enemy unprepared, and nearly in a state of security: and here is the occasion for Pallas's mirror: for it is common enough, before the danger presents itself, to see exactly into the state and posture of the enemy; but the principal use of the glass is, in the very instant of danger, to discover the manner thereof, and prevent consternation; which is the thing intended by Perseus's turning his head aside, and viewing the enemy in the glass.[2]

Two effects here follow the conquest: 1. The darting forth of Pegasus; which evidently denotes fame, that flies abroad, proclaiming the victory far and near. 2. The bearing of Medusa's head in the shield, which is the greatest possible defence and safeguard; for one grand and memorable enterprise, happily accomplished, bridles all the motions and attempts of the enemy, stupefies disaffection, and quells commotions.

VIII.—ENDYMION, OR A FAVORITE.

EXPLAINED OF COURT FAVORITES.

THE goddess Luna is said to have fallen in love with the shepherd Endymion, and to have carried on her amours with him in a new and singular manner; it being her custom, whilst he lay reposing in his native cave, under Mount Latmus, to descend frequently from her sphere, enjoy his company whilst he slept, and then go up to heaven again. And all this while, Endymion's fortune was no way prejudiced by his unactive and sleepy life, the goddess causing his flocks to thrive, and grow so exceeding numerous, that none of the other shepherds could compare with him.

EXPLANATION.—This fable seems to describe the tempers and dispositions of princes, who, being thoughtful and suspicious, do not easily admit to their

[2] Thus it is the excellence of a general, early to discover what turn the battle is likely to take; and looking prudently behind, as well as before, to pursue a victory so as not to be unprovided for a retreat.

privacies such men as are prying, curious, and vigi-
lant, or, as it were, sleepless; but rather such as are
of an easy, obliging nature, and indulge them in their
pleasures, without seeking anything further; but
seeming ignorant, insensible, or, as it were, lulled
asleep before them.[1] Princes usually treat such persons familiarly; and quitting their throne, like Luna,
think they may, with safety, unbosom to them. This
temper was very remarkable in Tiberius, a prince exceedingly difficult to please, and who had no favorites
but those that perfectly understood his way, and, at
the same time, obstinately dissembled their knowledge, almost to a degree of stupidity.

The cave is not improperly mentioned in the fable;
it being a common thing for the favorites of a prince
to have their pleasant retreats, whither to invite him,
by way of relaxation, though without prejudice to
their own fortunes; these favorites usually making a
good provision for themselves.

For though their prince should not, perhaps, pro-
mote them to dignities, yet, out of real affection, and
not only for convenience, they generally feel the en-
riching influence of his bounty.

---

[1] It may be remembered that the Athenian peasant voted for
the banishment of Aristides, because he was called the Just.
Shakespeare forcibly expresses the same thought:—

> "Let me have men about me that are fat;
> Sleek-headed men, and such as sleep o'nights:
> Yon Cassius has a lean and hungry look;
> He thinks too much: such men are dangerous."

If Bacon had completed his intended work upon "Sympathy
and Antipathy," the constant hatred evinced by ignorance of
intellectual superiority, originating sometimes in the painful
feeling of inferiority, sometimes in the fear of worldly injury
would not have escaped his notice.

IX.—THE SISTER OF THE GIANTS, OR FAME.

EXPLAINED OF PUBLIC DETRACTION.

THE poets relate, that the giants, produced from the earth, made war upon Jupiter, and the other gods, but were repulsed and conquered by thunder; whereat the earth, provoked, brought forth Fame, the youngest sister of the giants, in revenge for the death of her sons.

EXPLANATION.—The meaning of the fable seems to be this: the earth denotes the nature of the vulgar, who are always swelling, and rising against their rulers, and endeavoring at changes. This disposition, getting a fit opportunity, breeds rebels and traitors, who, with impetuous rage, threaten and contrive the overthrow and destruction of princes.

And when brought under and subdued, the same vile and restless nature of the people, impatient of peace, produces rumors, detractions, slanders, libels, &c., to blacken those in authority; so that rebellious actions and seditious rumors, differ not in origin and stock, but only, as it were, in sex; treasons and rebellions being the brothers, and scandal or detraction the sister.

X.—ACTEON AND PENTHEUS, OR A CURIOUS MAN.

EXPLAINED OF CURIOSITY, OR PRYING INTO THE SECRETS OF PRINCES AND DIVINE MYSTERIES.

THE ancients afford us two examples for suppressing the impertinent curiosity of mankind, in diving into secrets, and imprudently longing and endeavor-

ing to discover them. The one of these is in the person of Acteon, and the other in that of Pentheus.
Acteon, undesignedly chancing to see Diana naked,
was turned into a stag, and torn to pieces by his own
hounds. And Pentheus, desiring to pry into the hidden mysteries of Bacchus's sacrifice, and climbing a
tree for that purpose, was struck with a frenzy. This
frenzy of Pentheus caused him to see things double,
particularly the sun, and his own city, Thebes, so
that running homewards, and immediately espying
another Thebes, he runs towards that; and thus continues incessantly, tending first to the one, and then
to the other, without coming at either.

EXPLANATION.—The first of these fables may relate to the secrets of princes, and the second to divine
mysteries. For they who are not intimate with a
prince, yet, against his will, have a knowledge of his
secrets, inevitably incur his displeasure; and therefore, being aware that they are singled out, and all
opportunities watched against them, they lead the
life of a stag, full of fears and suspicions. It likewise
frequently happens that their servants and domestics
accuse them, and plot their overthrow, in order to
procure favor with the prince; for whenever the king
manifests his displeasure, the person it falls upon
must expect his servants to betray him, and worry
him down, as Acteon was worried by his own dogs.

The punishment of Pentheus is of another kind;
for they who, unmindful of their mortal state, rashly
aspire to divine mysteries, by climbing the heights
of nature and philosophy, here represented by climbing a tree,—their fate is perpetual inconstancy, per-
plexity, and instability of judgment. For as there is

one light of nature, and another light that is divine, they see, as it were, two suns. And as the actions of life, and the determinations of the will, depend upon the understanding, they are distracted as much in opinion as in will; and therefore judge very inconsistently, or contradictorily; and see, as it were, Thebes double; for Thebes being the refuge and habitation of Pentheus, here denotes the ends of actions; whence they know not what course to take, but remaining undetermined and unresolved in their views and designs, they are merely driven about by every sudden gust and impulse of the mind.

XI.—ORPHEUS, OR PHILOSOPHY.

EXPLAINED OF NATURAL AND MORAL PHILOSOPHY.

INTRODUCTION.—The fable of Orpheus, though trite and common, has never been well interpreted, and seems to hold out a picture of universal philosophy; for to this sense may be easily transferred what is said of his being a wonderful and perfectly divine person, skilled in all kinds of harmony, subduing and drawing all things after him by sweet and gentle methods and modulations. For the labors of Orpheus exceed the labors of Hercules, both in power and dignity, as the works of knowledge exceed the works of strength.

FABLE.—Orpheus having his beloved wife snatched from him by sudden death, resolved upon descending to the infernal regions, to try if, by the power of his harp, he could reobtain her. And, in effect, he so appeased and soothed the infernal powers by the melody and sweetness of his harp and voice, that they indulged him the liberty of taking her back, on condition that she should follow him behind, and he not turn to look upon her till they came into open day; but he, through the impatience of his care and affection, and thinking himself almost past danger, at length looked behind him, whereby the condition was violated, and she again precipitated to Pluto's regions. From this time Orpheus grew pensive and sad, a hater of the sex, and went into solitude, where, by the same sweetness of his harp and voice, he first drew the wild beasts of all sorts about him; so that, forgetting their natures, they were neither actuated by revenge, cruelty, lust, hunger, or the desire of prey, but stood gazing about him, in a tame and gentle manner, listening attentively to his music. Nay, so great was the power and efficacy of his harmony, that it even caused the trees and stones to remove, and place themselves in a regular manner about him. When he had for a time, and with great admiration, continued to do this, at length the Thracian women, raised by the instigation of Bacchus, first blew a deep and hoarse-sounding horn, in such an outrageous manner, that it quite drowned the music of Orpheus. And thus the power which, as the link of their society, held all things in order, being dissolved, disturbance reigned anew; each creature returned to its own nature, and pursued and preyed upon its fellow, as before. The rocks and woods also started back to their former places; and even Orpheus himself was at last torn to pieces by these female furies, and his limbs scattered all over the desert. But, in sorrow and revenge for his death, the River Helicon, sacred to the Muses, hid its waters under ground, and rose again in other places.

EXPLANATION.—The fable receives this explanation. The music of Orpheus is of two kinds; one that appeases the infernal powers, and the other that draws together the wild beasts and trees. The former properly relates to natural, and the latter to moral philosophy, or civil society. The reinstatement and restoration of corruptible things is the noblest work of natural philosophy; and, in a less degree, the preservation of bodies in their own state, or a prevention of their dissolution and corruption. And if this be possible, it can certainly be effected no other way than by proper and exquisite attemperations of nature; as it were by the harmony and fine touching of the harp. But as this is a thing of exceeding great difficulty, the end is seldom obtained; and that, probably, for no reason more than a curious and unseasonable impatience and solicitude.

And, therefore, philosophy, being almost unequal to the task, has cause to grow sad, and hence betakes itself to human affairs, insinuating into men's minds the love of virtue, equity, and peace, by means of eloquence and persuasion; thus forming men into societies; bringing them under laws and regulations; and making them forget their unbridled passions and affections, so long as they hearken to precepts and submit to discipline. And thus they soon after build themselves habitations, form cities, cultivate lands, plant orchards, gardens, &c. So that they may not improperly be said to remove and call the trees and stones together.

And this regard to civil affairs is justly and regularly placed after diligent trial made for restoring the mortal body; the attempt being frustrated in the end—because the unavoidable necessity of death, thus

evidently laid before mankind, animates them to
seek a kind of eternity by works of perpetuity, character, and fame.

It is also prudently added, that Orpheus was afterwards averse to women and wedlock, because the indulgence of the married state, and the natural affections which men have for their children, often prevent
them from entering upon any grand, noble, or meritorious enterprise for the public good; as thinking it
sufficient to obtain immortality by their descendants,
without endeavoring at great actions.

And even the works of knowledge, though the most
excellent among human things, have their periods;
for after kingdoms and commonwealths have flourished for a time, disturbances, seditions, and wars,
often arise, in the din whereof, first the laws are si-
lent, and not heard; and then men return to their own
depraved natures—whence cultivated lands and cities
soon become desolate and waste. And if this disorder
continues, learning and philosophy is infallibly torn
to pieces; so that only some scattered fragments thereof can afterwards be found up and down, in a few
places, like planks after a shipwreck. And barbarous
times succeeding, the River Helicon dips under-
ground; that is, letters are buried, till things having
undergone their due course of changes, learning rises
again, and shows its head, though seldom in the same
place, but in some other nation.[1]

[1] Thus we see that Orpheus denotes learning; Eurydice, things,
or the subject of learning; Bacchus, and the Thracian women,
men's ungoverned passions and appetites, &c. And in the same
manner all the ancient fables might be familiarly illustrated,
and brought down to the capacities of children.

XII.—CŒLUM, OR BEGINNINGS.

EXPLAINED OF THE CREATION, OR ORIGIN OF ALL THINGS.

THE poets relate, that Cœlum was the most ancient of all the gods; that his parts of generation were cut off by his son Saturn; that Saturn had a numerous offspring, but devoured all his sons, as soon as they were born; that Jupiter at length escaped the common fate; and when grown up, drove his father Saturn into Tartarus; usurped the kingdom; cut off his father's genitals, with the same knife wherewith Saturn had dismembered Cœlum, and throwing them into the sea, thence sprung Venus.

Before Jupiter was well established in his empire, two memorable wars were made upon him; the first by the Titans, in subduing of whom, Sol, the only one of the Titans who favored Jupiter, performed him singular service; the second by the giants, who being destroyed and subdued by the thunder and arms of Jupiter, he now reigned secure.

EXPLANATION.—This fable appears to be an enigmatical account of the origin of all things, not greatly differing from the philosophy afterwards embraced by Democritus, who expressly asserts the eternity of matter, but denies the eternity of the world; thereby approaching to the truth of sacred writ, which makes chaos, or uninformed matter to exist before the six days' works.

The meaning of the fable seems to be this: Cœlum denotes the concave space, or vaulted roof that incloses all matter, and Saturn the matter itself, which cuts off all power of generation from his father; as one and the same quantity of matter remains invariable in nature, without addition or diminution. But the agitations and struggling motions of matter, first produced certain imperfect and ill-joined compositions of things, as it were so many first rudiments, or essays of worlds; till, in process of time, there arose a fabric capable of preserving its form and structure. Whence the first age was shadowed out by the reign of Saturn; who, on account of the frequent dissolutions, and short durations of things, was said to devour his children. And the second age was denoted by the reign of Jupiter; who thrust, or drove those frequent and transitory changes into Tartarus—a place expressive of disorder. This place seems to be the middle space, between the lower heavens and the internal parts of the earth, wherein disorder, imperfection, mutation, mortality, destruction, and corruption, are principally found.

Venus was not born during the former generation of things, under the reign of Saturn; for whilst discord and jar had the upper hand of concord and uniformity in the matter of the universe, a change of the entire structure was necessary. And in this manner things were generated and destroyed, before Saturn was dismembered. But when this manner of generation ceased, there immediately followed another, brought about by Venus, or a perfect and established harmony of thing; whereby changes were wrought in the parts, whilst the universal fabric remained entire and undisturbed. Saturn is said to be thrust out and dethroned, not killed, and become extinct; because, agreeably to the opinion of Democritus, the world might relapse into its old confusion and disorder, which Lucretius hoped would not happen in his time.[a]

---

[a] "Quod procul a nobis flectat Fortuna gubernans:
Et ratio potius quam res persuadeat ipsa."

But now, when the world was compact, and held together by its own bulk and energy, yet there was no rest from the beginning; for first, there followed considerable motions and disturbances in the celestial regions, though so regulated and moderated by the power of the Sun, prevailing over the heavenly bodies, as to continue the world in its state. Afterwards there followed the like in the lower parts, by inundations, storms, winds, general earthquakes, &c., which, however, being subdued and kept under, there ensued a more peaceable and lasting harmony, and consent of things.

It may be said of this fable, that it includes philosophy; and again, that philosophy includes the fable; for we know, by faith, that all these things are but the oracle of sense, long since ceased and decayed; but the matter and fabric of the world being justly attributed to a creator.

XIII.—PROTEUS, OR MATTER.

EXPLAINED OF MATTER AND ITS CHANGES.

PROTEUS, according to the poets, was Neptune's herdsman; an old man, and a most extraordinary prophet, who understood things past and present, as well as future; so that besides the business of divination, he was the revealer and interpreter of all antiquity, and secrets of every kind. He lived in a vast cave, where his custom was to tell over his herd of sea-calves at noon, and then to sleep. Whoever consulted him, had no other way of obtaining an answer, but by binding him with manacles and fetters; when he, endeavoring to free himself, would change into all kind of shapes and miraculous forms; as of fire, water, wild beasts, &c.; till at length he resumed his own shape again.

EXPLANATION.—This fable seems to point at the secrets of nature, and the states of matter. For the person of Proteus denotes matter, the oldest of all things, after God himself;[1] that resides, as in a cave, under the vast concavity of the heavens. He is represented as the servant of Neptune, because the various operations and modifications of matter are principally wrought in a fluid state. The herd, or flock of Proteus, seems to be no other than the several kinds of animals, plants, and minerals, in which matter appears to diffuse and spend itself; so that after having formed these several species, and as it were finished its task, it seems to sleep and repose, without otherwise attempting to produce any new ones. And this is the moral of Proteus's counting his herd, then going to sleep.

This is said to be done at noon, not in the morning or evening; by which is meant the time best fitted and disposed for the production of species, from a matter duly prepared, and made ready beforehand, and now lying in a middle state, between its first rudiments and decline; which, we learn from sacred history, was the case at the time of the creation; when, by the efficacy of the divine command, matter directly came together, without any transformation or intermediate changes, which it affects; instantly obeyed the order, and appeared in the form of creatures.

And thus far the fable reaches of Proteus, and his flock, at liberty and unrestrained. For the universe,

_____
[1] Proteus properly signifies primary, oldest, or first.

with the common structures, and fabrics of the creatures, is the face of matter, not under constraint, or
as the flock wrought upon and tortured by human
means. But if any skilful minister of nature shall
apply force to matter, and by design torture and vex
it, in order to its annihilation, it, on the contrary,
being brought under this necessity, changes and trans-
forms itself into a strange variety of shapes and appearances; for nothing but the power of the Creator
can annihilate, or truly destroy it; so that at length,
running through the whole circle of transformations,
and completing its period, it in some degree restores
itself, if the force be continued. And that method of
binding, torturing, or detaining, will prove the most
effectual and expeditious, which makes use of manacles and fetters; that is, lays hold and works upon
matter in the extremest degrees.

The addition in the fable that makes Proteus a
prophet, who had the knowledge of things past, present, and future, excellently agrees with the nature
of matter; as he who knows the properties, the
changes, and the processes of matter, must, of necessity, understand the effects and sum of what it does,
has done, or can do, though his knowledge extends
not to all the parts and particulars thereof.

XIV.—MEMNON, OR A YOUTH TOO FORWARD.

EXPLAINED OF THE FATAL PRECIPITANCY OF YOUTH.

THE poets made Memnon the son of Aurora, and
bring him to the Trojan war in beautiful armor, and
flushed with popular praise; where, thirsting after

further glory, and rashly hurrying on to the greatest enterprises, he engages the bravest warrior of all the Greeks, Achilles, and falls by his hand in single combat. Jupiter, in commiseration of his death, sent birds to grace his funeral, that perpetually chanted certain mournful and bewailing dirges. It is also reported, that the rays of the rising sun, striking his statue, used to give a lamenting sound.

EXPLANATION.—This fable regards the unfortunate end of those promising youths, who, like sons of the morning, elate with empty hopes and glittering outsides, attempt things beyond their strength; challenge the bravest heroes; provoke them to the combat; and, proving unequal, die in their high attempts.

The death of such youths seldom fails to meet with infinite pity; as no mortal calamity is more moving and afflicting, than to see the flower of virtue cropped before its time. Nay, the prime of life enjoyed to the full, or even to a degree of envy, does not assuage or moderate the grief occasioned by the untimely death of such hopeful youths; but lamentations and bewailings fly, like mournful birds, about their tombs, for a long while after; especially upon all fresh occasions, new commotions, and the beginning of great actions, the passionate desire of them is renewed, as by the sun's morning rays.

XV.—TYTHONUS, OR SATIETY.

EXPLAINED OF PREDOMINANT PASSIONS.

IT is elegantly fabled by Tythonus, that being exceedingly beloved by Aurora, she petitioned Jupiter that he might prove immortal, thereby to secure herself the everlasting enjoyment of his company; but through female inadvertence she forgot to add, that he might never grow old; so that, though he proved immortal, he became miserably worn and consumed with age, insomuch that Jupiter, out of pity, at length transformed him to a grasshopper.

EXPLANATION.—This fable seems to contain an ingenious description of pleasure; which at first, as it were in the morning of the day, is so welcome, that men pray to have it everlasting, but forget that satiety and weariness of it will, like old age, overtake them, though they think not of it; so that at length, when their appetite for pleasurable actions is gone, their desires and affections often continue; whence we commonly find that aged persons delight themselves with the discourse and remembrance of the things agreeable to them in their better days. This is very remarkable in men of a loose, and men of a military life; the former whereof are always talking over their amours, and the latter the exploits of their youth; like grasshoppers, that show their vigor only by their chirping.

XVI.—JUNO'S SUITOR, OR BASENESS.

EXPLAINED OF SUBMISSION AND ABJECTION.

THE poets tell us, that Jupiter, to carry on his love-intrigues, assumed many different shapes; as of a bull, an eagle, a swan, a golden shower, &c.; but when he attempted Juno, he turned himself into the most ignoble and ridiculous creature,—even that of a wretched, wet, weather-beaten, affrighted, trembling and half-starved cuckoo.

EXPLANATION.—This is a wise fable, and drawn from the very entrails of morality. The moral is, that men should not be conceited of themselves, and imagine that a discovery of their excellences will always render them acceptable; for this can only succeed according to the nature and manners of the person they court, or solicit; who, if he be a man not of the same gifts and endowments, but altogether of a haughty and contemptuous behavior, here represented by the person of Juno, they must entirely drop the character that carries the least show of worth or gracefulness; if they proceed upon any other footing, it is downright folly; nor is it sufficient to act the deformity of obsequiousness, unless they really change themselves, and become abject and contemptible in their persons.

XVII.—CUPID, OR AN ATOM.

EXPLAINED OF THE CORPUSCULAR PHILOSOPHY.

THE particulars related by the poets of Cupid, or Love, do not properly agree to the same person, yet they differ only so far, that if the confusion of persons be rejected, the correspondence may hold. They say, that Love was the most ancient of all the gods, and existed before every thing else, except Chaos, which is held coeval therewith. But for Chaos, the ancients never paid divine honors, nor gave the title of a god thereto. Love is represented absolutely without progenitor, excepting only that he is said to have proceeded from the egg of Nox; but that himself begot the gods, and all things else, on Chaos. His attributes are four; viz: 1, perpetual infancy; 2, blindness; 3, nakedness; and 4, archery.

There was also another Cupid, or Love, the youngest son of the gods, born of Venus; and upon him the attributes of the elder are transferred, with some degree of correspondence.

EXPLANATION.—This fable points at, and enters, the cradle of nature. Love seems to be the appetite, or incentive, of the primitive matter; or, to speak more distinctly, the natural motion, or moving principle, of the original corpuscles, or atoms; this being the most ancient and only power that made and wrought all things out of matter. It is absolutely without parent, that is, without cause; for causes are as parents to effects; but this power or efficacy could have no natural cause; for, excepting God, nothing was before it; and therefore it could have no efficient in nature. And as nothing is more inward with nature, it can neither be a genus nor a form; and therefore, whatever it is, it must be somewhat positive, though inexpressible. And if it were possible to conceive its modus and process, yet it could not be known from its cause, as being, next to God, the cause of causes, and itself without a cause. And, perhaps, we are not to hope that the modus of it should fall, or be comprehended, under human inquiry. Whence it is properly feigned to be the egg of Nox, or laid in the dark.

The divine philosopher declares, that "God has made every thing beautiful in its season; and has given over the world to our disputes and inquiries; but that man cannot find out the work which God has wrought, from its beginning up to its end." Thus the

summary or collective law of nature, or the principle
of love, impressed by God upon the original particles of all things, so as to make them attack each
other and come together, by the repetition and multiplication whereof all the variety in the universe is
produced, can scarce possibly find full admittance
into the thoughts of men, though some faint notion
may be had thereof. The Greek philosophy is subtile, and busied in discovering the material principles
of things, but negligent and languid in discovering the
principles of motion, in which the energy and efficacy
of every operation consists. And here the Greek philosophers seem perfectly blind and childish; for the
opinion of the Peripatetics, as to the stimulus of matter, by privation, is little more than words, or rather
sound than signification. And they who refer it to
God, though they do well therein, yet they do it by
a start, and not by proper degrees of assent; for
doubtless there is one summary, or capital law, in
which nature meets, subordinate to God, viz: the law
mentioned in the passage above quoted from Solomon;
or the work which God has wrought from its beginning to its end.

Democritus, who further considered this subject,
having first supposed an atom, or corpuscle, of some
dimension or figure, attributed thereto an appetite,
desire, or first motion simply, and another compar-
atively, imagining that all things properly tended to
the centre of the world; those containing more matter falling faster to the centre, and thereby removing, and in the shock driving away, such as held less.
But this is a slender conceit, and regards too few
particulars; for neither the revolutions of the celestial bodies, nor the contractions and expansions of

things, can be reduced to this principle. And for the opinion of Epicurus, as to the declination and fortuitous agitation of atoms, this only brings the matter back again to a trifle, and wraps it up in ignorance and night.

Cupid is elegantly drawn a perpetual child; for compounds are larger things, and have their periods of age; but the first seeds or atoms of bodies are small, and remain in a perpetual infant state.

He is again justly represented naked; as all compounds may properly be said to be dressed and clothed, or to assume a personage; whence nothing remains truly naked, but the original particles of things.

The blindness of Cupid contains a deep allegory; for this same Cupid, Love, or appetite of the world, seems to have very little foresight, but directs his steps and motions conformably to what he finds next him, as blind men do when they feel out their way; which renders the divine and overruling Providence and foresight the more surprising; as by a certain steady law, it brings such a beautiful order and regularity of things out of what seems extremely casual, void of design, and, as it were, really blind.

The last attribute of Cupid is archery, viz: a virtue or power operating at a distance; for every thing that operates at a distance may seem, as it were, to dart, or shoot with arrows. And whoever allows of atoms and vacuity, necessarily supposes that the virtue of atoms operates at a distance; for without this operation, no motion could be excited, on account of the vacuum interposing, but all things would remain sluggish and unmoved.

As to the other Cupid, he is properly said to be the

youngest son of the gods, as his power could not take place before the formation of species, or particular bodies. The description given us of him transfers the allegory to morality, though he still retains some resemblance with the ancient Cupid; for as Venus universally excites the affection of association, and the desire of procreation, her son Cupid applies the affection to individuals; so that the general disposition proceeds from Venus, but the more close sympathy from Cupid. The former depends upon a near approximation of causes, but the latter upon deeper, more necessitating and uncontrollable principles, as if they proceeded from the ancient Cupid, on whom all exquisite sympathies depend.

XVIII.—DIOMED, OR ZEAL.

EXPLAINED OF PERSECUTION, OR ZEAL FOR RELIGION.

DIOMED acquired great glory and honor at the Trojan war, and was highly favored by Pallas, who encouraged and excited him by no means to spare Venus, if he should casually meet her in fight. He followed the advice with too much eagerness and intrepidity, and accordingly wounded that goddess in her hand. This presumptuous action remained unpunished for a time, and when the war was ended he returned with great glory and renown to his own country, where, finding himself embroiled with domestic affairs, he retired into Italy. Here also at first he was well received and nobly entertained by King Daunus, who, besides other gifts and honors, erected statues for him over all his dominions. But upon the first calamity that afflicted the people after the stranger's ar-

rival, Daunus immediately reflected that he entertained a devoted person in his palace, an enemy to
the gods, and one who had sacrilegiously wounded a
goddess with his sword, whom it was impious but to
touch. To expiate, therefore, his country's guilt, he,
without regard to the laws of hospitality, which were
less regarded by him than the laws of religion, directly slew his guest, and commanded his statues and
all his honors to be razed and abolished. Nor was it
safe for others to commiserate or bewail so cruel a
destiny; but even his companions in arms, whilst they
lamented the death of their leader, and filled all places
with their complaints, were turned into a kind of
swans, which are said, at the approach of their own
death, to chant sweet melancholy dirges.

EXPLANATION.—This fable intimates an extraordinary and almost singular thing, for no hero besides Diomed is recorded to have wounded any of the
gods. Doubtless we have here described the nature
and fate of a man who professedly makes any divine
worship or sect of religion, though, in itself vain and
light, the only scope of his actions, and resolves to
propagate it by fire and sword. For although the
bloody dissensions and differences about religion were
unknown to the ancients, yet so copious and diffusive was their knowledge, that what they knew not
by experience they comprehended in thought and representation. Those, therefore, who endeavor to reform or establish any sect of religion, though vain,
corrupt, and infamous (which is here denoted under
the person of Venus), not by the force of reason,
learning, sanctity of manners, the weight of arguments, and examples, but would spread or extirpate

it by persecution, pains, penalties, tortures, fire, and
sword, may, perhaps, be instigated hereto by Pallas,
that is, by a certain rigid, prudential consideration,
and a severity of judgment, by the vigor and efficacy
whereof they see thoroughly into the fallacies and fic-
tions of the delusions of this king; and through aversion to depravity and a well-meant zeal, these men
usually for a time acquire great fame and glory, and
are by the vulgar, to whom no moderate measures can
be acceptable, extolled and almost adored, as the
only patrons and protectors of truth and religion, men
of any other disposition seeming, in comparison with
these, to be lukewarm, mean-spirited, and cowardly.
This fame and felicity, however, seldom endures to
the end: but all violence, unless it escapes the reverses and changes of things by untimely death, is
commonly unprosperous in the issue; and if a change
of affairs happens, and that sect of religion which was
persecuted and oppressed gains strength and rises
again, then the zeal and warm endeavors of this sort
of men are condemned, their very name becomes
odious, and all their honors terminate in disgrace.

As to the point that Diomed should be slain by his
hospitable entertainer, this denotes that religious dissensions may cause treachery, bloody animosities,
and deceit, even between the nearest friends.

That complaining or bewailing should not, in so
enormous a case, be permitted to friends affected by
the catastrophe without punishment, includes this prudent admonition, that almost in all kinds of wickedness and depravity men have still room left for commiseration, so that they who hate the crime may yet
pity the person and bewail his calamity, from a principle of humanity and good-nature; and to forbid

the overflowings and intercourses of pity upon such occasions were the extremest of evils; yet in the cause of religion and impiety the very commiserations of men are noted and suspected. On the other hand, the lamentations and complainings of the followers and attendants of Diomed, that is, of men of the same sect or persuasion, are usually very sweet, agreeable, and moving, like the dying notes of swans, or the birds of Diomed. This also is a noble and remarkable part of the allegory, denoting that the last words of those who suffer for the sake of religion strongly affect and sway men's minds, and leave a lasting impression upon the sense and memory.

XIX.—DÆDALUS, OR MECHANICAL SKILL.

EXPLAINED OF ARTS AND ARTISTS IN KINGDOMS AND STATES.

THE ancients have left us a description of mechanical skill, industry, and curious arts converted to ill uses, in the person of Dædalus, a most ingenious but execrable artist. This Dædalus was banished for the murder of his brother artist and rival, yet found a kind reception in his banishment from the kings and states where he came. He raised many incomparable edifices to the honor of the gods, and invented many new contrivances for the beautifying and ennobling of cities and public places, but still he was most famous for wicked inventions. Among the rest, by his abominable industry and destructive genius, he assisted in the fatal and infamous production of the monster Minotaur, that devourer of promising youths. And then, to cover one mischief with another, and provide for the security of this monster, he invented and built a labyrinth; a work infamous for its end and design, but admirable and prodigious for art and workmanship. After this, that he might not only be celebrated for wicked inventions, but be sought after, as well for prevention, as for instruments of mischief, he formed that ingenious device of his clue, which led directly through all the windings of the labyrinth. This Dædalus was persecuted by Minos with the utmost severity, diligence, and inquiry; but he always found refuge and means of escaping. Lastly, endeavoring to teach his son Icarus the art of flying, the novice, trusting too much to his wings, fell from his towering flight, and was drowned in the sea.

EXPLANATION.—The sense of the fable runs thus. It first denotes envy, which is continually upon the watch, and strangely prevails among excellent artificers; for no kind of people are observed to be more implacably and destructively envious to one another than these.

In the next place, it observes an impolitic and improvident kind of punishment inflicted upon Dædalus—that of banishment; for good workmen are gladly received everywhere, so that banishment to an excellent artificer is scarce any punishment at all; whereas other conditions of life cannot easily flourish from home. For the admiration of artists is propagated and increased among foreigners and strangers; it being a principle in the minds of men to slight and despise the mechanical operators of their own nation.

The succeeding part of the fable is plain, concerning the use of mechanic arts, whereto human life stands greatly indebted, as receiving from this treasury numerous particulars for the service of religion, the ornament of civil society, and the whole provision and apparatus of life; but then the same magazine supplies instruments of lust, cruelty, and death. For, not to mention the arts of luxury and debauchery, we plainly see how far the business of exquisite poisons, guns, engines of war, and such kind of destructive inventions, exceeds the cruelty and barbarity of the Minotaur himself.

The addition of the labyrinth contains a beautiful allegory, representing the nature of mechanic arts in general; for all ingenious and accurate mechanical inventions may be conceived as a labyrinth, which, by reason of their subtilty, intricacy, crossing, and interfering with one another, and the apparent resemblances they have among themselves, scarce any power of the judgment can unravel and distinguish; so that they are only to be understood and traced by the clue of experience.

It is no less prudently added, that he who invented the windings of the labyrinth, should also show the use and management of the clue; for mechanical arts have an ambiguous or double use, and serve as well to produce as to prevent mischief and destruction; so that their virtue almost destroys or unwinds itself.

Unlawful arts and indeed frequently arts themselves, are persecuted by Minos, that is, by laws, which prohibit and forbid their use among the people; but notwithstanding this, they are hid, concealed, retained, and everywhere find reception and skulking-places; a thing well observed by Tacitus of the astrologers and fortune-tellers of his time. "These," says he, "are a kind of men that will always be prohibited, and yet will always be retained in our city."

But lastly, all unlawful and vain arts, of what kind soever, lose their reputation in tract of time; grow contemptible and perish, through their over-confidence, like Icarus; being commonly unable to perform what they boasted. And to say the truth, such arts are better suppressed by their own vain pretensions, than checked or restrained by the bridle of laws.[1]

XX.—ERICTHONIUS, OR IMPOSTURE.

EXPLAINED OF THE IMPROPER USE OF FORCE IN NATURAL PHILOSOPHY.

The poets feign that Vulcan attempted the chastity of Minerva, and impatient of refusal, had recourse to force; the consequence of which was the birth of Ericthonius, whose body from the middle upwards was comely and well-proportioned, but his thighs and legs small, shrunk, and deformed, like an eel. Conscious of this defect, he became the inventor of chariots, so as to show the graceful, but conceal the deformed part of his body.

Explanation.—This strange fable seems to carry this meaning. Art is here represented under the person of Vulcan, by reason of the various uses it makes of fire; and nature, under the person of Minerva, by reason of the industry employed in her works. Art, therefore, whenever it offers violence to nature, in order to conquer, subdue, and bend her to its purpose, by tortures and force of all kinds, seldom ob-

[1] Bacon nowhere speaks with such freedom and perspicuity as under the pretext of explaining these ancient fables; for which reason they deserve to be the more read by such as desire to understand the rest of his works.

tains the end proposed; yet upon great struggle and application, there proceed certain imperfect births, or lame abortive works, specious in appearance, but weak and unstable in use; which are, nevertheless, with great pomp and deceitful appearances, triumphantly carried about, and shown by impostors. A procedure very familiar, and remarkable in chemical productions, and new mechanical inventions; especially when the inventors rather hug their errors than improve upon them, and go on struggling with nature, not courting her.

XXI.—DEUCALION, OR RESTITUTION.

EXPLAINED OF A USEFUL HINT IN NATURAL PHILOSOPHY.

THE poets tell us, that the inhabitants of the old world being totally destroyed by the universal deluge, excepting Deucalion and Pyrrha, these two, desiring with zealous and fervent devotion to restore mankind, received this oracle for answer, that "they should succeed by throwing their mother's bones behind them." This at first cast them into great sorrow and despair, because, as all things were levelled by the deluge, it was in vain to seek their mother's tomb; but at length they understood the expression of the oracle to signify the stones of the earth, which is esteemed the mother of all things.

EXPLANATION.—This fable seems to reveal a secret of nature, and correct an error familiar to the mind; for men's ignorance leads them to expect the renovation or restoration of things from their corruption and remains, as the phœnix is said to be restored out of its ashes; which is a very improper procedure, because such kind of materials have finished their course, and are become absolutely unfit to supply the first rudiments of the same things again; whence, in cases of renovation, recourse should be had to more common principles.

XXII.—NEMESIS, OR THE VICISSITUDE OF THINGS.

EXPLAINED OF THE REVERSES OF FORTUNE.

NEMESIS is represented as a goddess venerated by all, but feared by the powerful and the fortunate. She is said to be the daughter of Nox and Oceanus.

She is drawn with wings, and a crown; a javelin of ash in her right hand; a glass containing Ethiopians in her left; and riding upon a stag.

EXPLANATION.—The fable receives this explanation. The word Nemesis manifestly signifies revenge, or retribution; for the office of this goddess consisted in interposing, like the Roman tribunes, with an "I forbid it," in all courses of constant and perpetual felicity, so as not only to chastise haughtiness, but also to repay even innocent and moderate happiness with adversity; as if it were decreed, that none of human race should be admitted to the banquet of the gods, but for sport. And indeed, to read over that chapter of Pliny wherein he has collected the miseries and misfortunes of Augustus Cæsar, whom, of all mankind, one would judge most fortunate,—as he had a certain art of using and enjoying prosperity, with a mind no way tumid, light, effeminate, confused, or melancholic—one cannot but think this a very great and powerful goddess, who could bring such a victim to her altar.[1]

The parents of this goddess were Oceanus and Nox; that is, the fluctuating change of things, and the obscure and secret divine decrees. The changes of things are aptly represented by the Ocean, on account of its perpetual ebbing and flowing; and secret providence is justly expressed by Night. Even the heathens have observed this secret Nemesis of the night, or the difference betwixt divine and human judgment.[2]

Wings are given to Nemesis, because of the sudden and unforeseen changes of things; for, from the earliest account of time, it has been common for great and prudent men to fall by the dangers they most despised. Thus Cicero, when admonished by Brutus of the infidelity and rancor of Octavius, coolly wrote back: "I cannot, however, but be obliged to you, Brutus, as I ought, for informing me, though of such a trifle."[3]

Nemesis also has her crown, by reason of the invidious and malignant nature of the vulgar, who generally rejoice, triumph, and crown her, at the fall of the fortunate and the powerful. And for the javelin in her right hand, it has regard to those whom she has actually struck and transfixed. But whoever escapes her stroke, or feels not actual calamity or misfortune, she affrights with a black and dismal sight in her left hand; for doubtless, mortals on the

---

[1] As she also brought the author himself.

[2] "—— cadit Ripheus, justissimus unus,
  Qui fuit ex Teucris, et servantissimus æqui:
  Diis aliter visum."—*Æneid*, lib. ii.

[3] Te autem mi Brute sicut debeo, amo, quod istud quicquid est nugarum me scire voluisti.

highest pinnacle of felicity have a prospect of death, diseases, calamities, perfidious friends, undermining enemies, reverses of fortune, &c., represented by the Ethiopians in her glass. Thus Virgil, with great elegance, describing the battle of Actium, says of Cleopatra, that "she did not yet perceive the two asps behind her;"[4] but soon after, which way soever she turned, she saw whole troops of Ethiopians still before her.

Lastly, it is significantly added, that Nemesis rides upon a stag, which is a very long-lived creature; for though perhaps some, by an untimely death in youth, may prevent or escape this goddess, yet they who enjoy a long flow of happiness and power, doubtless become subject to her at length, and are brought to yield.

XXIII.—ACHELOUS, OR BATTLE.

EXPLAINED OF WAR BY INVASION.

THE ancients relate, that Hercules and Achelous being rivals in the courtship of Deianira, the matter was contested by single combat; when Achelous having transformed himself, as he had power to do, into various shapes, by way of trial; at length, in the form of a fierce wild bull, prepares himself for the fight; but Hercules still retains his human shape, engages sharply with him, and in the issue broke off one of the bull's horns; and now Achelous, in great pain and fright, to redeem his horn, presents Hercules with the cornucopia.

[4] "Regina in mediis patrio vocat agmina sistro;
Necdum etiam geminos a tergo respicit angues."
Æneid, viii. 696.

EXPLANATION.—This fable relates to military expeditions and preparations; for the preparation of
war on the defensive side, here denoted by Achelous,
appears in various shapes, whilst the invading side
has but one simple form, consisting either in an army,
or perhaps a fleet. But the country that expects the
invasion is employed infinite ways, in fortifying
towns, blockading passes, rivers, and ports, raising
soldiers, disposing garrisons, building and breaking
down bridges, procuring aids, securing provisions,
arms, ammunition, &c. So that there appears a new
face of things every day; and at length, when the
country is sufficiently fortified and prepared, it represents to the life the form and threats of a fierce fight-
ing bull.

On the other side, the invader presses on to the fight,
fearing to be distressed in an enemy's country. And
if after the battle he remains master of the field, and
has now broke, as it were, the horn of his enemy, the
besieged, of course, retire inglorious, affrighted, and
dismayed, to their stronghold, there endeavoring to
secure themselves, and repair their strength; leaving, at the same time, their country a prey to the
conqueror, which is well expressed by the Amalthean
horn, or cornucopia.

XXIV.—DIONYSUS, OR BACCHUS.[1]

EXPLAINED OF THE PASSIONS.

THE fable runs, that Semele, Jupiter's mistress, having bound him by an inviolable oath to grant her an
unknown request, desired he would embrace her in the

[1] Ovid's Metamorphoses, b. iii., iv., and vi.; and Fasti, iii. 70.

same form and manner he used to embrace Juno; and the promise being irrevocable, she was burnt to death with lightning in the performance. The embryo, however, was sewed up, and carried in Jupiter's thigh till the complete time of its birth; but the burden thus rendering the father lame, and causing him pain, the child was thence called Dionysus. When born, he was committed, for some years, to be nursed by Proserpina; and when grown up, appeared with so effeminate a face, that his sex seemed somewhat doubtful. He also died, and was buried for a time, but afterwards revived. When a youth, he first introduced the cultivation and dressing of vines, the method of preparing wine, and taught the use thereof; whence becoming famous, he subdued the world, even to the utmost bounds of the Indies. He rode in a chariot drawn by tigers. There danced about him certain deformed demons called Cobali, &c. The Muses also joined in his train. He married Ariadne, who was deserted by Theseus. The ivy was sacred to him. He was also held the inventor and institutor of religious rites and ceremonies, but such as were wild, frantic, and full of corruption and cruelty. He had also the power of striking men with frenzies. Pentheus and Orpheus were torn to pieces by the frantic women at his orgies; the first for climbing a tree to behold their outrageous ceremonies, and the other for the music of his harp. But the acts of this god are much entangled and confounded with those of Jupiter.

EXPLANATION.—This fable seems to contain a little system of morality, so that there is scarce any better invention in all ethics. Under the history of Bacchus, is drawn the nature of unlawful desire or affection, and disorder; for the appetite and thirst of apparent good is the mother of all unlawful desire, though ever so destructive, and all unlawful desires are conceived in unlawful wishes or requests, rashly indulged or granted before they are well understood or considered, and when the affection begins to grow warm, the mother of it (the nature of good) is destroyed and burnt up by the heat. And whilst an unlawful desire lies in the embryo, or unripened in the mind, which is its father, and here represented by Jupiter, it is cherished and concealed, especially in the inferior part of the mind, corresponding to the thigh of the body, where pain twitches and depresses the mind so far as to render its resolutions and actions imperfect and lame. And even after this child of the mind is confirmed, and gains strength by consent and habit, and comes forth into action, it must still be nursed by Proserpina for a time; that is, it skulks and hides its head in a clandestine manner, as it were under ground, till at length, when the checks of shame and fear are removed, and the requisite boldness acquired, it either assumes the pretext of some virtue, or openly despises infamy. And it is justly observed, that every vehement passion appears of a doubtful sex as having the strength of a man at first, but at last the impotence of a woman. It is also excellently added, that Bacchus died and rose again; for the affections sometimes seem to die and be no more; but there is no trusting them, even though they were buried, being always apt and ready to rise again whenever the occasion or object offers.

That Bacchus should be the inventor of wine, carries a fine allegory with it; for every affection is cunning and subtle in discovering a proper matter to nourish and feed it; and of all things known to mortals, wine is the most powerful and effectual for exciting and inflaming passions of all kinds, being, indeed, like a common fuel to all.

It is again, with great elegance, observed of Bacchus, that he subdued provinces, and undertook endless expeditions, for the affections never rest satisfied with what they enjoy, but with an endless and insatiable appetite thirst after something further. And tigers are prettily feigned to draw the chariot; for as soon as any affection shall, from going on foot, be advanced to ride, it triumphs over reason, and exerts its cruelty, fierceness, and strength against all that oppose it.

It is also humorously imagined, that ridiculous demons dance and frisk about this chariot; for every passion produces indecent, disorderly, interchangeable and deformed motions in the eyes, countenance, and gesture, so that the person under the impulse, whether of anger, insult, love, &c., though to himself he may seem grand, lofty, or obliging, yet in the eyes of others appears mean, contemptible, or ridiculous.

The Muses also are found in the train of Bacchus, for there is scarce any passion without its art, science, or doctrine to court and flatter it; but in this respect the indulgence of men of genius has greatly detracted from the majesty of the Muses, who ought to be the leaders and conductors of human life, and not the handmaids of the passions.

The allegory of Bacchus falling in love with a cast mistress, is extremely noble; for it is certain that the affections always court and covet what has been rejected upon experience. And all those who by serving and indulging their passions immensely raise the value of enjoyment, should know, that whatever they covet and pursue, whether riches, pleasure, glory, learning, or anything else, they only pursue those things that have been forsaken and cast off with contempt by great numbers in all ages, after possession and experience.

Nor is it without a mystery that the ivy was sacred to Bacchus, and this for two reasons: first, because ivy is an evergreen, or flourishes in the winter; and secondly, because it winds and creeps about so many things, as trees, walls, and buildings, and raises itself above them. As to the first, every passion grows fresh, strong, and vigorous by opposition and prohibition, as it were by a kind of contrast or antiperistasis, like the ivy in the winter. And for the second, the predominant passion of the mind throws itself, like the ivy, round all human actions, entwines all our resolutions, and perpetually adheres to, and mixes itself among, or even overtops them.

And no wonder that superstitious rites and ceremonies are attributed to Bacchus, when almost every ungovernable passion grows wanton and luxuriant in corrupt religions; nor again, that fury and frenzy should be sent and dealt out by him, because every passion is a short frenzy, and if it be vehement, lasting, and take deep root, it terminates in madness. And hence the allegory of Pentheus and Orpheus being torn to pieces is evident; for every headstrong passion is extremely bitter, severe, inveterate, and revengeful upon all curious inquiry, wholesome admonition, free counsel, and persuasion.

Lastly; the confusion between the persons of Jupiter and Bacchus will justly admit of an allegory, because noble and meritorious actions may some-

times proceed from virtue, sound reason, and magnanimity, and sometimes again from a concealed
passion and secret desire of ill, however they may be
extolled and praised, insomuch that it is not easy to
distinguish betwixt the acts of Bacchus and the acts
of Jupiter.

XXV.—ATALANTA AND HIPPOMENES, OR GAIN.

EXPLAINED OF THE CONTEST BETWIXT ART AND NATURE.

ATALANTA, who was exceedingly fleet, contended
with Hippomenes in the course, on condition that, if
Hippomenes won, he should espouse her, or forfeit his
life if he lost. The match was very unequal, for Atalanta had conquered numbers, to their destruction.
Hippomenes, therefore, had recourse to stratagem.
He procured three golden apples, and purposely carried them with him; they started; Atalanta out-
stripped him soon; then Hippomenes bowled one of
his apples before her, across the course, in order not
only to make her stoop, but to draw her out of the
path. She, prompted by female curiosity, and the
beauty of the golden fruit, starts from the course to
take up the apple. Hippomenes, in the mean time,
holds on his way, and steps before her; but she, by
her natural swiftness, soon fetches up her lost ground,
and leaves him again behind. Hippomenes, however,
by rightly timing his second and third throw, at
length won the race, not by his swiftness, but his
cunning.

EXPLANATION.—This fable seems to contain a noble allegory of the contest betwixt art and nature. For art, here denoted by Atalanta, is much swifter, or more expeditious in its operations than nature, when all obstacles and impediments are removed, and sooner arrives at its end. This appears almost in every instance. Thus, fruit comes slowly from the kernel, but soon by inoculation or incision; clay, left to itself, is a long time in acquiring a stony hardness, but is presently burnt by fire into brick. So again, in human life, nature is a long while in alleviating and abolishing the remembrance of pain, and assuaging the troubles of the mind; but moral philosophy, which is the art of living, performs it presently. Yet this prerogative and singular efficacy of art is stopped and retarded to the infinite detriment of human life, by certain golden apples; for there is no one science or art that constantly holds on its true and proper course to the end, but they are all continually stopping short, forsaking the track, and turning aside to profit and convenience, exactly like Atalanta.[1] Whence it is no wonder that art gets not the victory over nature, nor, according to the condition of the contest, brings her under subjection; but, on the contrary, remains subject to her, as a wife to a husband.[2]

[1] "Declinat cursus, aurumque volubile tollit."

[2] The author, in all his physical works, proceeds upon this foundation, that it is possible, and practicable, for art to obtain the victory over nature; that is, for human industry and power to procure, by the means of proper knowledge, such things as are necessary to render life as happy and commodious as its mortal state will allow. For instance, that it is possible to lengthen the present period of human life; bring the winds under command: and every way extend and enlarge the dominion or empire of man over the works of nature.

XXVI.—PROMETHEUS, OR THE STATE OF MAN.

EXPLAINED OF AN OVERRULING PROVIDENCE, AND OF HUMAN NATURE.

THE ancients relate that man was the work of Prometheus, and formed of clay; only the artificer mixed in with the mass, particles taken from different animals. And being desirous to improve his workmanship, and endow, as well as create, the human race, he stole up to heaven with a bundle of birch-rods, and kindling them at the chariot of the Sun, thence brought down fire to the earth for the service of men.

They add that, for this meritorious act, Prometheus was repayed with ingratitude by mankind, so that, forming a conspiracy, they arraigned both him and his invention before Jupiter. But the matter was otherwise received than they imagined; for the accusation proved extremely grateful to Jupiter and the gods, insomuch that, delighted with the action, they not only indulged mankind with use of fire, but moreover conferred upon them a most acceptable and desirable present, viz: perpetual youth.

But men, foolishly overjoyed hereat, laid this present of the gods upon an ass, who, in returning back with it, being extremely thirsty, strayed to a fountain. The serpent, who was guardian thereof, would not suffer him to drink, but upon condition of receiving the burden he carried, whatever it should be. The silly ass complied, and thus the perpetual renewal of youth was, for a drop of water, transferred from men to the race of serpents.

Prometheus, not desisting from his unwarrantable practices, though now reconciled to mankind, after they were thus tricked of their present, but still continuing inveterate against Jupiter, had the boldness to attempt deceit, even in a sacrifice, and is said to have once offered up two bulls to Jupiter, but so as in the hide of one of them to wrap all the flesh and fat of both, and stuffing out the other hide only with the bones; then, in a religious and devout manner, gave Jupiter his choice of the two. Jupiter, detesting this sly fraud and hypocrisy, but having thus an opportunity of punishing the offender, purposely chose the mock bull.

And now giving way to revenge, but finding he could not chastise the insolence of Prometheus without afflicting the human race (in the production whereof Prometheus had strangely and insufferably prided himself), he commanded Vulcan to form a beautiful and graceful woman, to whom every god presented a certain gift, whence she was called Pandora.[1] They put into her hands an elegant box, containing all sorts of miseries and misfortunes; but Hope was placed at the bottom of it. With this box she first goes to Prometheus, to try if she could prevail upon him to receive and open it; but he being upon his guard, warily refused the offer. Upon this refusal, she comes to his brother Epimetheus, a man of a very different temper, who rashly and inconsiderately opens the box. Finding all kinds of miseries and misfortunes issued out of it, he grew wise too late, and with great hurry and struggle tried to clap the cover on again; but with all his endeavor could scarce keep in Hope, which lay at the bottom.

[1] "All-gift."

Lastly, Jupiter arraigned Prometheus of many heinous crimes; as that he formerly stole fire from heaven; that he contemptuously and deceitfully mocked him by a sacrifice of bones; that he despised his present,[2] adding withal a new crime, that he attempted to ravish Pallas; for all which, he was sentenced to be bound in chains, and doomed to perpetual torments. Accordingly, by Jupiter's command, he was brought to Mount Caucasus, and there fastened to a pillar, so firmly that he could no way stir. A vulture or eagle stood by him, which in the daytime gnawed and consumed his liver; but in the night the wasted parts were supplied again; whence matter for his pain was never wanting.

They relate, however, that his punishment had an end; for Hercules sailing the ocean, in a cup, or pitcher, presented him by the Sun, came at length to Caucasus, shot the eagle with his arrows, and set Prometheus free. In certain nations, also, there were instituted particular games of the torch, to the honor of Prometheus, in which they who ran for the prize carried lighted torches; and as any one of these torches happened to go out, the bearer withdrew himself, and gave way to the next; and that person was allowed to win the prize, who first brought in his lighted torch to the goal.

EXPLANATION.—This fable contains and enforces many just and serious considerations; some whereof have been long since well observed, but some again remain perfectly untouched. Prometheus clearly and expressly signifies Providence; for of all the things in nature, the formation and endowment of man was

[2] Viz: that by Pandora.

singled out by the ancients, and esteemed the peculiar work of Providence. The reason hereof seems: 1. That the nature of man includes a mind and understanding, which is the seat of Providence. 2. That it is harsh and incredible to suppose reason and mind should be raised, and drawn out of senseless and irrational principles; whence it becomes almost inevitable, that providence is implanted in the human mind in conformity with, and by the direction and the design of the greater overruling Providence. But, 3. The principal cause is this: that man seems to be the thing in which the whole world centres, with respect to final causes; so that if he were away, all other things would stray and fluctuate, without end or intention, or become perfectly disjointed, and out of frame; for all things are made subservient to man, and he receives use and benefit from them all. Thus the revolutions, places, and periods, of the celestial bodies, serve him for distinguishing times and seasons, and for dividing the world into different regions; the meteors afford him prognostications of the weather; the winds sail our ships, drive our mills, and move our machines; and the vegetables and animals of all kinds either afford us matter for houses and habitations, clothing, food, physic; or tend to ease, or delight, to support, or refresh us so that everything in nature seems not made for itself, but for man.

And it is not without reason added, that the mass of matter whereof man was formed, should be mixed up with particles taken from different animals, and wrought in with the clay, because it is certain, that of all things in the universe, man is the most compounded and recompounded body; so that the ancients, not improperly, styled him a Microcosm, or little world within himself. For although the chemists have absurdly, and too literally, wrested and perverted the elegance of the term microcosm, whilst they pretend to find all kind of mineral and vegetable matters, or something corresponding to them, in man, yet it remains firm and unshaken, that the human body is, of all substances, the most mixed and organical; whence it has surprising powers and faculties; for the powers of simple bodies are but few, though certain and quick; as being little broken, or weakened, and not counterbalanced by mixture; but excellence and quantity of energy reside in mixture and composition.

Man, however, in his first origin, seems to be a defenceless, naked creature, slow in assisting himself, and standing in need of numerous things. Prometheus, therefore, hastened to the invention of fire, which supplies and administers to nearly all human uses and necessities, insomuch that, if the soul may be called the form of forms, if the hand may be called the instrument of instruments, fire may, as properly, be called the assistant of assistants, or the helper of helps; for hence proceed numberless operations, hence all the mechanic arts, and hence infinite assistances are afforded to the sciences themselves.

The manner wherein Prometheus stole this fire is properly described from the nature of the thing; he being said to have done it by applying a rod of birch to the chariot of the Sun; for birch is used in striking and beating, which clearly denotes the generation of fire to be from the violent percussions and collisions of bodies; whereby the matters struck are subtilized, rarefied, put into motion, and so prepared to receive the heat of the celestial bodies; whence they, in a clandestine and secret manner, collect and snatch fire, as it were by stealth, from the chariot of the Sun.

The next is a remarkable part of the fable, which represents that men, instead of gratitude and thanks, fell into indignation and expostulation, accusing both Prometheus and his fire to Jupiter,—and yet the accusation proved highly pleasing to Jupiter; so that he, for this reason, crowned these benefits of mankind with a new bounty. Here it may seem strange that the sin of ingratitude to a creator and benefactor, a sin so heinous as to include almost all others, should meet with approbation and reward. But the allegory has another view, and denotes, that the accusation and arraignment, both of human nature and human art among mankind, proceeds from a most noble and laudable temper of the mind, and tends to a very good purpose; whereas the contrary temper is odious to the gods, and unbeneficial in itself. For they who break into extravagant praises of human nature, and the arts in vogue, and who lay themselves out in admiring the things they already possess, and will needs have the sciences cultivated among them, to be thought absolutely perfect and complete, in the first place, show little regard to the divine nature, whilst they extol their own inventions almost as high as his perfection. In the next place, men of this temper are unserviceable and prejudicial in life, whilst they imagine themselves already got to the top of things, and there rest, without further inquiry. On the contrary, they who arraign and accuse both nature and art, and are always full of complaints against them, not only preserve a more just and modest sense of mind, but are also perpetually stirred up to fresh industry and new discoveries. Is not, then, the ignorance and fatality of mankind to be extremely pitied, whilst they remain slaves to the arrogance of a few of their own fellows, and are dotingly fond of that scrap of Grecian knowledge, the Peripatetic philosophy; and this to such a degree, as not only to think all accusation or arraignment thereof useless, but even hold it suspect and dangerous? Certainly the procedure of Empedocles, though furious—but especially that of Democritus (who with great modesty complained that all things were abstruse; that we know nothing; that truth lies hid in deep pits; that falsehood is strangely joined and twisted along with truth, &c.)—is to be preferred before the confident, assuming, and dogmatical school of Aristotle. Mankind are, therefore, to be admonished, that the arraignment of nature and of art is pleasing to the gods; and that a sharp and vehement accusation of Prometheus, though a creator, a founder, and a master, obtained new blessings and presents from the divine bounty, and proved more sound and serviceable than a diffusive harangue of praise and gratulation. And let men be assured that the fond opinion that they have already acquired enough, is a principal reason why they have acquired so little.

That the perpetual flower of youth should be the present which mankind received as a reward for their accusations, carries this moral; that the ancients seem not to have despaired of discovering methods, and remedies, for retarding old age, and prolonging the period of human life; but rather reckoned it among those things which, through sloth and want of diligent inquiry, perish and come to nothing, after having been once undertaken, than among such as are absolutely impossible, or placed beyond the reach of the human power. For they signify and intimate from the true use of fire, and the just and strenuous accusation and conviction of the errors of art, that the divine bounty is not wanting to men in such kind of presents, but that men indeed are wanting to themselves, and lay such an inestimable gift upon the back of a slow-paced ass; that is, upon the back of the heavy, dull, lingering thing, experience; from whose sluggish and tortoise-pace proceeds that ancient complaint of the shortness of life, and the slow advancement of arts. And certainly it may well seem, that the two faculties of reasoning and experience are not hitherto properly joined and coupled together, but to be still new gifts of the gods, separately laid, the one upon the back of a light bird, or abstract philosophy, and the other upon an ass, or slow-paced practice and trial. And yet good hopes might be conceived of this ass, if it were not for his thirst and the accidents of the way. For we judge, that if any one would constantly proceed, by a certain law and method, in the road of experience, and not by the way thirst after such experiments as make for profit or ostentation, nor exchange his burden, or quit the original design for the sake of these, he might be an useful bearer of a new and accumulated divine bounty to mankind.

That this gift of perpetual youth should pass from men to serpents, seems added by way of ornament, and illustration to the fable; perhaps intimating, at the same time, the shame it is for men, that they, with their fire, and numerous arts, cannot procure to themselves those things which nature has bestowed upon many other creatures.

The sudden reconcilation of Prometheus to mankind, after being disappointed of their hopes, contains a prudent and useful admonition. It points out the levity and temerity of men in new experiments, when, not presently succeeding, or answering to expectation, they precipitantly quit their new undertakings, hurry back to their old ones, and grow reconciled thereto.

After the fable has described the state of man, with regard to arts and intellectual matters, it passes on to religion; for after the inventing and settling of arts, follows the establishment of divine worship, which hypocrisy presently enters into and corrupts. So that by the two sacrifices we have elegantly painted the person of a man truly religious, and of an hypocrite. One of these sacrifices contained the fat, or the portion of God, used for burning and incensing; thereby denoting affection and zeal, offered up to his glory. It likewise contained the bowels, which are expressive of charity, along with the good and useful flesh. But the other contained nothing more than dry bones, which nevertheless stuffed out the hide, so as to make it resemble a fair, beautiful, and magnificent sacrifice; hereby finely denoting the external and empty rites and barren ceremonies, wherewith men burden and stuff out the divine worship,— things rather intended for show and ostentation than conducing to piety. Nor are mankind simply content with this mock-worship of God, but also impose and further it upon him, as if he had chosen and ordained it. Certainly the prophet, in the person of God, has a fine expostulation, as to this matter of choice: "Is this the fasting which I have chosen, that a man should afflict his soul for a day, and bow down his head like a bulrush?"

After thus touching the state of religion, the fable

next turns to manners, and the conditions of human life. And though it be a very common, yet is it a just interpretation, that Pandora denotes the pleasures and licentiousness which the cultivation and luxury of the arts of civil life introduce, as it were, by the instrumental efficacy of fire; whence the works of the voluptuary arts are properly attributed to Vulcan, the God of Fire. And hence infinite miseries and calamities have proceeded to the minds, the bodies, and fortunes of men, together with a late repentance; and this not in each man's particular, but also in kingdoms and states; for wars and tumults and tyrannies, have all arisen from this same fountain, or box of Pandora.

It is worth observing, how beautifully and elegantly the fable has drawn two reigning characters in human life, and given two examples, or tablatures of them, under the persons of Prometheus and Epimetheus. The followers of Epimetheus are improvident, see not far before them, and prefer such things as are agreeable for the present; whence they are oppressed with numerous straits, difficulties, and calamities, with which they almost continually struggle; but in the meantime gratify their own temper, and, for want of a better knowledge of things, feed their minds with many vain hopes; and with so many pleasing dreams, delight themselves, and sweeten the miseries of life.

But the followers of Prometheus are the prudent, wary men, that look into futurity, and cautiously guard against, prevent, and undermine many calamities and misfortunes. But this watchful, provident temper, is attended with a deprivation of numerous pleasures, and the loss of various delights, whilst such men debar themselves the use even of innocent things, and what is still worse, rack and torture themselves with cares, fears, and disquiets; being bound fast to the pillar of necessity, and tormented with numberless thoughts (which for their swiftness are well compared to an eagle), that continually wound, tear, and gnaw their liver or mind, unless, perhaps, they find some small remission by intervals, or as it were at nights; but then new anxieties, dreads, and fears, soon return again, as it were in the morning. And, therefore, very few men, of either temper, have secured to themselves the advantages of providence, and kept clear of disquiets, troubles, and misfortunes.

Nor indeed can any man obtain this end without the assistance of Hercules; that is, of such fortitude and constancy of mind as stands prepared against every event, and remains indifferent to every change; looking forward without being daunted, enjoying the good without disdain, and enduring the bad without impatience. And it must be observed, that even Prometheus had not the power to free himself, but owed his deliverance to another; for no natural inbred force and fortitude could prove equal to such a task. The power of releasing him came from the utmost confines of the ocean, and the sun; that is, from Apollo, or knowledge; and again, from a consideration of the uncertainty, instability, and fluctuating state of human life, which is represented by sailing the ocean. So, Virgil has joined these two together, accounting him happy who knows the causes of things, and has conquered all his fears, apprehensions, and superstitions.[3]

It is added, with great elegance, for supporting and

---

[3] "Felix qui potuit rerum cognoscere causas,
   Quique metus omnes et inexorabile fatum
   Subjecit pedibus, strepitumque Acherontis avari."
                                              Georg. ii, 490.

confirming the human mind, that the great hero who thus delivered him sailed the ocean in a cup, or pitcher, to prevent fear, or complaint; as if, through the narrowness of our nature or a too great fragility thereof, we were incapable of that fortitude and constancy to which Seneca finely alludes, when he says: "It is a noble thing, at once to participate in the frailty of man and the security of a god."

We have hitherto, that we might not break the connection of things, designedly omitted the last crime of Prometheus—that of attempting the chastity of Minerva—which heinous offence it doubtless was, that caused the punishment of having his liver gnawed by the vulture. The meaning seems to be this,—that when men are puffed up with arts and knowledge, they often try to subdue even the divine wisdom and bring it under the dominion of sense and reason, whence inevitably follows a perpetual and restless rending and tearing of the mind. A sober and humble distinction must be made betwixt divine and human things and betwixt the oracles of sense and faith, unless mankind had rather choose an heretical religion, and a fictitious and romantic philosophy.[4]

The last particular in the fable is the Games of the Torch, instituted to Prometheus, which again relates to arts and sciences, as well as the invention of fire, for the commemoration and celebration whereof these games were held. And here we have an extremely prudent admonition, directing us to expect the perfection of the sciences from succession, and not from the swiftness and abilities of any single person; for he who is fleetest and strongest in the course may perhaps be less fit to keep his torch alight, since

[4] *De Augmentis Scientiarum*, sec. xxviii. and supplem. xv.

there is danger of its going out from too rapid as well as from too slow a motion.[5] But this kind of contest, with the torch, seems to have been long dropped and neglected; the sciences appearing to have flourished principally in their first authors, as Aristotle, Galen, Euclid, Ptolemy, &c.; whilst their successors have done very little, or scarce made any attempts. But it were highly to be wished that these games might be renewed, to the honor of Prometheus, or human nature, and that they might excite contest, emulation, and laudable endeavors, and the design meet with such success as not to hang tottering, tremulous, and hazarded, upon the torch of any single person. Mankind should be admonished to rouse themselves, and try and exert their own strength and chance, and not place all their dependence upon a few men, whose abilities and capacities are not greater than their own.

These are the particulars which appear to us shadowed out by this trite and vulgar fable, though without denying that there may be contained in it several intimations that have a surprising correspondence with the Christian mysteries. In particular, the voyage of Hercules, made in a pitcher, to release Prometheus, bears an allusion to the word of God, coming in the frail vessel of the flesh to redeem mankind. But we indulge ourselves no such liberties as these, for fear of using strange fire at the altar of the Lord.

[5] An allusion which, in Plato's writings, is applied to the rapid succession of generations, through which the continuity of human life is maintained from age to age; and which are perpetually transferring from hand to hand the concerns and duties of this fleeting scene. Γεννῶντες τε καὶ ἐκτρέφοντες παῖδας, καθάπερ λαμπάδα τὸν βίον παραδιδόντες ἄλλοις ἐξ ἄλλων—Plato, Leg. b. vi. Lucretius also has the same metaphor:—

"Et quasi cursores vitai lampada tradunt."

XXVII.—ICARUS AND SCYLLA AND CHA-RYBDIS, OR THE MIDDLE WAY.

EXPLAINED OF MEDIOCRITY IN NATURAL AND MORAL PHILOSOPHY.

MEDIOCRITY, or the holding a middle course, has been highly extolled in morality, but little in matters of science, though no less useful and proper here; whilst in politics it is held suspected, and ought to be employed with judgment. The ancients described mediocrity in manners by the course prescribed to Icarus; and in matters of the understanding by the steering betwixt Scylla and Charybdis, on account of the great difficulty and danger in passing those straits.

Icarus, being to fly across the sea, was ordered by his father neither to soar too high nor fly too low, for, as his wings were fastened together with wax, there was danger of its melting by the sun's heat in too high a flight, and of its becoming less tenacious by the moisture if he kept too near the vapor of the sea. But he, with a juvenile confidence, soared aloft, and fell down headlong.

EXPLANATION.—The fable is vulgar, and easily interpreted; for the path of virtue lies straight between excess on the one side, and defect on the other. And no wonder that excess should prove the bane of Icarus, exulting in juvenile strength and vigor; for excess is the natural vice of youth, as defect is that of old age; and if a man must perish by either, Icarus chose the better of the two; for all defects are justly esteemed more depraved than excesses. There is some magnanimity in excess, that, like a bird, claims kindred with the heavens; but defect is a reptile, that basely

crawls upon the earth. It was excellently said by
Heraclitus: "A dry light makes the best soul:" for if
the soul contracts moisture from the earth, it perfectly degenerates and sinks. On the other hand,
moderation must be observed, to prevent this fine
light from burning, by its too great subtility and dryness. But these observations are common.

In matters of the understanding, it requires great
skill and a particular felicity to steer clear of Scylla
and Charybdis. If the ship strikes upon Scylla, it is
dashed in pieces against the rocks; if upon Charybdis,
it is swallowed outright. This allegory is pregnant
with matter; but we shall only observe the force of it
lies here, that a mean be observed in every doctrine
and science, and in the rules and axioms thereof, between the rocks of distinctions and the whirlpools of
universalities: for these two are the bane and shipwreck of fine geniuses and arts.

XXVIII.—SPHINX, OR SCIENCE.

EXPLAINED OF THE SCIENCES.

THEY relate that Sphinx was a monster, variously
formed, having the face and voice of a virgin, the
wings of a bird, and the talons of a griffin. She resided on the top of a mountain, near the city Thebes,
and also beset the highways. Her manner was to
lie in ambush and seize the travellers, and having
them in her power, to propose to them certain dark
and perplexed riddles, which it was thought she received from the Muses, and if her wretched captives
could not solve and interpret these riddles, she, with
great cruelty, fell upon them, in their hesitation and

confusion, and tore them to pieces. This plague having reigned a long time, the Thebans at length offered their kingdom to the man who could interpret her riddles, there be:ng no other way to subdue her. Œdipus, a penetrating and prudent man, though lame in his feet, excited by so great a reward, accepted the condition, and with a good assurance of mind, cheerfully presented himself before the monster, who directly asked him: "What creature that was, which, being born four-footed, afterwards became two-footed, then three-footed, and lastly four-footed again?" Œdipus, with presence of mind, replied it was man, who, upon his first birth and infant state, crawled upon all fours in endeavoring to walk; but not long after went upright upon his two natural feet; again, in old age walked three-footed, with a stick; and at last, growing decrepit, lay four-footed confined to his bed; and having by this exact solution obtained the victory, he slew the monster, and, laying the carcass upon an ass, led her away in triumph; and upon this he was, according to the agreement, made king of Thebes.

EXPLANATION.—This is an elegant, instructive fable, and seems invented to represent science, especially as joined with practice. For science may, without absurdity, be called a monster, being strangely gazed at and admired by the ignorant and unskilful. Her figure and form is various, by reason of the vast variety of subjects that science considers; her voice and countenance are represented female, by reason of her gay appearance and volubility of speech; wings are added, because the sciences and their inventions run and fly about in a moment, for knowledge like light communicated from one torch to another, is

presently caught and copiously diffused; sharp and
hooked talons are elegantly attributed to her, because
the axioms and arguments of science enter the mind,
lay hold of it, fix it down, and keep it from moving or
slipping away. This the sacred philosopher observed,
when he said: "The words of the wise are like goads
or nails driven far in."[1]   Again, all science seems
placed on high, as it were on the tops of mountains
hard to climb; for science is justly imagined a sublime
and lofty thing, looking down upon ignorance from an
eminence, and at the same time taking an extensive
view on all sides, as is usual on the tops of mountains.
Science is said to beset the highways, because through
all the journey and peregrination of human life there
is matter and occasion offered of contemplation.

Sphinx is said to propose various difficult questions
and riddles to men, which she received from the
Muses; and these questions, so long as they remain
with the Muses, may very well be unaccompanied with
severity, for while there is no other end of contemplation and inquiry but that of knowledge alone, the
understanding is not oppressed, or driven to straits
and difficulties, but expatiates and ranges at large,
and even receives a degree of pleasure from doubt and
variety; but after the Muses have given over their
riddles to Sphinx, that is, to practice, which urges and
impels to action, choice, and determination, then it is
that they become torturing, severe, and trying, and,
unless solved and interpreted, strangely perplex and
harass the human mind, rend it every way, and perfectly tear it to pieces. All the riddles of Sphinx,
therefore, have two conditions annexed, viz: dilacera-

[1] Eccles. xii. 11.

tion to those who do not solve them, and empire to those that do. For he who understands the thing proposed, obtains his end, and every artificer rules over his work.[2]

Sphinx has no more than two kinds of riddles, one relating to the nature of things, the other to the nature of man; and correspondent to these, the prizes of the solution are two kinds of empire,—the empire over nature, and the empire over man. For the true and ultimate end of natural philosophy is dominion over natural things, natural bodies, remedies, machines, and numberless other particulars, though the schools, contented with what spontaneously offers, and swollen with their own discourses, neglect, and in a manner despise, both things and works.

But the riddle proposed to Œdipus, the solution whereof acquired him the Theban kingdom, regarded the nature of man; for he who has thoroughly looked into and examined human nature, may in a manner command his own fortune, and seems born to acquire dominion and rule. Accordingly, Virgil properly makes the arts of government to be the arts of the Romans.[3] It was, therefore, extremely apposite in Augustus Cæsar to use the image of Sphinx in his signet, whether this happened by accident or by design; for he of all men was deeply versed in politics, and through the course of his life very happily solved abundance of new riddles with regard to the nature of

[2] This is what the author so frequently inculcates in the *Novum Organum,* viz: that knowledge and power are reciprocal; so that to improve in knowledge is to improve in the power of commanding nature, by introducing new arts, and producing works and effects.

[3] "Tu regere imperio populos, Romane, memento:
Hæ tibi erunt artes."

Æneid, vi. 851.

man; and unless he had done this with great dexterity and ready address, he would frequently have been involved in imminent danger, if not destruction.

It is with the utmost elegance added in the fable, when Sphinx was conquered, her carcass was laid upon an ass; for there is nothing so subtile and abstruse but after being once made plain, intelligible, and common, it may be received by the slowest capacity.

We must not omit that Sphinx was conquered by a lame man, and impotent in his feet; for men usually make too much haste to the solution of Sphinx's riddles; whence it happens, that she prevailing, their minds are rather racked and torn by disputes, than invested with command by works and effects.

XXIX.—PROSERPINE, OR SPIRIT.

EXPLAINED OF THE SPIRIT INCLUDED IN NATURAL BODIES.

THEY tell us, Pluto having, upon that memorable division of empire among the gods, received the infernal regions for his share, despaired of winning any one of the goddesses in marriage by an obsequious courtship, and therefore through necessity resolved upon a rape. Having watched his opportunity, he suddenly seized upon Proserpine, a most beautiful virgin, the daughter of Ceres, as she was gathering narcissus flowers in the meads of Sicily, and hurrying her to his chariot, carried her with him to the subterraneal regions, where she was treated with the highest reverence, and styled the Lady of Dis. But Ceres, missing her only daughter, whom she extremely loved, grew pensive and anxious beyond measure, and taking a lighted torch in her hand, wandered the world over in quest of her daughter,—but all to no purpose, till, suspecting she might be carried to the infernal regions, she, with great lamentation and abundance of tears, importuned Jupiter to restore her; and with much ado prevailed so far as to recover and bring her away, if she had tasted nothing there. This proved a hard condition upon the mother, for Proserpine was found to have eaten three kernels of a pomegranate. Ceres, however, desisted not, but fell to her entreaties and lamentations afresh, insomuch that at last it was indulged her that Proserpine should divide the year betwixt her husband and her mother, and live six months with the one and as many with the other. After this, Theseus and Perithous, with uncommon audacity, attempted to force Proserpine away from Pluto's bed, but happening to grow tired in their journey, and resting themselves upon a stone in the realms below, they could never rise from it again, but remain sitting there forever. Proserpine, therefore, still continued queen of the lower regions, in honor of whom there was also added this grand privilege, that though it had never been permitted any one to return after having once descended thither, a particular exception was made, that he who brought a golden bough as a present to Proserpine, might on that condition descend and return. This was an only bough that grew in a dark grove, not from a tree of its own, but like the mistletoe from another, and when plucked a fresh one always shot out in its stead.

EXPLANATION.—This fable seems to regard natural philosophy, and searches deep into that rich and fruitful virtue and supply in subterraneous bodies, from whence all the things upon the earth's surface spring, and into which they again relapse and return. By Proserpine, the ancients denoted that ethereal spirit shut up and detained within the earth, here represented by Pluto,—the spirit being separated from the superior globe, according to the expression of the poet.[1] This spirit is conceived as ravished, or snatched up by the earth, because it can in no way be detained, when it has time and opportunity to fly off, but is only wrought together and fixed by sudden intermixture and comminution, in the same manner as if one should endeavor to mix air with water, which cannot otherwise be done than by a quick and rapid agitation, that joins them together in froth whilst the air is thus caught up by the water. And it is added, Proserpine was ravished whilst she gathered narcissus flowers, which have their name from numbedness or stupefaction; for the spirit we speak of is in the fittest disposition to be embraced by terrestrial matter when it begins to coagulate, or grow torpid.

It is an honor attributed to Proserpine and not to any other wife of the gods, that of being the lady or mistress of her husband, because this spirit performs all its operations in the subterraneal regions, whilst Pluto, or earth, remains stupid, or ignorant of them.

The ether, or the efficacy of the heavenly bodies, denoted by Ceres, endeavors with infinite diligence to force out this spirit, and restore it to its pristine state. And by the torch in the hand of Ceres, or the ether, is doubtless meant the sun, which disperses light over the whole globe of the earth, and if the thing were possible, must have the greatest share in recovering

---

[1] "Sive recens tellus, seductaque nuper ab alta
Æthere, cognati retinebat semina coeli."—*Metam.* i. 80.

Proserpine, or reinstating the subterraneal spirit. Yet Proserpine still continues and dwells below, after the manner excellently described in the condition betwixt Jupiter and Ceres. For first, it is certain that there are two ways of detaining the spirit, in solid and terrestrial matter,—the one by condensation or obstruction, which is mere violence and imprisonment; the other by administering a proper aliment, which is spontaneous and free. For after the included spirit begins to feed and nourish itself, it is not in a hurry to fly off, but remains as it were fixed in its own earth. And this is the moral of Proserpine's tasting the pomegranate; and were it not for this, she must long ago have been carried up by Ceres, who with her torch wandered the world over, and so the earth have been left without its spirit. For though the spirit in metals and minerals may perhaps be, after a particular manner, wrought in by the solidity of the mass, yet the spirit of vegetables and animals has open passages to escape at, unless it be willingly detained, in the way of sipping and tasting them.

The second article of agreement, that of Proserpine's remaining six months with her mother and six with her husband, is an elegant description of the division of the year; for the spirit diffused through the earth lives above-ground in the vegetable world during the summer months, but in the winter returns under ground again.

The attempt of Theseus and Perithous to bring Proserpine away denotes that the more subtile spirits which descend in many bodies to the earth, may frequently be unable to drink in, unite with themselves, and carry off the subterraneous spirit, but on the contrary be coagulated by it, and rise no more, so as to increase the inhabitants and add to the domination of Proserpine.[2]

The alchemists will be apt to fall in with our interpretation of the golden bough, whether we will or no, because they promise golden mountains, and the restoration of natural bodies from their stone, as from the gates of Pluto; but we are well assured that their theory had no just foundation, and suspect they have no very encouraging or practical proofs of its soundness. Leaving, therefore, their conceits to themselves, we shall freely declare our own sentiments upon this last part of the fable. We are certain, from numerous figures and expressions of the ancients, that they judged the conservation, and in some degree the renovation, of natural bodies to be no desperate or impossible thing, but rather abstruse and out of the common road than wholly impracticable. And this seems to be their opinion in the present case, as they placed this bough among an infinite number of shrubs, in a spacious and thick wood. They supposed it of gold, because gold is the emblem of duration. They feigned it adventitious, not native, because such an effect is to be expected from art, and not from medicine or any simple or mere natural way of working.

XXX.—METIS, OR COUNSEL.

EXPLAINED OF PRINCES AND THEIR COUNCIL.

THE ancient poets relate that Jupiter took Metis to wife, whose name plainly denotes counsel, and that

[2] Many philosophers have certain speculations to this purpose. Sir Isaac Newton, in particular, suspects that the earth receives its vivifying spirit from the comets. And the philosophical chemists and astrologers have spun the thought into many fantastical distinctions and varieties.—See Newton, *Princip.* lib. iii. p. 473, &c.

he, perceiving she was pregnant by him, would by no means wait the time of her delivery, but directly devoured her; whence himself also became pregnant, and was delivered in a wonderful manner; for he from his head or brain brought forth Pallas armed.

EXPLANATION.—This fable, which in its literal sense appears monstrously absurd, seems to contain a state secret, and shows with what art kings usually carry themselves towards their council, in order to preserve their own authority and majesty not only inviolate, but so as to have it magnified and heightened among the people. For kings commonly link themselves, as it were, in a nuptial bond to their council, and deliberate and communicate with them after a prudent and laudable custom upon matters of the greatest importance, at the same time justly conceiving this no diminution of their majesty; but when the matter once ripens to a decree or order, which is a kind of birth, the king then suffers the council to go on no further, lest the act should seem to depend upon their pleasure. Now, therefore, the king usually assumes to himself whatever was wrought, elaborated, or formed, as it were, in the womb of the council (unless it be a matter of an invidious nature, which he is sure to put from him), so that the decree and the execution shall seem to flow from himself.[1] And as this decree or execution proceeds with prudence and power, so as to imply necessity, it is elegantly wrapped up under the figure of Pallas armed.

[1] This policy strikingly characterized the conduct of Louis XIV., who placed his generals under a particular injunction, to advertise him of the success of any siege likely to be crowned with an immediate triumph, that he might attend in person and appear to take the town by a *coup de main*.

Nor are kings content to have this seem the effect of their own authority, free will, and uncontrollable choice, unless they also take the whole honor to themselves, and make people imagine that all good and wholesome decrees proceed entirely from their own head, i.e., their own sole prudence and judgment.

XXXI.—THE SIRENS, OR PLEASURES.

EXPLAINED OF MEN'S PASSION FOR PLEASURES.

INTRODUCTION.—The fable of the Sirens is, in a vulgar sense, justly enough explained of the pernicious incentives to pleasure; but the ancient mythology seems to us like a vintage ill-pressed and trod; for though something has been drawn from it, yet all the more excellent parts remain behind in the grapes that are untouched.

FABLE.—The Sirens are said to be the daughters of Achelous and Terpsichore, one of the Muses. In their early days they had wings, but lost them upon being conquered by the Muses, with whom they rashly contended; and with the feathers of these wings the Muses made themselves crowns, so that from this time the Muses wore wings on their heads, except only the mother to the Sirens.

These Sirens resided in certain pleasant islands, and when, from their watch-tower, they saw any ship approaching, they first detained the sailors by their music, then, enticing them to shore, destroyed them.

Their singing was not of one and the same kind, but they adapted their tunes exactly to the nature of each person, in order to captivate and secure him.

And so destructive had they been, that these islands of the Sirens appeared, to a very great distance, white with the bones of their unburied captives.

Two different remedies were invented to protect persons against them, the one by Ulysses, the other by Orpheus. Ulysses commanded his associates to stop their ears close with wax; and he, determining to make the trial, and yet avoid the danger, ordered himself to be tied fast to a mast of the ship, giving strict charge not to be unbound, even though himself should entreat it; but Orpheus, without any binding at all, escaped the danger, by loudly chanting to his harp the praises of the gods, whereby he drowned the voices of the Sirens.

EXPLANATION.—This fable is of the moral kind, and appears no less elegant than easy to interpret. For pleasures proceed from plenty and affluence, attended with activity or exultation of the mind.[1] Anciently their first incentives were quick, and seized upon men as if they had been winged, but learning and philosophy afterwards prevailing, had at least the power to lay the mind under some restraint, and make it consider the issue of things, and thus deprived pleasures of their wings.

This conquest redounded greatly to the honor and ornament of the Muses; for after it appeared, by the example of a few, that philosophy could introduce a contempt of pleasures, it immediately seemed to be a sublime thing that could raise and elevate the soul, fixed in a manner down to the earth, and thus render

[1] The one denoted by the river Achelous, and the other by Terpsichore, the muse that invented the cithara and delighted in dancing.

men's thoughts, which reside in the head, winged as it were, or sublime.

Only the mother of the Sirens was not thus plumed on the head, which doubtless denotes superficial learning, invented and used for delight and levity; an eminent example whereof we have in Petronius, who, after receiving sentence of death, still continued his gay frothy humor, and as Tacitus observes, used his learning to solace or divert himself, and instead of such discourses as give firmness and constancy of mind, read nothing but loose poems and verses.[2] Such learning as this seems to pluck the crowns again from the Muses' heads, and restore them to the Sirens.

The Sirens are said to inhabit certain islands, because pleasures generally seek retirement, and often shun society. And for their songs, with the manifold artifice and destructiveness thereof, this is too obvious and common to need explanation. But that particular of the bones stretching like white cliffs along the shores, and appearing afar off, contains a more subtile allegory, and denotes that the examples of others' calamity and misfortunes, though ever so manifest and apparent, have yet but little force to deter the corrupt nature of man from pleasures.

The allegory of the remedies against the Sirens is not difficult, but very wise and noble; it proposes, in effect, three remedies, as well against subtile as

---

[2] "Vivamus, mea Lesbia, atque amemus;
Rumoresque senum severiorum
Omnes unius estimemus assis."—*Catull. Eleg.* v.

And again—

"Jura senes norint, et quod sit fasque nefasque
Inquirant tristes; legumque examina servent."
Metam. ix. **550.**

violent mischiefs, two drawn from philosophy and one from religion.

The first means of escaping is to resist the earliest temptation in the beginning, and diligently avoid and cut off all occasions that may solicit or sway the mind; and this is well represented by shutting up the ears, a kind of remedy to be necessarily used with mean and vulgar minds, such as the retinue of Ulysses.

But nobler spirits may converse, even in the midst of pleasures, if the mind be well guarded with constancy and resolution. And thus some delight to make a severe trial of their own virtue, and thoroughly acquaint themselves with the folly and madness of pleasures, without complying or being wholly given up to them; which is what Solomon professes of himself when he closes the account of all the numerous pleasures he gave a loose to, with this expression: "But wisdom still continued with me." Such heroes in virtue may, therefore, remain unmoved by the greatest incentives to pleasure, and stop themselves on the very precipice of danger; if, according to the example of Ulysses, they turn a deaf ear to pernicious counsel, and the flatteries of their friends and companions, which have the greatest power to shake and unsettle the mind.

But the most excellent remedy, in every temptation, is that of Orpheus, who, by loudly chanting and resounding the praises of the gods, confounded the voices, and kept himself from hearing the music of the Sirens; for divine contemplations exceed the pleasures of sense, not only in power but also in sweetness.